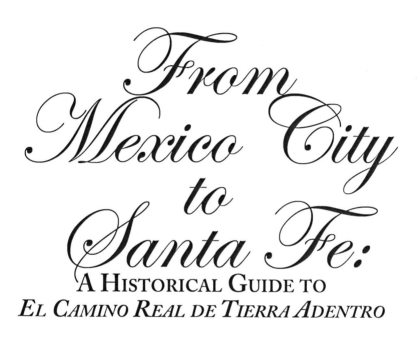

# From Mexico City to Santa Fe:
## A HISTORICAL GUIDE TO
### EL CAMINO REAL DE TIERRA ADENTRO

Compiled and Edited by
Joseph P. Sánchez and Bruce A. Erickson

# From Mexico City to Santa Fe:

## A Historical Guide to
## El Camino Real de Tierra Adentro

Compiled and Edited by
Joseph P. Sánchez and Bruce A. Erickson

Río Grande Books
Los Ranchos, NM

Published by Río Grande Books
925 Salamanca NW
Los Ranchos, NM 87107-5647
505-344-9382
www.nmsantos.com

Printed in the United States of America

Book Design: Paul Rhetts

Library of Congress Cataloging-in-Publication Data

Sánchez, Joseph P.
From Mexico City to Santa Fe : a historical guide to El Camino Real
de Tierra Adentro / compiled and edited by Joseph P. Sánchez and
Bruce A. Erickson.
p. cm.
Includes bibliographical references and index.
ISBN 978-1-890689-89-6 (pbk. : alk. paper)
1. Chihuahua Trail--Guidebooks. 2. Chihuahua Trail--History.
3. Chihuahua Trail--History, Local. 4. Historic sites--Chihuahua Trail.
5. Names, Geographical--Chihuahua Trail.
I. Erickson, Bruce A. II. Title.
F799.S264 2011
972'.16--dc23
2011030379

For Helen, Anna, Tom, Corine and Mary Jane,
whose ancestors traveled *El Camino Real de Tierra Adentro*
to New Mexico in 1598

For Genoa Wilson, Lewis and Glenn Erickson,
and for all the contributors, and centuries of travelers and writers
who made the work possible

# Contents

# Maps

# Preface

On October 13, 2000, the United States Congress designated 404 miles of *El Camino Real de Tierra Adentro* (The Royal Road of the Interior) within the United States (Texas and New Mexico), as a National Historic Trail.[1] Thus El Camino Real de Tierra Adentro National Historic Trail entered the pantheon of national historic trails that have forged our nation's history. Equally so, Spain and Mexico share in the history and heritage of the *Camino Real*. At least 1,200 miles of the trail are located between Mexico City and Juarez. As a binational trail, *El Camino Real de Tierra Adentro*, or Royal Road of the Interior, has a history of its own. Adding to the significance of the trail, on August 1, 2010, UNESCO designated that the Mexican portion of the Camino Real de Tierra Adentro as a World Heritage Site. With the two designations, the Camino Real has entered the realm of a modern-day, binational Wonder of the World.

The purpose of this book is to provide a reference guide for the rich heritage evident in the many place names that align with *El Camino Real de Tierra Adentro*. To that end, this book is aimed at recounting the history of the *Camino Real* and its significance to our national story as well as

---

1    See Appendix A, El Camino Real de Tierra Adentro National Historic Trail Establishment Act (P.L. 106-307).

the associated histories of Spain and Mexico. Certainly, as a travel guide and as a sourcebook of place names along the *Camino Real* it is hoped that this book will encourage the preservation and protection of the Camino Real as well as the study of its history. Equally so, this guide will add to the enjoyment of the recreational and touristic exploration of places named herein.

The Introduction to this book serves to place *El Camino Real de Tierra Adentro* within an historical perspective that explains how the route developed across time between 1540 and 1821 as well as its aftermath during the Mexican Territorial Period of present southwestern United States between 1821 and 1848 and the acquisition of that region by the United States after 1848. This sourcebook offers brief histories of place names associated with *El Camino Real de Tierra Adentro* during those periods.

*El Camino Real de Tierra Adentro* is much more than an historic road for it was forged from earlier indigenous foot trails that crisscrossed the length of Mexico's *meseta central* which is bordered by two enormous parallel mountain ranges running north to south. Those ranges are the Sierra Madre Oriental on the east side of the *meseta central* and the Sierra Madre Occidental on the west. The rugged terrain, which is oriented on a south to north axis, is beset by a series of cross mountain ranges some of which run either perpendicular to or are transversal to the *Sierra Madres*. The meandering route of *El Camino Real de Tierra Adentro* from Mexico City to its terminus in Santa Fe, New Mexico, is over 1,500 miles.

The historical origins of the *Camino Real,* aside from indigenous primitive trails, begin with the first silver strikes north of Mexico City at places between Querétaro and Durango. In the middle 1500s, Spanish forty-niners poured into the mining areas and began to found towns and places, like *haciendas* and *estancias* and other establishments. In the sixteenth century, the *Camino Real* from Mexico City to the silver mines as far north as Durango was called *El Camino de la Plata*, the Silver Road. As new mines were established farther north and as cattle ranching, town founding, and missionary activity expanded beyond the last settlement, so too, did the *Camino Real* inch northward in an historical process that took nearly sixty years to complete in terms of its length and in the context of the settlement patterns that sprang up along it.

Overall, *El Camino Real de Tierra Adentro* was its own frontier—albeit linear in character. The culture that developed along it carried out its main business of trade, transport of things and animals that went north or south along it, as well as cultural institutions and traditions brought forth by the general migration of people. The history of *El Camino Real de Tierra Adentro* was somewhat different than that of the settlements that grew up miles from it in deep mountain canyons, or ranges. Indeed, the settlers along *El Camino Real de Tierra Adentro* had their own history, their own culture, and their own way of doing things.

Significantly, *El Camino Real de Tierra Adentro* is about people. Today, descendants of the early settlers of many places along the route still live on or near the historic route that brought their ancestors there. In New Mexico, 1598 marks the year that Spanish-Mexican frontiersmen established the first settlement at San Juan de los Caballeros. Descendants of early pioneers, share a kinship, for many of their ancestors not only knew each other, they had walked much of the Camino Real together, camped for seemingly endless nights, and reached their destination together after six months of travel from Santa Barbara to San Juan de los Caballeros. Spanish settlers into New Mexico traveled the route, marrying along the way and creating relationships between families that remained in towns such as Zacatecas, San Luis Potosí, Santa Barbara, Albuquerque, Santa Fe and others. Four hundred years later, the Hispanic culture that evolved, between El Paso and Santa Fe as "typically New Mexican," was forged from many migrations over the *Camino Real.*

As a migration route, *El Camino Real de Tierra Adentro* is a transmitter of European culture. Today, Spanish is the spoken language along the entire route of the *Camino Real,* just as it was in the Spanish Colonial Period, 1521-1821. Spanish settlers introduced Christianity, law, a system of governance, land grants, technologies, industries, music, food, folklore and other cultural practices, customs, and institutions via the *Camino Real* that, today, prevail along the historic corridor from Mexico City to Santa Fe.

Continuity and change is evident in the form of governance that evolved over time along the *Camino Real.* By the early the sixteenth century, the cabildo, the basic unit of self-governance, had been established earlier in the Caribbean Islands (Santo Domingo, Cuba, and Puerto Rico), Mexico City, and San Agustin in Florida. In 1598, Governor Juan de Oñate introduced the *cabildo* into New Mexico. The *cabildo*, or town council, comprised of elected and appointed members. As it had evolved from Greek to Roman to European towns and finally the Americas, the *cabildo* advised the governor on issues concerning the business of the colony. In time the *cabildo* de Santa Fe, also referred to in the late Spanish period as the *ayuntamiento*, evolved into the *asamblea* (assembly) de Santa Fe during the Mexican Territorial period. Under the United States, the *asamblea* evolved as the Territorial Legislature; and, after statehood was proclaimed in 1912, the legislative body became the New Mexico State Legislature. From *cabildo* to state legislature, the assembly only moved a few blocks from the Plaza de Santa Fe to the Round House. Indeed, Santa Fe is the ony capital that remained in its orginal place contrasted with the Spanish colonial capitals that were moved from San Antonio, Texas, Tucson, Arizona and Monterey, Californa. The direct line of evolution from *cabildo* to the state legislature is one of the enduring legacies of *El Camino Real de Tierra Adentro*.

Spanish law influenced the character of all *caminos reales* throughout the empire. The word *real* is rooted in the word *regalía*, meaning privileges granted by the king. In principle and in theory, the *real* was a privilege or set of privileges conceded by the king of Spain to a person or group that carried a documentation that a *real* had been granted to them. *Reales* granted to townships, such as villas, carried town charters that indicated their privileges. In general, *caminos reales* connected villas, but more importantly ran from one Spanish capital to another. In the colonial world, a *camino real* would likely not have connected Indian villages, although colonial roads ran to them as well. Thus, Spanish law defined towns, land grants, and other places as well as *caminos reales*.[2] For further discussion of the definition of a *camino real*, see Appendix B.

The earliest writings of the segment of the Camino Real de Tierra Adentro in New Mexico are found in the *Itinerario* of Juan de Oñate's expedition to establish New Mexico as a Spanish Colony in 1598 and Gaspar Pérez de Villagra's *Historia* de la Nueva Mexico which is an epic

---

2   Joseph P. Sánchez, María Luisa Pérez González, Bruce A. Erickson, Toward a Definition of the Spanish *Camino Real: Cabañas, Villas,* Armies, and the Spanish Crown (Original copy in the Spanish Colonial Research Center, see Appendix I).

poem. The *Itineriario* offers detailed historical documentation, while Villagra's *Historia* is an epic poem in point of fact and take poetic license in revealing the day to day struggle to survive on the waterless portions of the Camino Real north of Santa Barbara.[3]

In 1598, Juan de Oñate blazed a segment of the trail directly north from Santa Barbara to El Paso del Norte. Today, that segment is called "La Ruta de Oñate" or Oñate's Route. With 600 settlers and thousands of head of sheep, cattle, and horses, Oñate's settlers crossed the Río Grande at El Paso, which they named. Leaving the river for flatter land, they headed north along a route northeast of Las Cruces known as the *Jornada del Muerto*, Dead Man's Journey. Eighty miles in length, the nearly waterless *Jornada del Muerto* stretched beyond the horizon to a place called Socorro. Their the settlers and their long wagon train returned to the Río Grande and stopped for water, rest, and food which was provided by local Indians. The settlers remembered the place of safety and help and called it "*Socorro.*" Their descendants are a part of the long history of *El Camino Real de Tierra Adentro* for many of them still live along the route in places like Las Cruces, Socorro, Belen, Los Lunas, Albuquerque, Santa Fe and Española as well as other points in between such as Abiquiu, Cuba, Las Trampas, Truchas, Mora, Anton Chico, Santa Rosa and southward past Vaughn, Corona, Carrizozo, and El Paso. Their lore, language, and historical past merge in the telling of each place name along *El Camino Real de Tierra Adentro*.

During the Mexican Territorial Period, 1821-1848 in present southwestern United States, the *Camino Real* continued in use. While the *Camino Real* ceased to be "royal" as it was the "King's Road" and Mexico had won its independence from Spain in 1821, the road was still dubbed, "El *Camino Real.*" Sometimes the name was segmented. For example, from Chihuahua, it was called *"el camino de Nuevo México."* From New

---

3    Joaquín Francisco Pacheco, Francisco de Cárdenas y Espejo, and Luis Torres deMendoza (eds.). *Colección de documentos ineditos, relativos al descubrimiento, conquista y organización de las antiguas posesiones españolas de América y Oceania, sacados de los archivos del reino, y muy especialmente del de Indias. Competemente autorizada.* Madrid: Ministerio de Ultramar, 1864-84. Miguel Encinias, Alfred Rodríguez and Joseph P. Sánchez (Trans. and eds.). *Gaspar Pérez de Villagrá's historia de la Nueva Mexico, 1610.* Albuquerque: University of New Mexico Press, 1992.

Mexico, the segment south was called *"el camino de Chihuahua."* But, in general, it was still the "Royal Road."

Finally, in 1848, by dint of war and the Treaty of Guadalupe Hidalgo, the United States annexed a portion of Mexican territory that became the states of New Mexico, Colorado, Arizona, Utah, Nevada, and California. *El Camino Real de Tierra Adentro* from El Paso to Santa Fe now belonged to the United States. In time, it linked with the Santa Fe Trail from Missouri to Santa Fe when Anglo-American traders began trading with Chihuahua. Then, a new era began for the *Camino Real*, for a portion of it became known as the Santa Fe-Chihuahua Trail. Another trail, Old Spanish Trail, emanated from the Camino Real at Santa Fe threaded its way to Los Angeles via southern Utah. It, too, was designated by Congress as a National Historic Trail in 2002. For that reason, nineteenth-century sources were used in this historical-geographical dictionary to prove the existence of places along the route of the Camino Real used by travelers in previous centuries and to compare their descriptions of them in the evolving historical process as it and other trails came into being.

There are many people to thank in assisting to develop the historical dictionary that follows. A debt of gratitude is owed the staff at the Spanish Colonial Research Center at the University of New Mexico. Among those who contributed assistance to this effort are Dr. Angelica Sánchez-Clark, Carrie Finnance and Dr. Jerry L. Gurule. Dr. Ramon Olivas of the "old" National Park Service's Mexico Affairs Office in Las Cruces, deserves special mention for his efforts and his tireless work with INAH directors in Mexico to preserve the history of the Camino Real. A debt is also owed to the Institutio Nacional de Antropología e Historia (INAH) and the many INAH directors along the route of the Camino Real who assisted to promote the significance of the trail in Mexico. Mexican historians Chantal Cramaussel and Salvador Alvarez as well as Anthropologist José Luis Perea, then director de INAH Centro Chihuahua and Dr. José de la Cruz Pacheco, then director de INAH Centro Zacatecas, are especially recognized for their assistance in contributing to this historical guide. The staff at the Center for Southwest Research, Zimmerman Library, University of New Mexico, were especially generous of their time in assisting our research efforts. Additionally, the staffs of the Archivo General de Indias (AGI), Sevilla, Spain, the Archivo General de la Nación

(AGN), Mexico City, and the State of New Mexico Record Center and Archive, Santa Fe, New Mexico provided assistance in the research of this book. Finally, a special word of acknowledgment and gratitude is owed to Paul Rhetts of LPD Press and Rio Grande Books. His special and caring work as publisher has brought out the best attributes of this book.

Joseph P. Sánchez
Albuquerque, New Mexico
July 18, 2011

## Map 1: *El Camino Real de Tierra Adentro*—Mexico City to San Juan de los Caballeros

# El Camino Real de Tierra Adentro
by
Joseph P. Sánchez

The development of roads is, of necessity, a significant function in the historical evolution of nation states. The historic roads of New Spain, present Mexico, are as much prehistoric in character and purpose, and their development prior to European intrusions, influenced the location of many colonial roads that were established between 1521 and 1821. Aside from Spanish military needs, the colonial economic development of New Spain led to the continual development of roads throughout the Viceregal Period, 1535-1821. During the colonial period, internal and external economic developments were intricately tied to indigenous routes that similarly had been used for trade, transportation of people and things as well as for war. Although Pre-Columbian roads were not well developed beyond the central highlands, routes and corridors from the Central Valley to places lying beyond the edges of the Aztec domain were well-defined for travel. Unlike the roads developed by Europeans for wagons and animals of burden, indigenous trails were relatively primitive and generally used for foot traffic. In contrast, late sixteenth century Spanish colonial roads combined primitive trails with ones newly constructed, some with bridges, to areas with economic potential. Historically, the east-west and south-north pathways from Mexico City followed the pattern of conquest, economic expansion to mining areas, and the transhumance of the livestock industry. Very early in the colonial period, roads which connected major cities became part of a network of trunk roads known as *caminos reales*. One such road was *El Camino Real de Tierra Adentro* which ran from Mexico City to Santa Fe in New Mexico. In its historical development, it followed the paths of miners, ranchers, soldiers, missionaries and native and European emigrants who settled places along the way. Narrative accounts of the route describe its variants throughout the 16th, 17th, 18th, and 19th centuries. They contain a wealth of information about the topography as well as onomastic forms of place names along the trail. The scholarship of the selected literature examined herein focuses on one specific problem: the tracing of the route and the variants of *El Camino Real de Tierra Adentro* throughout its colonial history.

## The Four Principal *Caminos Reales* of New Spain

The significant historical longevity of the *caminos reales* in New Spain is easily tested through contemporary descriptions of them from the earliest times to the end of Spanish colonial rule in the early nineteenth century. In his *Ensayo Político*, published in 1808, Alejandro de Humboldt, identified four major *caminos reales* that had played significant roles in the economic and demographic development of New Spain and its frontier areas.[1] The first was the road from Mexico City to Veracruz which ran through Puebla de Xalapa; the second was the one that ran from Mexico City to Acapulco by way of Chilpanzingo; the third ran from Mexico City to Guatemala via Oaxaca; and the fourth ran a long course from Mexico City to Durango and beyond Chihuahua, then known as Nueva Vizcaya, to Santa Fe in New Mexico.[2] That road, wrote Humboldt, "is popularly called *El Camino*

---

1   Alejandro de Humboldt, *Ensayo Político sobre el reyno de Nueva España*, 1808 (Madrid: Imprenta de Núñez, 1818), I:296.

2   The four roads are discussed in Woodrow Borah, "Early Colonial Trade and Navigation Between Mexico and Peru," *Ibero-Americana* (1954), 38:27; John K. Chance, *Race and Class in Colonial Oaxaca* (Stanford: Stanford University Press:1978), 54; Philip Wayne Powell, *Soldiers, Indians & Silver* (Berkeley: University of California Press, 1952), 20; Peter William Rees, "Route Inertia and Route Competition: An Historical Geography of Transportation Between Mexico City and Vera Cruz," Ph.D. diss.

*Real de Tierra Adentro,*"³ the royal road of the interior.

The road from Mexico City eastward to Veracruz, considered to be the first *camino real,* was established very early in the colonial history of Mexico. By 1590, an alternate route, the one mentioned by Humboldt, had been established from Veracruz through Orizaba and Puebla to Mexico City.⁴ The original route with its indigenous precedences ran from Veracruz to Jalapa, Chalco, Texcoco, Venta de Caceras (present Oriental), and finally, Mexico City. Both routes continued to serve Mexico City from Veracruz on the east coast throughout the colonial period.

The route westward from Mexico City to Acapulco was opened by 1547. The road began in Mexico City and ran to Cuernavaca and Tuspa whence it crossed the Río de las Balsas through Chilpancingo, and finally to Acapulco. It was not until the 1570s when the Manila trade got underway that the route gained in importance.⁵ Although the road did not accommodate wagons during the sixteenth century, it was adequate for pack trains.

The southern route from Mexico City to Oaxaca to Guatemala was begun in 1529.⁶ Its route was varied, and it passed through many towns. By the mid-sixteenth century, it connected Mexico City via several routes. One route went south through Cuernavaca, thence southeast to Izúcar. From Izúcar the route turned southeast through Acatlan and the valleys of Tamazualapan, Teposcolula, and Nochixtlan to the Valley of Oaxaca. Another road from Mexico City ran from Puebla to Tepeaca, Tecamachalco, Tehuacan, Cuicatlan and Seda. The segments of these roads were constructed between 1531 and 1548.

The route from Mexico City northward represented the historical development of mining, ranching and farming that accompanied the push into the Gran Chichimeca. The period between 1545 and 1555 witnessed

---

University of California at Berkeley, 1971, 112; and William Lytle Schurz, *The Manila Galleon* (New York: E.P. Dutton and Co. 1939), 385.

3    Humboldt, *Ensayo Político,* 296.

4    Humboldt, *Ensayo Político,* 296. Also see, Rees, "Route Inertia and Route Competition: An Historical Geography of Transportation Between Mexico City and Vera Cruz," p. 112.

5    Schurz, *The Manila Galleon,* p. 385.

6    Chance, *Race and Class,* p. 54.

the opening of roads that led to the mining areas between Querétaro and Zacatecas.[7] In the early 1540s, as Spanish miners expanded northward, Viceroy Antonio de Mendoza made land grants for settlers in the area, mostly for pasturelands for livestock. The discovery of silver in Zacatecas in 1546 was the impetus for construction of new roads. During that time, the *camino real* was extended from Mexico City to Querétaro to Zacatecas. The expansion of the road during that period allowed for passage of pack trains and caravans of large wagons as well as made possible the opening of supply routes between Zacatecas, Guadalajara, and Michoacán.

Humboldt, moreover, recalled that *El Camino Real de Tierra Adentro* in its historical denouement ran from Mexico to Querétaro to Guanajuato and Durango beyond to Guautitlan, Huehuetoca, and the Puerto de los Reyes close to the hills near Bata "which rise 80 meters above the level of the Plaza Mayor of Mexico."[8] All roads led to and from Mexico City, and the *caminos reales* were the main thoroughfares of the colonial traffic to all parts of the Mexican viceroyalty.

## The Sixteenth Century *Camino Real*

The longest of the four *caminos reales* in New Spain was *El Camino Real de Tierra Adentro* that ran from Mexico City to Santa Fe in New Mexico. As an emigrant trail in the sixteenth century, *El Camino Real de Tierra Adentro*, as it came to be known because it traversed nearly the entire length of the interior of present Mexico, took on significance as the first step in the northward expansion of Spanish settlements and the development of a mining frontier.

The first phases of the march northward from Mexico City took place in the late 1540s as silver mines were discovered in Querétaro, Guanajuato, San Luis Potosí, and Zacatecas. The first silver rush, the first wagon trains of settlers, and the first cattle drives in North America took place along this trail. Indeed, the first Forty-niners in North American history were those who rushed to the silver mines before the decade of the 1540s was over. The establishment of Zacatecas in 1546 represented an important phase of the development of the trail as Spanish settlers pushed northward

---

7    Powell, *Soldiers, Indians & Silver*, p. 20.

8    Humboldt, *Ensayo político*, 144.

to other fields, thus expanding the settlement pattern beyond the Zacate-cas-Durango frontier line. With expansion came demands for protection and pacification of the area. To that end, missionaries and soldiers moved forward to establish religious and military institutions along the route.

Significantly, the silver strike at Zacatecas served as the cause for ex-pansion northward. By 1549, the well-traveled road from Mexico City to Zacatecas attracted the attention of Viceroy Antonio de Mendoza as new roads from the agricultural fields of Michoacán, Guanajuato, and Queré-taro developed to supply workers in the mines. In 1952, Philip Wayne Powell defined the historical route from Querétaro to Zacatecas by exam-ining the principal settlements and stopping places (*parajes)* for the evolv-ing *camino real* as follows:

> Going north from Mexico City, the route of travel was already well defined as far as Querétaro by the time of the Zacatecas discovery. There was a regular traffic of merchants, officials, cattlemen, and livestock through this province of Jilotepec, a region that did not offer great travel difficulties. The principal settlements and stopping places for the traffic were Cuautitlán, Tepejí, Jilotepec, and San Juan del Río. Between Querétaro and the later foundation of San Felipe there were two main roads toward Zacate-cas. One went northwest direct to San Miguel, then along the east bank of the San Miguel River toward San Felipe. The other went north from Querétaro passed just to the east of the Nieto Pass (where a road branched off to San Miguel, then turned northwest through Jofre Pass (near the later San Luis de la Paz), passing through the llanos called La Mohina, and joining with the other road at a point between the Río de los Sauces and San Felipe. The combined road then went north west through the *portezu-elo* of San Felipe to Ojuelos. Just beyond Ojuelos it passed a point known as Encinillas, which was considered to be the dividing line on the Zacatecas highway between the *audiencias* of Nueva Galicia and Mexico. From Encinillas the road passed through Las Bocas and Ciénega Grande (both fortified by the viceregal government during the

1570s), then on to the *paraje* del Cuicillo, nine leagues from Zacatecas, where it joined another road going north from Michoacán.[9]

The Spanish league, particularly in the eighteenth century, is generally reckoned to be 2.6 miles. Travelers were often surprisingly accurate in their measurement of distance traveled in a day.

By 1575, the frontier line had, moved as far north as the Santa Barbara-Parral in present Chihuahua. Presidios between Querétaro and Durango dotted the road and defined the importance of protecting the settlement pattern. For example, during the period 1570 to 1600, presidios between Querétaro and Guanajuato at Maxcala, Jofre, and Atotonilco marked the beginning of the route. In that same period, the progression of the presidial line moved north of there to Jasó, Portezuelo, Ojuelos, Bocas, Cíenega Grande, Cuicillo, and Palmillas reaching Zacatecas. Beyond Zacatecas, just south of Durango, the presidial garrisons at San Martín and Llerena for a while marked the northernmost end of *El Camino Real de Tierra Adentro*. Then, with the establishment of New Mexico by Juan de Oñate in 1598, the trail took a major jump from Santa Bárbara to the confluence of the Río Chama and the Río Grande.

In 1595, Viceroy Velasco and Juan de Oñate agreed on a formal contract for the settlement of New Mexico.[10] Under the terms of the contract, which developed a history of its own owing to several disputes between Oñate and the Viceroy Velasco, Oñate would pay all expenses for the expeditionary force, except for the Franciscan missionaries who were subsidized by the *Patronato Real* [the royal patronage], a special fund for missionaries. In return for underwriting certain expenses, Oñate would receive a salary, and hold the title of *adelantado*. Additionally, he would serve as governor and captain general in command of all troops within his jurisdiction, and he would administer the *encomienda*, a feudal collection of tribute from Indians under Spanish control. Generally, if Indians could not pay the tribute, the amount due was converted to payment in servitude. There were

---

9    Powell, *Soldiers, Indians & Silver*, pp. 17-18.

10   Herbert E. Bolton, ed., *Spanish Exploration in the Southwest, 1542-1706* (New York: Charles Scribner's Son, 1916). 201.

other provisions stipulated in his contract.[11] Even so, Oñate hoped to develop an entailed estate (*mayorazgo*) from lands acquired in New Mexico. On January 26, 1598, after much delay and great expenditure to Oñate, the expedition was permitted to leave for New Mexico. In a great cloud of dust, the slow-moving, oxen-pulled *carreta* caravan creaked out of the Valle de San Bartolomé in Nueva Vizcaya, present Chihuahua. Driving thousands of sheep, pigs, goats, cattle, mules, and horses, the soldiers and settlers began the trek to their new homeland far to the north. Scouts, led by the Sargento Mayor Vicente de Zaldívar, nephew of Oñate, wandered far ahead of the wagon to find an easier route with water and pasturage.[12] As they approached the Río Grande, light snow had fallen in the area as a cold wind swept the desert of northern Chihuahua.

For months on end, the air of northern Chihuahua resounded with the sharp cracks made by the whips of drivers as they pushed the caravan farther into the *tierra adentro*. By the end of April 1598, they had reached the Río Grande. Of the event, the author of the "Itinerario," the main diary of the expedition, wrote:

> On April 30, 1598, day of the Ascension of our Lord, at this Río del Norte Governor Don Juan de Oñate took possession of all the kingdoms and provinces of New Mexico, in the name of King Felipe [II], our lord, in the presence of Juan Pérez de Donis, royal notary and secretary of the jurisdiction and expedition. There was a sermon, a great ecclesiastical and secular celebration, a great salute and rejoicing, and in the afternoon, a comedy. The royal standard was blessed and placed in charge of Francisco de Sosa Peñalosa, the royal ensign.[13]

They followed the river to a point where the mountains came down

11  Bolton, ed., *Spanish Exploration*, 201.
12  Joseph P. Sánchez, *The Río Abajo Frontier, 1540-1692: A History of Early Colonial New Mexico* (Albuquerque: Albuquerque Museum History Monograph Series, 1987), 54.
13  Itinerario in Pacheco, Joaquín F., Cárdenas, Francisco de, y Torres de Mendoza, Luis, eds., *Colección de Documentos Inéditos Relativos al Descubrimiento, Conquista y Organización de las Antiguas Posesiones Españoles de América y Oceanía* (hereinafter cited as *CDI*) (Madrid, 1864-1865, 42 vols.), XVI:242.

to form "the pass of the river and the ford." The crossing was named "Los Puertos,"[14] although later it would be known as El Paso. In that desolate land, the warm spring sun of May 4 witnessed the activity as Oñate's army and forty Indians moved their cargo, carts, and livestock across the river. It was near there that they met the first Indians from New Mexico. It was there they stopped to give thanks to their God, for bringing them safely to that point in their travel northward. It was the first European thanksgiving in North America.

Looking northward into the *tierra adentro* beyond the river crossing of El Paso, Oñate realized, "There is no other road for carts for many leagues."[15] The Spaniards would have to blaze their own road. He asked the Indians about Cíbola, and they responded "very clearly by signs that the settlements were six days distant, or eight days along the route of travel" for the carts. But Oñate's opinion about there being "no other road" was soon contradicted. Before the day was over, "we passed the ruts made by ten carts that Castaño and Morlete took out from New Mexico"[16] about six years earlier. Indeed, some of Oñate's men had been with Morlete.

Ten days later, they moved up the desolate trail, now stopping to repair their carts; now stopping to observe a holy day of obligation; now stopping to wonder about the place "where it is said that Captain Morlete hanged four Indians because they had stolen some horses."[17] The summer rains and heat alternated as often as the thirst and hunger that afflicted the slow-moving wagon train that passed below the Sierra del Olvido with its craggy spirals which rose a short distance to the east of the Río del Norte. The range, present Organ Mountains, received its name because Oñate's men who had been with Morlete could not remember ever having seen them. Eight decades later, the Sierra del Olvido, named for the forgetfulness of Oñate's men upon entering New Mexico, would be renamed "Los Organos" by Spaniards fleeing the province in the Pueblo Revolt of 1680.

At this point, near the vicinity of present Las Cruces, Oñate, the Father Commissary Friar Cristóbal de Salazar, Juan de Zaldívar, Vicente de

---

14   Itinerario, *CDI*, XVI:244. The date was 4 May 1598.

15   Itinerario, *CDI*, XVI:244. The date was 4 May 1598.

16   Itinerario, *CDI*, XVI:244-45. The date was 11 May 1598.

17   Itinerario, *CDI*, XVI:235. The date was 11 May 1598.

Zaldívar and a complement of sixty horsemen set out for the Indian settlements far to the north. They rode ahead of the caravan to prepare the pueblos for their coming;[18] and, as the expedition was in need of supplies, Oñate hoped to replenish the supplies.

Beyond the Sierra del Olvido to the east lay a plain that would be easier for the carts to travel despite its lack of water. The writer of the "Itinerario" noted that "We all fared badly on account of the river, toward the west. On this day, when a dog appeared with muddy paws and hind feet, we searched for some water holes. At a place commemorated as *El Perrillo* [the little dog], Captain Gaspar de Villagrá found one and Cristóbal Sánchez another, not far from where we were, toward the river."[19]

The trail away from the river was overcome after much hardship to man and beast. "We were exploring and feeling our way along the entire route for the first time, and we suffered a great deal because of not knowing it....We went six leagues to the marsh of the *mesilla guinea*, so-called because [the rock on] it was black."[20] The date was 27 May 1598; they were near present San Marcial on a flat, marshy plain below a round top of black rock. They had crossed a plain, later known as the Jornada del Muerto, deadman's journey, which is about eighty miles long. After one more day, they camped at a pueblo called Qualacú on the northern end of the jornada and at the southern end of the Río Abajo, a relative geographical reference meaning the lower part of the Río Grande which ran from Cochití Pueblo in the north to a point near San Marcial.

The cart train moved out along the east bank of the Río Abajo and by mid-June reached the pueblo of Teypana, which the Spaniards called Socorro because the people there "furnished us with much maiz." One of the Teypana leaders, Letoc, spoke Piro and communicated to the Spaniards about the other pueblos they would pass on their trek northward. Most of them, however, were abandoned in fear of the Spaniards and their terrible weapons and horses. The caravan passed by the abandoned pueblos north of Socorro and left them undisturbed. Somewhere north of Socorro, the Spaniards recrossed the river and traveled along the east bank on slight-

---

18   Itinerario, *CDI*, XVI:247. The date was 22 May 1598.
19   Itinerario, *CDI*, XVI:248. The date was 23 May 1598.
20   Itinerario, *CDI*, XVI:249.

ly flatter terrain. Shortly they reached an abandoned pueblo they called Nueva Sevilla, which later maps would show as Sevilleta. There, in the abandoned pueblo, the settlers camped for a week.[21]

Meanwhile, Oñate's nephews, the Maese de Campo Juan de Zaldívar and the Sargento Mayor Vicente de Zaldívar, explored the nearby pueblos northeast of the camp. Although some of the pueblos they visited were on the Río Grande, the Zaldívar brothers were attracted to those east of the large Sierra Morena, present Manzano Mountain Range. Where today's Abó Pass—which the Spaniards later called *el portuelo* [the little gateway]—comes into view from the river, the small scouting party turned east. At the southern end of the Manzanos, they visited other pueblos, doubtless seen by Antonio de Espejo in 1583 and probably by Sánchez Chamuscado in 1581. Upon their return to Nueva Sevilla, the Zaldívars reported having seen many pueblos on the other side of the mountain. One of them they identified by the fascinating name of "Aboó."[22] It was around 22 June 1598, when the Zaldívar brothers "discovered" the ancient pueblo. Soon after, they rejoined the expedition.

From their camp at Nueva Sevilla, Oñate led a detachment of some sixty horsemen northward once again. Passing through the valley of Puaray, they saw many pueblos and cultivated fields on both sides of the Río Abajo within the area of present Albuquerque. Most of the pueblos of Puaray, located along the river, had been abandoned, for they lived in fear of a returning Spanish army. Their lore constantly reminded them of the war of "fire and sword" waged on them by Francisco Vázquez de Coronado almost six decades earlier. By 1598, their fear, caused by having killed Friar Agustín Rodríguez and his missionary companions in 1581, seemed to loom over Puaray like a curse. Almost every time a Spanish expedition passed by, the people fled to the Sandia Mountains or to nearby pueblos. Although Oñate had no such intentions, the people of Puaray and those of other pueblos believed that the Spaniards would seek revenge for the deaths of the missionaries.

Oñate and his horsemen, nonetheless, rode past the abandoned Puaray

21   Itinerario, *CDI*, XVI:251.

22   Itinerario, *CDI*, XVI:252.

to the Keres pueblo known as Santo Domingo.[23] They knew of the pueblo because of the eventful arrest of Gaspar Castaño de Sosa by Juan de Mor-lete in 1592. There the Spaniards sought out two of the Mexican Indians, Tomás and Cristóbal, who had been with Castaño and had decided to remain at Santo Domingo. Oñate needed them as translators. Although Spanish activities along the Río Abajo between Nueva Sevilla and Santo Domingo had been peaceful, Tomás and Cristóbal were taken by surprise[24] and quickly impressed into service as interpreters.

Although the Santo Domingo Indians looked on with guarded dis-pleasure, they soon realized that Oñate intended them no harm. Oñate, through his Mexican Indian interpreters, called a general council at Santo Domingo and invited the seven nearby pueblos to send representatives. Once the council was assembled, Governor Oñate, speaking through Tomás and Cristóbal, explained the purpose of the new Spanish presence among them and asked each leader to pledge obedience to the Spanish Crown, an act which he believed they comprehended.[25] Then he announced that Santo Domingo would be the site of a Franciscan convent dedicated to Nuestra Señora de la Asunción and that the patron saints of the pueblo would be Peter and Paul.[26] Convinced that peace had been established among the pueblos of the Río Abajo and the Spaniards, Oñate departed Santo Domingo in a northward direction.

Seeking a place to settle, Oñate and his men pushed their horses along the Río Arriba, the geographic reference to the upper Río Grande between Cochiti and Taos pueblos, where Castaño de Sosa and his men had been eight years before. En route, Oñate passed the pueblo called Bove, which he named San Ildefonso in honor of the expedition's father commissary, Fray Alonso Martínez.[27] Having passed much of the land which Castaño de Sosa had described, they reached the confluence of the Río Grande and the Río Chama. There, on 4 July 1598, at a small pueblo called Caypa, Oñate set up camp. He renamed the pueblo San Juan de los Caballeros

23 Itinerario, *CDI*, XVI:252-53.
24 Itinerario, *CDI*, XVI:253.
25 Itinerario, *CDI*, XVI:256.
26 Itinerario, *CDI*, XVI:254.
27 Itinerario, *CDI*, XVI:256.

and ordered the Maese de Campo Juan de Zaldívar and a small contingent of soldiers to return to Nueva Sevilla and bring up the settlers.[28] By mid-August the settlers and sixty-one carts had arrived at San Juan. Of the eighty-three wagons that had begun the expedition, twenty-two had been left along the trail between El Paso and Nueva Sevilla. Because of their value to colonial transportation, they would be retrieved at a later date.[29] The expedition to settle New Mexico had taken nearly eight months. The route they established would extend *El Camino Real de Tierra Adentro* nearly 650 miles. It would become the major road connecting the New Mexican outpost with the rest of the Spanish empire for the rest of the colonial period.

The expedition of Juan de Oñate had blazed a new segment to the *camino real*. Unlike miners and ranchers who pushed the frontier northward from Mexico City by establishing towns, haciendas and mining districts, virtually taking one step at a time, Juan de Oñate and his expedition of settlers to New Mexico in 1598 were users of an established trail lined with Spanish settlements and presidios. Beyond Santa Barbara, Oñate's scouts blazed a direct route almost due north to the Río Grande. Their descriptions were usually in the form of day to day reports of what they had seen when they followed rutted portions of the *camino real* or when they blazed a new direct route to the Río Grande from Santa Barbara to a point near present El Paso before moving northward to the pueblo world of New Mexico.

## The Seventeenth Century *Camino Real*

After 1600 and before 1700, the presidial line followed the settlement pattern along the Royal Road as it turned northeast toward El Pasaje, then zagged northwest to El Gallo, south of Mapimí, then northerly to Cerro Gordo south of Parral and the presidio of Conchos north of there. Before the century ended, the northernmost garrison was at El Paso.

Spanish frontiersmen depended on the presidial line to defend their properties. Land grants, *estancias*, farmlands, and other estates specifying land tenure developed along the *Camino Real*. By the end of the 1600s, a

---

28  Itinerario, *CDI*, XVI:254-56.
29  Itinerario, *CDI*, XVI:254-56.

new definition operated along the Royal Road. The word *hacienda*, which once meant moveable property such as harvest and livestock haciendas, now extended to include mining haciendas.[30] The mill, animal driven or water powered, characterized the harvest and mining haciendas. The words mill and hacienda became interchangeable. Along the *Camino Real* countless mills were constructed and, because of their economic importance, became associated with place names along the route. In time, haciendas with their mills were associated with extensive land holding patterns characterized by large fortified houses. So impressive were certain haciendas that they became towns on the *Camino Real*. Travelers on the Royal Road depended on haciendas for shelter and protection.

Presidios, haciendas, mines, frontier settlements and Indian pueblos dotted the route of the *Camino Real*. In 1940, Joaquín Ramírez Cabañas edited *Descripción Geográfica de los Reinos de Nueva Galicia, Nueva Vizcaya y Nueva Leon por D. Alonso de la Mota y Escobar*. Through the eyes of Bishop Alonso Mota y Escobar, one is able to see how life on the linear frontier of the *Camino Real* operated as Spain expanded its effective claim deeper and deeper into the interior of New Spain in the early seventeenth century. The development of the road as seen by Bishop Mota y Escobar reveals the route along the *Camino Real* between Lagos and Cuencamé. The widest east-west extension of his pastoral *visita* presents a panoramic guide to a frontier stretching from the west coast of Sinaloa eastward to Nuevo Leon near the Gulf of Mexico. The long south to north extension of his travels ran from Colima to Nueva Vizcaya, present Chihuahua.[31]

Bishop Mota y Escobar was born in Mexico City, on May 18, 1546, of Captain Gerónimo Ruíz de la Mota and Catalina Iñiguez de Escobar.[32] Having spent his life as a churchman, Mota y Escobar became bishop of Guadalajara in 1597. Later, in 1606, he was appointed to the bishopric of Puebla where he served until his death in 1625.[33] Following an Indian uprising at Topia in Nueva Galicia in 1601, Mota y Escobar, as bishop of Guadalajara, undertook a pastoral inspection of the province. With his

30  François Chevalier, *Land and Society in Colonial Mexico: The Great Hacienda* (Berkeley: University of California Press, 1963), 266.

31  Ramírez Cabañas, ed., *Descripción Geográfica*, p. 15.

32  Ramírez Cabañas, ed., *Descripción Geográfica*, pp. 9-10.

33  Ramírez Cabañas, ed., *Descripción Geográfica*, p. 14.

known zeal, he traveled extensively throughout Nueva Galicia and recorded from his detailed notes his *Descripción Geográfica de la Nueva Galicia*,
between 1602 and 1605.[34]

In his eyewitness account, Bishop Mota y Escobar gave information
about towns, their founding, and their purpose. Everywhere Bishop Mota
y Escobar went, he noted which towns had mills, which had cattle, which
had mines, which had stores, and which religious orders ministered sacra-
ments to frontiersmen in peril of losing their souls. His descriptions of
small villages or settlements, his scrupulously kept statistics about people
and animals, his observations about the land, mines, mills, commerce, eth-
nography, and politics along the route painted an extraordinary picture
of the line of settlement along the *Camino Real* and other areas in Nueva
Galicia.

He noted, for example, that Lagos was situated on the *Camino Real*
that went from Mexico City to Zacatecas, one of the most traveled roads of
the period. Lagos, wrote Bishop Mota y Escobar, was established in 1561
as a defensive post against Indians, but equally so, because of the fertility of
the soil, the two rivers and a large lake in the area which contributed to its
agricultural potential. Bishop Mota y Escobar pointed out that firewood
was scarce because Lagos was so far from the wooded mountains in the
vicinity.[35] Cerro Gordo, a nearby mountain, was a haven for enemy Indian
tribes which included the Copuces, the Zacatecas, and the Guachichiles
who raided Spanish settlements including Lagos. The structures at Lagos, he wrote, were architecturally more like towers and fortifications than
well ordered residences. Lagos had twenty Spanish citizens, who appeared
quite wealthy compared to others in the vicinity. A parish church was fi-
nanced through tithing. Well situated along the *Camino Real*, Lagos was
blessed by two rivers nearby that provided catfish and other fish. A large
lake close to Lagos provided wildlife that supplemented the village diet.[36]
On the *Camino Real*, Lagos was well supplied with all kinds of clothes,

---

34   Ramírez Cabañas, ed., *Descripción Geográfica*, pp. 14-15.
35   Joaquín Ramírez Cabañas, editor, *Descripción Geográfica de los Reinos de Nueva
     Galicia, Nueva Vizcaya y Nueva Leon por d. Alonso de la Mota y Escobar* (Mexico,
     D.F.: Editorial Pedro Robredo, 1940), pp. 121-123.
36   Ramírez Cabañas, ed., *Descripción Geográfica*, p. 122.

wine, vinegar, raisins, and almonds from Mexico and other provisions.[37] Bishop Mota y Escobar felt Lagos was one of the best situated towns in Nueva Galicia.[38]

In contrast, he saw the Villa of Aguascalientes when it was still a growing village with adobe houses badly laid out. In its midst was a parish church. Then, Aguascalientes was mostly inhabited by poor, but rugged, mestizo frontiersmen who herded cattle.[39] Aguascalientes, wrote Bishop Mota y Escobar, was so named "for some hot springs which are near there; a year around arroyo runs past the houses from which all the neighbors drink, and although the water runs hot, it neither tastes like *asufre, alumbre* nor *herrumbre*, when it is chilled, the water is very sweet and salubrious."[40] The people were poor and served the large landowners by herding their large herds of varied livestock. At Aguascalientes the people did not farm. When they did trade it was only for mares, horses, mules, and cattle.[41] Zacatecas was not far from there.

Regarding Zacatecas, Bishop Mota y Escobar, revealed something about daily life in towns on the *Camino Real*. Rich in gold and silver,[42] the hills around Zacatecas formed a fabulous treasure waiting to be excavated. They were discovered in 1540 by Juan de Tolosa, a Basque.[43] La Bufa, a large hill, held rich deposits which made Zacatecas one of the wealthiest areas on the *Camino Real*. The common language of Zacatecas was Spanish, but many indigenous tongues were spoken owing to the presence of a sizeable population of *"mexicanos, otomíes, tarascos* and other nations."[44] Zacatecas was filled with various mechanics, tailors, carpenters, and smiths.[45] Among other resources in Zacatecas, he noted that firewood was expensive because settlers had denuded the vicinity of trees. Firewood was carted in on the

---

37  Ramírez Cabañas, ed., *Descripción Geográfica*, p. 123.

38  Ramírez Cabañas, ed., *Descripción Geográfica*, p. 122.

39  Ramírez Cabañas, ed., *Descripción Geográfica*, p. 124.

40  Ramírez Cabañas, *Descripción Geográfica*, 124.

41  Ramírez Cabañas, *Descripción Geográfica*, 124.

42  Ramírez Cabañas, *Descripción Geográfica*, 139.

43  Ramírez Cabañas, *Descripción Geográfica*, 140.

44  Ramírez Cabañas, *Descripción Geográfica*, 145.

45  Ramírez Cabañas, *Descripción Geográfica*, 146.

large, solid wheel *carretas* and sold at the highest price. The situation was similar at Lagos. In Zacatecas, Spaniards, Mestizos, Indian laborers, black and mulatto slaves lived in many of the 300 adobe houses, which were nothing more than hovels, with a few stone structures. He described four plazas that were connected by one main road. Franciscans, Jesuits and Augustinians competed in Zacatecas, for there was only one parish church. Among his many observations, Bishop Mota y Escobar wrote about the history and politics of the mines in Zacatecas.[46]

At Fresnillo, he saw 12 mills and, at the *Hacienda de Medina* on the northern edge of the Zacatecas mining frontier, he headed toward Nueva Vizcaya (present Chihuahua), where he saw cultivated fields, livestock, and mills for processing silver.[47] Beyond there, at Pueblo de Sain, he saw livestock in the area and two water-run mills for processing ore, indications of an incipient economy based on mining.[48] At Sombrerete, which he called Real de Minas de Sombrerete and Villa de Llerena, he wrote that the richest ores had already been extracted although five or six haciendas with their mills were still in operation along with a Franciscan *convento*.[49] Just west of Sombrerete, Bishop Mota y Escobar found *Real de Minas de San Martín,* in mountainous terrain. He noted its economic decline as a mining area with five or six Spanish residents sustained by groves of apple trees, a product in demand among miners in the area.[50]

Traveling northward past Chalchihuites to Valle de Suchil, located between Sombrerete and Nombre de Dios in present Durango, Bishop Mota y Escobar was impressed with its fertility and its eight productive farms.[51] Beyond there, he veered west toward Nombre de Dios. Once there, Mota y Escobar described the town as hot and humid with a stream that carried water year around. Nombre de Dios, he wrote had been founded to defend the road from Chichimeca raiders. At that time, Nombre de Dios was a *paraje*, or stopping place on the *Camino Real* situated on the northern edge

---

46 Ramírez Cabañas, ed., *Descripción Geográfica,* 139-155.
47 Ramírez Cabañas, ed., *Descripción Geográfica,* p. 174.
48 Ramírez Cabañas, ed., *Descripción Geográfica,* p. 175.
49 Ramírez Cabañas, ed., *Descripción Geográfica,* p. 176-177.
50 Ramírez Cabañas, ed., *Descripción Geográfica,* p. 177.
51 Ramírez Cabañas, ed., *Descripción Geográfica,* p. 179.

of Nueva Galicia. At the time of his *visita*, Nombre de Dios had fifteen or twenty resident Spaniards living in small adobe houses who owned large farmlands nearby. Near there, 50-70 Indians lived in a small pueblo with a Franciscan convent.[52]

In the vicinity of Nombre de Dios at Asiento del Capitán Loiz, Bishop Mota y Escobar found four water-driven mills, some for processing ore and others for grinding wheat. He also observed livestock and an abundance of wildlife in the area. From there, he went to Real de Minas de las Nieves and saw much livestock, plentiful water, and large cultivated fields. There, he saw four or five mills for processing ore and a mule-driven mill.

West of there was the working Estancia del Comendador Rodrigo del Río with large numbers of slaves, Indian servants and mulattoes who worked as herders and field hands.[53] Beyond Real de Joachín and San Juan de Mezquital, inhabited by 100 Chichimecas, Bishop Mota y Escobar reached Gracián, which was known for its coal mines.[54]

On to La Punta by way of Valle de las Poanas, Bishop Mota y Escobar mentioned crossing a large stream called Los Berros.[55] From there, Mota y Escobar traveled to Tunal, a pueblo of peaceful Chichimeca farmers. A Franciscan priest attended to their spiritual needs.[56] At this point Mota y Escobar had meandered in and around present Durango and, barely six miles from there, had turned southwest. Not far from Avino, Mota y Escobar passed through Peñol Blanco, a place with several mines and two water-driven mills.[57]

From there, Bishop Mota y Escobar, again changing directions, meandered to Cuencamé. Of the mines there, he wrote that they had been recently discovered, sometime in 1601. Most of the mines were on one mountain. A parish church had already been constructed there to serve over a hundred Spanish residents. Franciscan missionaries worked among

52  Ramírez Cabañas, ed., *Descripción Geográfica*, pp. 179-180.
53  Ramírez Cabañas, ed., *Descripción Geográfica*, pp. 182-183.
54  Ramírez Cabañas, ed., *Descripción Geográfica*, p. 184.
55  Ramírez Cabañas, ed., *Descripción Geográfica*, pp. 180 and 185.
56  Ramírez Cabañas, ed., *Descripción Geográfica*, p. 193.
57  Ramírez Cabañas, ed., *Descripción Geográfica*, p. 194.

the Chichimecas after whom the town was named.[58]

Beyond there, Bishop Mota y Escobar's next stop was in the Valle de San Bartolomé. There he saw all kinds of crops and livestock owing to an irrigation system. Industrious frontiersmen had built mills for flour to sell to nearby miners. Wildlife abounded and Mota y Escobar reported seeing geese, ducks, and cranes at a marsh not far from the Spanish settlement. At that time, Franciscans from Santa Barbara made weekly visitations to the parish church there.[59] Nearby, at Todos Santos, Bishop Mota y Escobar noted eight to ten Spaniards running a mule driven mill there. Aside from an abundance of water and wildlife, they raised wheat and other crops as well as livestock for sustenance. Mota y Escobar wrote that Todos Santos was the last settlement in the northwestern part of Nueva Vizcaya. Beyond that point began the large expanse leading to New Mexico.[60]

Were it not for the diligent eye of Alonso de Benavides, the Franciscan prelate and custodian of the Holy Office of the Inquisition in New Mexico in 1626, a panoramic view of the *Camino Real* in New Mexico would be lacking. In his *Memorial of 1630* and his *Revised Memorial of 1634*, Benavides recorded invaluable descriptions of villages and people north of El Paso, which by now was the recognized gateway to New Mexico. Like Bishop Mota y Escobar, Benavides traveled the land and recorded his observations for his superiors to use in promoting the missionary field in *"la conversión de San Pablo en la provincia de Nuevo México."* Of the southern limit of New Mexico, Benavides, writing through Spanish colonial eyes, wrote,

"The kingdom of the provinces of New Mexico are situated four hundred leagues beyond the City of Mexico, to the north at 37⁰. And, although the settlements are situated there, the district really begins two hundred leagues before that point, that is, in the Valley of Santa Bárbara, the last pueblo of New Spain in that direction. The dividing line is the Conchos River, so named because of the Concha nation which dwells there. From here we travel

---

58  Ramírez Cabañas, ed., *Descripción Geográfica*, p. 195.
59  Ramírez Cabañas, ed., *Descripción Geográfica*, pp. 199-200.
60  Ramírez Cabañas, ed., *Descripción Geográfica*, pp. 199-201.

on for a distance of one hundred leagues in search of the
Río del Norte, and we do this at very great risk, because the
route passes through the territory inhabited by the Tobosos, Tarahumares, Tepioanes, Tomites, Sumas, Hanos and
other very ferocious, barbarous and indomitable tribes....
We have made every effort to convert and pacify these nations, both for the good of their souls and the safety of the
road....Having traversed these hundred leagues, we arrive
at the famous Río del Norte."[61]

Beyond the ford of the Río del Norte, it appears that Benavides traveled through an area inhabited by the Apaches del Perrillo, which was
obviously present Jornada del Muerto. El Perrillo, the water hole named
during the Oñate expedition of 1598 which found water in a seemingly
waterless plain by following the tracks of a small dog, had given way to a
toponym as well to the designation of an Apache tribe, probably part of the
Mescaleros or Mimbreños.[62] A ways up present Jornada del Muerto, Benavides passed present San Marcial before reaching Socorro. In his *Memorial*,
he described mines south of Socorro, and mission sites at San Antonio de
Senecú and San Luis de Sevilleta. North of Socorro, along a stretch of the
*Camino Real*, Benavides followed the Río Grande to San Antonio de la
Isleta and then to San Francisco de Sandia, thence north of there to San
Felipe and on to Santa Fe, which was founded in 1610. Benavides provided
yet another glimpse of the *Camino Real* through New Mexico which would
be replicated by prospectors, miners, soldiers, friars, settlers, and governors
who settled in New Mexico. The colorful onomastic development of New
Mexican place names was still in its developmental stage.

By the middle 1600s, the *Camino Real* was in constant use between
Santa Fe, El Paso, and Mexico City. One of the most notable governors
in New Mexico during the seventeenth century was Governor Bernardo
López de Mendizábal (1659-1661), and his first lady, Doña Teresa de
Aguilera de la Rocha. López would travel the *Camino Real* twice: first as

---

61    Peter P. Forrestal, translator, and Cyprian J. Lynch, ed., *Benavides' Memorial of 1630*
(Washington, D.C.: Academy of American Franciscan History, 1954), pp. 9-10.

62    Forrestal, trans., and Lynch, ed., *Memorial of 1630*, 14.

governor, then as prisoner of the Holy Office of the Inquisition.[63] Their trip to New Mexico, nonetheless, is noteworthy because it is one of the very few descriptions presented in seventeenth century documents about travel along the Royal Road.

The Lópezes left Mexico city with the yearly supply caravan of 1658 bound for New Mexico in December of that year. As the caravan moved along the dusty *Camino Real de Tierra Adentro*, passing mining camps, towns and ranches, it was obvious that the governor and his wife were accustomed to a high standard of living. Among the creaking *carretas*, their large *carossa*, a covered wagon with bedding and curtains, appeared quite distinct. In a separate wagon rode their servants, including the mulatta Clarilla and the negress Ana de la Cruz, who would serve the Lópezes in Santa Fe. The servants attended the *carossa* at every stop.

The journey on the *Camino Real* was not only long and tiring but dangerous. Caravans were sometimes waylaid by robbers or some catastrophe could occur on winding hillsides. The Lópezes endured the journey by reading or by some other diversion. It was said they never left their *carossa*, not even to attend Mass. By spring 1659, after several months on the trail the caravan had reached Parral on the southern end of Chihuahua's mining frontier. Wending its way from water hole to water hole across the desert, the caravan finally reached the crossing of the Río Grande near present-day El Paso. Not far from there, missionaries at the *Conversión de los Mansos y Sumas*, a mission serving two semi sedentary Indian tribes, had the Royal Road lined with natives holding branches to form an archway in honor of the new governor.[64]

Proceeding northward through the *Jornada del Muerto*, they reached the *Convento de Nuestra Señora de Socorro* on June 30, 1659. With church bells ringing and trumpets blaring, the father guardian, Fray Benito de la Natividad, sprinkled holy water on the governor and the caravan and directed them to the church. That evening, one of the settlers in the area invited the governor and his wife to supper. Doña Luisa Díaz de Betansos

---

63   For an account of the governorship of Bernardo López de Mendizábal, see Sánchez, *Río Abajo Frontier*, 110-119.

64   Primera Audiencia de don Bernardo López de Mendizábal, 1663, Archivo General de la Nación, Sección Inquisición (hereinafter cited as AGN, Inq.) 594

y Castro, an eighty-year old widow, but a very spry frontierswoman,[65] and her daughter Doña Isabel de Salazar, had prepared a sumptuous dinner in honor of the dignitaries.

The next day the caravan broke camp and resumed the journey northward. They stopped at many of the haciendas, estancias and missions along the *Camino Real* in the Province of New Mexico before reaching Santa Fe sometime in mid-July.

Toward the end of the century, an event occurred that would give the Jornada del Muerto its name. The naming of the Jornada del Muerto occurred as a result of the persecution of a German, Bernardo Gruber, by the Holy Office of the Inquisition.[66] Between 1668 and 1670, the Inquisition in New Mexico investigated its last case in the Jurisdiction of Las Salinas in the Manzano Mountains. Facing charges of superstition, Bernardo Gruber, a trader from Sonora, suffered an ordeal at the hands of frontier Inquisition authorities that later cost him his life. Aware that Gruber had been mistreated, officials of the Holy Tribunal in Mexico City moved to lessen the powers of local agents of the Holy Office in outlying provinces like New Mexico. By that time, Gruber was dead and his case closed. Along the dry wastelands northeast of El Paso, two place-names, *Jornada del Muerto* and *Alemán,* survived to remind travelers on the *Camino Real* of Bernardo Gruber's final test.

Charged with superstition involving claims of immortality, Gruber, referred to as *El Alemán* [the German] was arrested at Quarai and eventually jailed at Sandia Pueblo where he spent nearly two years as a prisoner.[67] Meanwhile, his herds, his goods, and his trading contacts dissipated before him as the hard winters and drought-stricken summers took high toll of his animals, and his goods became prey to local frontiersmen who made off with some of Gruber's trade items. Finally, with no word about whether he would be set free or kept imprisoned at Sandia, Gruber plotted with his loyal Apache servant, Atanasio, to escape. Local frontiersman including

65  Testigo de Luisa Díaz de Betansos y Castro, Socorro, April 30, 1662, AGN, Inq. 593.
66  The following narrative about Bernardo Gruber is taken from Joseph P. Sánchez, "Bernardo Gruber and the New Mexican Inquisition," in Sánchez, *The Río Abajo Frontier,* 120-128.
67  Autos sent by Fray Juan Bernal to Mexico City, AGN, Inq. 608, f. 333. Also see, AGN, Inq. 666, f. 406.

Juan Martín Serrano assisted in the escape by providing Gruber with supplies and several horses.[68] Feigning illness, Gruber was able to distract his jailers into thinking he was not much of an escape risk.[69] At midnight of June 22, 1670, Gruber, having loosened the bars to his jail cell, made his escape.[70] Riding south through the *bosques* of the Sandia Jurisdiction, Gruber and Atanasio followed the *Camino Real* past present Albuquerque toward Belen.[71] Near there they rode near the Hacienda of Thomé Domingues de Mendoza on their way toward Isleta and Socorro

Meanwhile, his jailer at Sandia discovered the escape. Quickly, a posse was organized under orders of the governor to chase down the escapee and his accomplice. Their efforts proved fruitless, for no trace of them could be found. Nine days later, Captain Cristóbal de Anaya had pursued the fugitives as far as El Paso del Norte without result. Far to the north of them another event unraveled.[72] It appears that Bernardo Gruber's life had already come to an end. A lone Atanasio rode into Mission Senecú not far from Socorro. There, he was later apprehended by Anaya, who received a message about Atanasio's surrender. The young Apache confessed his story to Fray Francisco Nicolás Hurtado, *ministro de doctrina del Convento de Senecú* not far from Socorro. The Apache picked up the narrative at the *Camino Real* near Thomé Domínguez Mendoza's hacienda. Riding day and night through Tuesday, June 24, they passed the feast day of San Juan on the trail somewhere near Senecú. That night they camped at a place called Fray Cristóbal. The next day they pulled their tired horses through the hot wasteland to Las Peñuelas, which was waterless. They arrived there about 4 p.m., when the sun was still high. Exhausted, thirsty and dusty, Gruber, unable to travel any further, sent young Atanasio in search of water. "Bring it back in a *jícara*," he said hoarsely. In case of danger, he gave his harquebus to the Apache, who traveled a full day to the water hole at San Diego, reaching it at midday on Thursday.[73]

---

68   Declaration of Atanasio, Sandia, July 8, 1670, AGN, Inq. 666, f. 404.
69   Testimony of Captain Francisco de Ortega, Pecos, June 30, 1670, AGN, Inq. 666, f. 406.
70   Undated letter of Fray Juan Bernal, AGN, Inq. 666, f. 404.
71   Undated letter of Fray Juan Bernal, AGN, Inq. 666, f. 404.
72   Statement by Fray Juan Bernal, June 30, 1670, AGN, Inq. 666, f. 408.
73   Declaration of Atanasio, Sandia, July 8, 1670, AGN, Inq. 666, ff. 411-412.

At the water hole, he filled the *jícara* and rode back toward Las Peñuelas. But on the way the *jícara* broke and Atanasio returned to San Diego for water. The only way to carry water back to his master, he reasoned, was to soak his *sudador* [saddle blanket]. When Atanasio finally arrived at Las Peñuelas on Friday morning, Gruber was gone! He had taken only one horse south along the *Camino Real*, the other three horses were still there. The youth spent the rest of Friday and Saturday in an unsuccessful search for El Alemán, the German. Returning to Senecú, Atanasio went to the *convento* to report Gruber's disappearance.[74]

After listening to the young Apache, Fray Francisco ordered four Indians to take Atanasio to Pedro de Leyba, the *alcalde mayor* of the Jurisdiction of Senecú, who lived in Socorro. From there, he was transferred to Sandia Pueblo where he was interrogated by Fray Pedro de Ayala and Padre Juan Bernal. At first Atanasio claimed to be the sole accomplice in the escape of Bernardo Gruber. But Fray Pedro, who was aware of other testimony, implicated Juan Martín Serrano as well. Soon after his interrogation, Atanasio escaped. Father Ayala believed that he had returned to Sonora. Later, it would be said, without proof, that Atanasio had killed Gruber.[75]

Although the *despoblado* was continually searched for Gruber over the next few months, what were believed to be the German's remains were found quite by accident by travelers near what would bear the place name Alemán. New Mexican lore would commemorate the trail as *La Jornada del Muerto* [The Dead Man's Journey]. Almost three weeks after Gruber's escape, five traders on their way to Parral in present Chihuahua, passed between Las Peñuelas and El Perillo. One of them, Captain Andrés de Peralta, strayed from the group, then called out to his companions that he had found something. Francisco del Castillo Betancur, who knew Gruber well, was with them. Writing from Parral in September 1670, to a friend in New Mexico, Castillo described what he had seen:

> I went to him and found a roan horse tied to a tree by a halter. It was dead and near it was a doublet or coat of

74 Declaration of Atanasio, Sandia, July 8, 1670. AGN, Inq. 666, ff. 411-412.
75 Francisco del Castillo Betancur to Dr. Juan de Ortega, El Parral, September 1, 1670. AGN, Inq. 666, f. 402.

blue cloth lined with otter skin. There were also a pair of trousers of the same material, and other remnants of clothing that had decayed. I examined them, and it seemed that they belonged to Bernardo Gruber, the fugitive. I made a search which did not result in vain, for I found at once all of his hair and the remnants of clothing which he had worn. I and my companions searched carefully for the bones, and found in very widely separated places the skull, three ribs, two long bones, and two other little bones which had been gnawed by animals. This, sir, occurred on Wednesday the thirtieth of the month of July of this present year. It is supposed that an Indian who was traveling with Bernardo Gruber killed him.[76]

Castillo and his companions took Gruber's remains to El Paso del Norte. There, outside a mission site, *La Conversión de los Mansos y Sumas*, the bones of Gruber were buried by the resident priest.[77] The Gruber story, which appeared closed to his contemporaries, quietly resurrected itself in New Mexico lore. Since then, the name *Jornada del Muerto* haunted every colonial and modern map of New Mexico. It would be one of hundreds of stories that emerged from the historical development of the *Camino Real* north of El Paso.

As the seventeenth century neared its end, the great Pueblo Revolt of 1680 exploded in the face of New Mexico settlers, sending them reeling to El Paso where they remained for twelve years. The Pueblo Revolt is part of the history of the *Camino Real*, for it resulted in an event in which Hispanic refugees, using the Royal Road, fled southward from Santa Fe past the pueblos of the lower Río Grande to Socorro, then through the Jornada del Muerto, to El Paso.

From El Paso, Spanish officials led sorties northward along the *Camino Real* to reconnoiter the damage done to the land they had occupied since 1598. Some expeditions hoped to retake New Mexico, but it was not until 1692 that the "Reconquest" began. That year, Diego de Vargas led an army

---

76    Francisco del Castillo Betancur to Dr. Juan de Ortega, El Parral, September 1, 1670, Archivo General de la Nación, Sección Inquisición 666, f. 402. Translated by Joseph P. Sánchez.

77    Ibid.

northward along the *Camino Real* and succeeded in gaining a foothold in Santa Fe which led to the recolonization of New Mexico. The *Camino Real* had witnessed a pageantry of settlers, soldiers, friars, fugitives, and refugees in Colonial New Mexico's history.

## The Eighteenth Century *Camino Real*

The eighteenth century unfurled with a stream of activity along the *Camino Real* as Spain sought to strengthen its holdings. The *Camino Real*, as an emigrant route from New Spain, once again saw a series of wagon trains headed northward as new settlers and missionaries moved to reoccupy New Mexico.

By the 1720s, New Mexico was back in Spanish hands, but a new threat loomed on the horizon. French traders who had pushed onto the Great Plains and East Texas posed a challenge to the Spanish occupation of New Mexico. The need to bolster defenses along the northern frontier prompted Spanish officials to review the situation on the frontier. To that end, in 1724, Brigadier Pedro de Rivera was commissioned to lead a two-year inspection of military installations along the northern frontier. His cartographer Francisco Barreiros mapped much of the territory along the *Camino Real.*

As the military inspection moved along *El Camino Real de Tierra Adentro*, Rivera and his entourage retraced the ancient road that was reaching a new cycle of development. By his time, many of the adobe villages seen by Bishop Mota y Escobar had become large towns or cities. Some of the places seen by Mota y Escobar had disappeared. Along the way, Rivera described other new places that had been established since then.

Traveling on *El Camino Real de Tierra Adentro* through Mexico's interior, the expedition took many side trips off the road in its inspection as it virtually zig-zagged throughout the frontier. Rivera's report *Diario y Derrotero de lo caminado, visto y observado en la visita que hizo a los presidios de la Nueva España septentrional el Brigadier Pedro de Rivera*, edited by Vito Alessio Robles in 1946, describes the purpose of the inspection and the various routes taken by the expedition. From Mexico City, Rivera marched north toward the Basílica of Nuestra Señora de Guadalupe, thence to the ancient Toltec ruins at Tula, and finally picking up the road to Querétaro and Zacatecas, the old mining frontier of yesteryear. Tracing the *Camino*

EL CAMINO REAL

*Real,* Rivera headed toward Durango and Ciudad Chihuahua, then north to El Paso and lastly, the old presidial settlement at Santa Fe.

The military inspection by Rivera revealed many weaknesses in the defense of the north for which he made recommendations. Similarly, Rivera's cartographer, Barreiros, left a graphic outline in several maps of the frontier and its many colonial roads, including the *Camino Real.* The entries in *Diario y Derrotero* describe an active linear frontier along the *Camino Real* filled with hard working, but poor, frontiersmen who served as farmers and militiamen, friars who tended their ministries, miners who depended on local ranchers and farmers to sustain them, black slaves and Indian servants whose miserable lives and labor left their mark etched in mine shafts of places like Querétaro, Guanajuato, Zacatecas, Durango, and Santa Barbara, merchants who traveled the royal road, and woman and children who perpetuated the cultural life along a 1200 mile corridor that stretched from Mexico City to Santa Fe in New Mexico. Significantly, two new places had been added to the map of northern New Spain. The Villa de Alburquerque, New Mexico, founded in 1706, and the Villa de Chihuahua (present Ciudad Chihuahua), founded in 1709, added new life, by way of a revived commerce, to the *Camino Real.* The establishment of these villas resulted in new names for that segment of the royal road between the two places. The *Camino de Chihuahua* as seen from New Mexico and the *Camino de Nuevo Mexico* as seen from Chihuahua were duly noted in Spanish colonial cartography. Later, in the nineteenth century, when the Santa Fe Trail from Missouri was established, it incorporated the *Camino de Chihuahua* into its name, the Santa Fe-Chihuahua Trail, thus extending the length of the network of immigration and commercial routes in North America and joining two frontier cultures: Hispanic America and Anglo America. In 1808, Alejandro de Humboldt, included, in his *Ensayo Político,* maps of the Rivera expedition along *El Camino Real de Tierra Adentro* demonstrating the impressive length of the route with all of its historical development from Mexico City to Santa Fe.

The next forty years saw but little change in military life along the *Camino Real* with exception of new installations that were established along the way to bolster defenses and, coincidentally, creating new place names. Not until the Seven Years' War did Spanish officials take up a new military inspection of the northern frontier of New Spain. Spawned by the

Peace of Paris in 1763, which resulted in a new map for North America which gave Great Britain strategic advantages, Spain undertook reform of its defense system under the Bourbon Reforms. Under the reforms, King Carlos III of Spain ordered the reorganization of military units.

In the midst of the whirlwind activity, the marquees de Ruby, a field marshal, began a general inspection of the north.[78] For two years, 1764-66, Ruby and his small escort inspected the entire presidial system of the Provincials Internals, that is, the northern frontier of New Spain, from Guanajuato to Santa Fe in New Mexico and from Sonora to Texas. The result of the Ruby *inspection* was *Regalement de 1772*, a set of military regulations that provided a plan of defense as well as rules governing the deportment of military personnel while on duty. The 1772 regulations served to set the tone and pattern for soldiering on New Spain's northern frontier.

In 1935, Vito Alessio Robles edited one of the reports of the Rubí mission to the north: *Nicolás de Lafora, Relación del Viaje que Hizo a los Presidios Internos Situados en la Frontera de la America Septentrional.* Lafora served as the expedition's cartographer. His maps, like those of Barreiro before him, graphically described *El Camino Real de Tierra Adentro.* In 1766 Lafora visited El Paso from 18 July to 5 August. Like all travelers before him, he realized he was at the gateway to New Mexico on the *Camino Real.* At that time the Presidio de Nuestra Señora de Pilar del Paso del Río del Norte housed a company of cavalry that was below strength at forty-six men. Nearby were five missions in the area ministered by Franciscans. The village of El Paso, the presidio, the missions, and an hacienda in the vicinity contained 5000 people. Lafora's colleague, José Urrútia, a military engineer, drew the plan of El Paso and its cultivated fields along with that of the presidio and location of the missions. Urrútia drew a similar plan for Santa Fe, the terminus of the *Camino Real* and the northern extent of the Rubí mission.

In the 1770s and 1780s, renewed interest in New Mexico among Spanish officials resulted in the appointment of Juan Bautista de Anza, a legendary soldier and capable administrator, as governor of New Mexico. Anza's march from Sonora past Fronteras took him to the Río Grande.

---

78  Joseph P. Sánchez, *Spanish Bluecoats: The Catalonian Volunteers in Northwestern New Spain, 1767-1810* (Albuquerque: University of New Mexico Press, 1990), 6-7.

EL CAMINO REAL

His inspection of New Mexico along the *Camino Real* resulted in a number of changes to the age-old problem of frontier defenses in New Mexico. Ultimately, Anza led a march northward of Santa Fe in pursuit of Cuernoverde, the Comanche chieftain, who had plundered New Mexican farms and Indian pueblos. Anza finally trapped and killed his adversary in southern Colorado, forcing a peace on the Comanche.

The cartography produced by Bernardo Miera y Pacheco, during the 1770s and 1780s, continued a tradition of mapping the *Camino Real* in New Mexico. In New Mexico, the settlement pattern stretched from El Paso past the Jornada del Muerto to Sevilleta, Socorro, Belen, Isleta, Pajarito, Los Chaves, Alburquerque, Alameda, Corrales, Bernalillo, Sandia, San Felipe, Santo Domingo, Cochiti, Los Golondrinas, La Cienega, and Santa Fe. The places that appeared on Miera y Pacheco's maps demonstrated the continued existence of places on the *Camino Real* since the days of Oñate.

The eighteenth century also witnessed ecclesiastical *visitas* made by Bishop Pedro Tamarón y Romeral (1760), Fray Atanasio Domínguez (1776), Fray Juan Agustín Morfí (1777), and other important churchmen who described, as Bishop Mota y Escobar before them, the frontier people who lived along the *Camino Real* as well as their economies, their homes, and their culture. The significance of their *visitas* is that they left a written record of life along a linear frontier that was always in communication with all points along it through commerce, immigration, and the general movement of people and things. These reports include the geographical range from Mexico City to Santa Fe in New Mexico. Particular descriptions of the *Camino Real* through New Mexico add knowledge regarding the antiquity of place names between El Paso and Santa Fe.

As New Mexico gained in importance, visibility and stature as an established frontier area in the eighteenth century, Spanish officials recognized its military and ecclesiastical values. It was, after all, part of the Spanish empire. After nearly two centuries, Spanish officials began to acknowledge the imperial investment in New Mexico. Even though New Mexico still had a way to go in terms of its economic development, the military inspections and the ecclesiastical *visitas* reflected a renewed interest in its strategic importance. In many ways the *Camino Real* had served as the umbilical cord that had nurtured New Mexico's progress through trade, immigration, and imperial support. But the times were changing too rapidly for the realization of Spanish plans for New Mexico.

Between 1810 and 1821, the *Camino Real* soon became a thoroughfare for insurgent and royalist forces locked in mortal combat in the wave of independence movements that plagued a dying Spanish empire. Indeed, as the first phase of rebellion ended, the Hidalgo Revolt had been quelled by royalist armies, and Father Miguel Hidalgo fled along the *Camino Real* to Ciudad Chihuahua, near where he was captured, and where he was imprisoned, tried, and executed in 1811. Out of the independence movement emerged an incipient Mexican nation. With it, the *Camino Real* entered a new era.

## The Nineteenth Century *Camino Real*

Toward the end of the independence movement in Mexico, Anglo-American Mountain Men entered New Mexico to trap fur bearing animals and trade with New Mexicans. By 1821, the Santa Fe Trail from Missouri had been established. It ran its course from 1821 to the 1890s, when railroad lines displaced oxen-drawn freighting trails. The advent of the railroad spelled the slow demise of *El Camino Real de Tierra Adentro* as the principal means for commerce, as railroad lines would soon extend throughout the southwestern United States and the central corridor of Mexico. But before that happened, the *Camino Real* realized an historical transition that spelled change.

Perhaps the earliest Anglo-American description of the *Camino Real* is that of Zebulon Montgomery Pike, who, captured by Spanish troops in 1807, was taken to Santa Fe. Pike was taken to Ciudad Chihuahua so that officials could determine whether to punish Pike and his men for trespassing on Spanish soil or release them. In the end, Pike was released by way of San Antonio in Texas, but not before he was inadvertently given a tour along *El Camino Real de Tierra Adentro* and the colonial road to Saltillo and San Antonio. His journals were subsequently published, revealing, to the outside world, a view of the *Camino Real* and the Spanish frontiers of New Mexico, Chihuahua, Coahuila, and Texas.

Between 1821 and 1846, Anglo-American traders engaged in trade with Santa Fe. Notable among them was Josiah Gregg, whose account *Commerce of the Prairies: The Journal of a Santa Fé Trader* described New

Mexico during the 1830s and 1840s. As a trader, Gregg had plied his business acumen on the *Camino Real*. Dr. Adolph Wislizenus, who accompanied the U.S. Army to New Mexico during the Mexican War, left his *Memoir of a Tour to Northern Mexico, Connected with Col. Doniphan's Expedition, in 1846-1847*. Wizlizenus's descriptions of the *Camino Real* are of particular interest because of the attention he gave to locations and distances along the route.

The Anglo-American intrusion into Spanish, and later Mexican, territories represented the historical progression of change along the *Camino Real*. Ultimately, the United States would become a shareholder in the history of the *Camino Real* for it would become intricately intertwined with that of Mexico.

In its long history, the *Camino Real* developed as Mexico's frontier extended along a south to north line until it stretched from Mexico City to Santa Fe in New Mexico. It served as a line of communication between settlements for trade, defense, and further expansion. By the nineteenth century, the *Camino Real* connected two frontiers, one Spanish, the other Anglo-American. The significance of the *Camino Real* is based on its historic use and the resulting demographic pattern that evolved in the history of two countries as well as the evolution of the *Camino Real* as an interconnecting network of modern roads and railroads that are international in scope and character. In the broad facets of U.S. history and Mexican history, the *Camino Real* played a role in trade and commerce, settlement patterns, war, and transmission of culture. In its historical denouement, the *Camino Real* transcends time, place, and culture.

# Historical Events in New Mexico along the *Camino Real* during the Mexican Territorial Period, 1821-1848

During the Mexican Period, 1821-1846, *El Camino Real* de *Tierra Adentro* continued to serve New Mexico as the main transportation route in the territory. Running from Mexico City to Santa Fe as it had during the Spanish Colonial Period, the Mexican independence movement did little to change the tempo and rhythm of trade and migration along it. If anything, it ceased to be a "Royal Road" and, instead became a national road of Mexico. Still, it continued to be called "El Camino Real" or locally "El Camino de Chihuahua," or, as the people of Chihuahua called it, "El Camino de Nuevo México." *El Camino Real de Tierra Adentro* in New Mexico during the Mexican period had a history of its own. Along its path events unfolded that ushered New Mexico into a new and unexpected period of change culminating in its annexation to the United States in 1848.

The new history unveiled when, in early winter 1821, New Mexicans learned about Mexican Independence. Earlier in October, the Mexican government had sent a circular throughout the nation instruction its citizens to celebrate "Independence" immediately. Official news of the celebration, however, did not reach New Mexico until late December 1821 because the rugged terrain between Mexico City and Santa Fe made overland mail service along *El Camino Real de Tierra Adentro* slow and dangerous. For over two centuries, New Mexico, as a remote colony of Spain, had been a distant outpost from the center of power. That aspect changed little under Mexico.

Although they were aware of Mexico's struggle for independence from Spain, New Mexicans did not realize the impact of the revolution till the end of 1821. Until a mounted courier passed along the Camino Real through the Villa de Alburquerque, as he had along other villages of the Río Abajo, on his way to Santa Fe, New Mexicans had only heard rumors about the creation of the new government. On December 26, 1821, at the Palace of the Governors, the courier dismounted and handed a mail pouch to Governor Facundo Melgares. The pouch contained official correspondence demanding that New Mexico's governor and other officials take an oath of allegiance to the recently established Mexican government.[79] Five days later, New Mexicans celebrated the event despite the cold weather that had blown in over the Sangre de Cristo Mountains.

Two festivities, a week apart, marked the event in the *Plaza de Santa Fe*. Virtually in the dead of winter, New Mexicans braved the freezing temperatures to celebrate into the wee hours of the night. The celebration included parades, orations, patriotic dramas, music, masses, ringing

---

79  David J. Weber, editor, "An Unforgettable Day: Facundo Melgares on Independence," *New Mexico Historical Review* (1973), 48:27. Also see, Joseph P. Sánchez and Janet LeCompte, "When Santa Fe was a Mexican Town," in David Noble *Santa Fe: A History of an Ancient City* (Santa Fe: School of American Research, 2007).

of church bells, firing of muskets, dancing of Pueblo Indians, and a ball in the governor's palace.[80] Thus, the tradition for commemorating Mexican Independence (also known as Diez y Seis de Septiembre) in New Mexico, had its origins in Santa Fe during the winter of 1821-1822.

Once independence from Spain had been achieved in 1821, New Mexicans received other official notices concerning political reform throughout Mexico. New Mexicans adjusted to the changing times as a new order unfurled with new laws largely regarding the reorganization of political and economic institutions. For the most part,[81] the structure of the budding Mexican Nation would have more of an effect on the political organization of settlements as participating units in national politics. Anxiously, New Mexicans wondered how New Mexico would fit into the larger picture of Mexican rule which, in perspective, evolved quickly in a brief, but active, twenty-five years or so.

Only two long roads led to Santa Fe in 1821. One, *El Camino Real de Tierra Adentro* from Mexico City passed through the central plateau of Mexico with the many scattered Mexican villages situated throughout the extremely rugged terrain. En route, the traveler often passed long periods of time through long lonely stretches of hostile and empty land with deep canyons before reaching Santa Fe. The other road, still evolving, came from Missouri in the United States. Known as the Santa Fe Trail, it connected in Santa Fe with the Camino Real, and later became known as the Santa Fe-Chihuahua Trail.

Established by William Becknell in 1821, the Santa Fe Trail was not only a commercial route used by Anglo-American and New Mexican merchants, it was an immigrant trail used by U.S. citizens who moved to New Mexico. The Mexican colonization acts of the 1820s and 1830s encouraged migration from the United States via the Santa Fe Trail. Thus, citizens in the United States also took an interest in the changes made by the Mexican national government in areas like Texas, New Mexico and California.

The Santa Fe-Chihuahua Trail became a significant pathway in the history of New Mexico, especially during the War of 1846 when the Army of the West invaded and occupied New Mexico. The life of the Santa Fe-Chi-

---

80   *Ibid.* Weber, p. 32.
81   *Ibid.* Weber, p. 33.

huahua Trail coincided with the short-lived Mexican Period in the present Greater Southwest. Another trail, blazed in 1829 by Antonio Armijo, led from Santa Fe to Los Angeles in California. With a small group of men, Armijo opened a trail known as Old Spanish Trail via southern Utah to Los Angeles. It, too, became a commercial and migrant route that connected with the Santa Fe Trail and the Camino Real in Santa Fe.

During the first years of transition from Spanish Colonial to Mexican national power, the Mexican government defined its authority throughout Mexico. The National Congress defined Mexican sovereignty as the "Supreme Power" of the new nation formed by the legislative, executive, and judicial branches. The government announced that the territories of Mexico were an integral part of the emerging nation state

The Constitution of 1836, furthermore, provided that the Congress could create departments or states.[82] With the Decree of December 29, 1836, the Republic was divided into Departments, which, in turn, were sub-divided into districts, and those, in turn, were divided further into precincts. Through the Law of December 30, 1836, New Mexico, among other territories, effectively became a department.[83] Santa Fe would, of course, host the Departmental Junta. The *partido* governments would have their own capitals: San Ildefonso (Hispanic settlement) and Taos (Hispanic settlement) in the north; and, Alburquerque and Los Padillas in the south which took in settlements around Los Lunas, Tome, Belén, and other villages to Socorro. They would serve as capitals akin to seats of government with an *ayuntamiento* and an *alcalde constitucional*.

By 1843, the Departments underwent one more revision before the end of the Mexican Period. The Decree of June 13, 1843, created as*ambleas* or Departmental Assemblies, such as the one in Santa Fe, composed of eleven members with a minimum of seven allowed. To serve in the a*samblea*, members had to be twenty-five years of age.

In the new system, governors reported directly to the central government. They served at the pleasure of the President of the Republic who appointed all the governors who, theoretically, according to the law, were to be nominated by the *Asambleas*.

---

82   Decree of December 29, 1836 in SMLL, pp. 203-204.
83   Law of December 30th, 1836 in SMLL, p. 209.

Between 1830 and 1840, the political atmosphere created by a vigorous Mexican authority in a frontier circumstance proved stressful to New Mexicans. Frustrated and angry about changes that appeared abusive to them, New Mexicans, in 1837, openly rebelled against the Centralist Mexican government. At the time, New Mexicans living along the Camino Real had no idea that they would participate in events surrounding the restoration of New Mexico in the wake of the rebellion against Pérez.

Appointed to the military-governorship of New Mexico by Antonio López de Santa Anna in 1835, Albino Pérez, a native of Veracruz, was an outsider to Santa Fe's politics.[84] Consequently New Mexicans opposed Pérez in public. Having arrived in New Mexico in April 1835, Pérez, with hopes of improving the situation which confronted him, succeeded only in encouraging the resentment harbored against him by those who considered him an outsider. Appointed by Mexican Dictator Antonio López de Santa Anna, Pérez' objective was to prepare the people of New Mexico for the change from an outlying provincial frontier territory to a department or state. Instead, he inspired opposition from New Mexican frontiersmen who interpreted the change to mean that they would surrender local power to a distant central government. Consequently, an explosive political issue regarding home rule worked to undermine his mission. The undercurrent of opposition began to move swiftly gathering the discontented and opportunistic elements of New Mexico's political society. Slowly Pérez' political enemies revealed themselves.

In the backlands of northern New Mexico, meanwhile, trouble brewed for the Pérez faction. On August 3, 1837, a revolutionary junta was formed;[85] it consisted of twelve persons who called their district the Cantón de La Cañada. The Hispanic rebels gathered at an encampment near La Cañada with their counterparts "the principal warriors of al the northern pueblos."[86]

Meanwhile as word reached Pérez of impending trouble he hastened to gather a militia but could muster only "a hundred and fifty men in-

---

84  Lansing B. Bloom, "New Mexico Under Mexican Administration" *Old Santa Fe*, Vol. II (July 1914-April 1915), p. 4.
85  *Ibid.*
86  *Ibid.*

cluding the warriors of the Pueblo of Santo Domingo."[87] With his small force, Pérez left the capital on August 7, 1837, to suppress the rebels. Having spent the night at the Indian Pueblo of Pojoaque, they continued the march to Santa Cruz, while en route they were attacked by the rebels, reported Francisco Sarracino, "in a disorderly manner giving us a lively fire."[88] With the battle lost, most of Pérez' men either defected to the rebels or were captured. Pérez was chased back to the outskirts of Santa Fe where on August 9 he was caught and brutally killed.

The rebel forces, two thousand strong, almost all Pueblo warriors, marched on Santa Fe. Preparing for the worst, the inhabitants fortified themselves in their homes. The rabble entered the city and elected a governor, José Gonzales.[89] Two days after their entry into Santa Fe, they left. With Gonzales and the rebels at large, New Mexico was in the state of rebellion.

News of the rebellion reached the Hispanic villages south of Santa Fe along the Camino Real between Bernalillo, Belen and Socorro. On September 8, 1837, concerned citizens held a meeting at Tomé, south of Albuquerque, and called for the suppression of the rebellion which, by then, was centered in Santa Fe. Aware of the danger to the stability of New Mexico and sensing that the tide of sentiment for rebellion had ended, the Albuquerquean Manuel Armijo joined them in announcing his opposition to the uprising.[90] At the meeting at Tomé, the representatives of each town chose Manuel Armijo as the leader of the army. Despite their dislike of the Pérez administration, the people of Peña Blanca, Algodones, Bernalillo, Albuquerque, Alameda, Corrales, Ranchos de Alburquerque, Atrisco, Pajarito, Tomé, and Cubero formed an army.

Armijo reported the situation to Mexico City and asked for reinforcements. Mexican officials sent 300 men under Colonel Justiniani in command of the Escuadrón de Veracruz and presidial troops from Chihuahua[91] by the end of the year. Moving quickly, Armijo attacked the rebels

87    Depositions and certificates testifying to the loyalty of Donaciano Vigil in the fight with the insurrectionists in August, 1837, Ritch Paptes, reel 24, frame 169.

88    Ibid.

89    Josiah Gregg, Commerce of the Prairies, pp. 131-132.

90    Marc Simmons, Hispanic Albuquerque, 1706-1846 (2003), p. 139.

91    Hubert Howe Bancroft, History of Arizona and New Mexico1530-1888 (1889) 17:318.

just north of the Santa Cruz Valley and routed them. On January 27, 1838, in the fight at La Cañada, Armijo captured and executed Gonzales, thus crushing the revolt. Next, he reported to the central government that the situation was under control, and there was no need to send more troops northward. Armijo, already recognized as commander-in-chief, petitioned for the governorship and received it. Granted that concession, New Mexico was restored to its native sons. With Pérez dead and Armijo in power, New Mexicans could ignore directives from the central government in Mexico City.

In the wake of rebellion, a strange event took place that would solidify Armijo's powers with the central government in Mexico City. Tending their sheep and farms, New Mexicans along the Camino Real were unaware that their lives would be touched by an historical event that historians would later call the "Texas Invasion of New Mexico." Far away, in Texas, a group of adventurers decided to invade New Mexico and make it part of Texas. The Río Grande, they claimed, was the boundary, and the entire east bank, from the Gulf of Mexico to the San Luis Valley belonged to the Lone Star Republic. In general, the Texans theorized that New Mexicans awaited an opportunity to declare independence from Mexico. If true, therefore, then it would be their duty to release New Mexicans from Mexican tyranny, especially those living on the east bank of the Río Grande.[92] The Texans also theorized that if the invasion were successful, the Santa Fe-Chihuahua Trail trade could be diverted through Texas channels.

In spring 1841, President Mirabeau Buonaparte Lamar, without the support of the congress of Texas, approved an expedition of about 300 men in six companies. Under Colonel Hugh McLeod, the expedition advanced toward New Mexico. Three commissioners accompanied the expedition to make proclamations[93] explaining the advantages of freedom from Mexico. Other men on the expedition were traders, adventurers, and travelers who did not understand the purpose of the expedition.

The anonymous author of the note to *The Journal of the Santa Fe Expedition* by Peter Gallagher, a member of the ill-fated expedition, wrote:

---

92  Bancroft, Arizona and New Mexico, XVII:320.

93  Alos habitantes de Santa Fe y los demas pueblos de Nuevo Mexico al Oriental del Rio Grande [1841], Daughters of the Republic of Texas (DRT) Library, San Antonio Texas.

This 'wild goose chase' was sponsored by President Lamar for the express purpose of territorial expansion, of acquiring control of New Mexico—by peaceful means if possible; by military force if necessary. The expedition was assembled within the shadow of the Texas capital and with the advice and aid of the Texas President himself.[94]

Pretending to be traders along the Santa Fe-Chihuahua Trail, McLeod led his men across the arid lands of west Texas.[95] On the morning of June 19, 1841, they left Brushy Creek, fifteen miles north of Austin, bound for New Mexico. Poorly supplied and equipped, they planned to live off the land. After a week, the expedition travelled through unfamiliar land. By the first week in September, they had reached the vicinity of present Amarillo. The men, fatigued from the march through a treeless plain, were discontented and wanted to abandon the expedition. One had committed suicide, a few others suffered a fever, some had been killed by Indians, and morale was low. By the time the expedition reached New Mexico, the survivors were near starvation, dehydrated and their clothes, ragged and dirty.

On September 17, the arrival of New Mexicans with messages from Armijo electrified the camp.[96] The next day, they followed the guides through the waterless Llano Estacado for nearly two weeks. On October 4, a Mexican escort, fully armed, commanded by Coronel Damasio Salazar met them at Laguna Colorado. Lieutenant Colonel Juan Andrés Archuleta presented the terms of capitulation. They included that the Texans surrender under the following conditions. First, that they lay down their arms; second, that they would be protected of life, liberty, and their personal property; and, third, that they would be escorted to San Miguel, several days hence. Believing that their arms would be returned to them, the Texans capitulated.

Meanwhile, Governor Armijo personally attended to the Texas invasion.[97] Armijo had already informed New Mexicans that it was the intent

---

94   Peter Gallagher, Journal of the Santa Fe Expedition, DRT Library, San Antonio, Texas.

95   Bancroft, *Arizona and New Mexico*, XVII:320.

96   Gallagher, *Journal*, p. 31.

97   Bancroft, *Arizona and New Mexico*, XVII:322.

of the Texans to "burn, slay and destroy"[98] on their march through the Department. At first, Lewis tried to tell Armijo that they were merchants from the United States. Having dealt with merchants along the Santa Fe-Chihuahua Trail, Armijo pointed to the star and the word Texas on Lewis's uniform. Turning to the Texans, he said, "You cannot deceive me; United States merchants do not wear Texas uniforms."[99] Armijo's ire was evident; his patience thin. Too, Armijo had confiscated and read through McLeod's "Order Book," which explained the intent of the Texas invaders.

Armijo dealt with the invasion for what it was. Some members of the expedition were executed. The majority were sent to Mexico City for trial and imprisonment. Among them was José Antonio Navarro, who had supported the Texas Rebellion against Mexico. He was treated as a traitor by Antonio López de Santa Anna and imprisoned for nearly four years.

Damasio Salazar was the officer in charge of the prisoners. He marched them south from Santa Fe along the old Camino Real to Albuquerque, then southward through Atrisco, Pajarito, and Los Padillas, past Isleta through Los Lunas, Tomé, and Belén to Socorro. Most of the *hispanos* felt sorry for them, gave them food, and making the sign of the cross, wished them well and prayed for them. "*Pobrecitos*" (poor things) was the word most commonly heard by the Texans as they headed south.

George W. Kendall, a Louisiana newpaper reporter and prisoner, recalled that they entered Albuquerque (on October 22) along the Camino Real about noon[100] "famed for the beauty of its women, besides being the largest place in the province of New Mexico, and the residence of Armijo a part of the year." The people turned out to see the *estrangeros*. Kendall wrote, "As we were marched directly through the principal streets the inhabitants were gathered on either side to gaze at the *estrangeros*, as we were called. The women, with all kindness of heart, gave our men corn, pumpkins, bread, and everything they could spare from their scanty store as we passed."[101] Kendall wrote that after they departed Albuquerque, they passed near a succession of cultivated fields and pastures, undoubtedly

98   A.J. Sowell, The Santa Fe Expedition (Houston: The Union National Bank, 1929), p.3.
99   Sowell, *The Santa Fe Expedition*, p. 3.
100  George Wilkins Kendall, Narrative of the Texan Santa Fe Expedition (1850), I:382.
101  Kendrick, *Narrative*, I:383.

those of Atrisco, Los Padillas, Armijo, and Pajarito. Of the route, Kendall wrote, "After leaving Albuquerque, we continued our march through a succession of cultivated fields and pastures[102] until we reached a small rancho called Los Placeres, and here we camped for the night"—a short distance from Albuquerque. By late evening of October 24, 1841, they had reached Valencia. Everywhere along the Camino Real, settlers approached the prisoners and gave the food, mostly corn and bread, and water for sustenance. After they had left the last settlements, beyond Socorro, the road became a living nightmare.

The Camino Real to Mexico City was filled with death. Those who could not stand up and march were executed; the ears of dead prisoners were cut off as proof that they had not escaped. Especially after having passed Socorro, lack of water, food, and the desert heat took its toll on the Texans as they were forced to march through the Jornada del Muerto before reaching the Las Cruces area. The Texans had been brutally treated by their captors. Thirsty, starving, fatigued, beaten, they arrived in El Paso. There, as in the valley of Albuquerque, and later, Ciudad Chihuahua, compassionate people came out to give them food and water. In the end, they marched the entire length of the Camino Real to Mexico City, where many of them were released; a few of them would be found guilty of sedition and treachery and sentenced to imprisonment in Mexico City or in San Juan de Ulloa, the island in the harbor of Veracruz.

As for Governor Armijo, he emerged as a patriot for having dealt with the invasion in a heroic manner, limiting the loss of life for Mexican citizens who resided in New Mexico. Santa Fe Trail merchants kept away from the prisoners lest they be identified with the invaders. Within three weeks after the attempted Texan invasion, *Atrisqueños* and other New Mexicans read a circular containing Armijo's Proclamation of November 10, 1841. In it, he declared that it was necessary to confuse the Texans, apprehend them, and manipulate their surrender with minimal risk to New Mexicans and, in so doing, protect Mexico's honor. He emphasized that the nation's integrity had been challenged by Texans who wished to extend their claim to include New Mexico.[103] Then, and in all future relations, Armijo kept a

---

102 Kendrick, *Narrative*, I:386.
103 Manuel Armijo, Proclamation, November 10, 1841, Santa Fe. Ina Sizer Cassidy Col-

wary watch on all foreigners. In Santa Fe, Armijo was greatly applauded. As a native of Albuquerque, doubtless, the citizens there and in the neighboring settlements between Bernalillo, Alameda, Albuquerque, Atrisco, Los Padillas, and Pajarito down to Socorro, looked on with pride on their governor. Even though Armijo did rule New Mexico with an iron hand, Kendall's biased writings, unfairly, began an historiographical legacy that would malign Armijo in stereotypical terms. Later historians acknowledged that Armijo, who had confiscated Captain McLeod's Order Book, which revealed his plan, had appropriately handled the invasion for what it was.[104]

Still, Mexican authorities had long anticipated an invading army from Texas. They had issued warnings and strengthened reinforcements. When an invasion did occur, they praised Governor Armijo for the way he had handled the situation. Armijo had emerged as the man of the hour.

In New Mexico, especially during the 1840s, New Mexican officials used land grants to influence private enterprises and create defensive barriers against marauding Indians, Texans, and Anglo-American intruders. New Mexicans were encouraged to settle lands in river valleys on the northeastern and eastern peripheries bordering the Republic of Texas.

Buoyed by the Mexican government's desire to colonize the northern frontier by anyone who would swear allegiance to the Mexican government, become a Roman Catholic, and promise to bring additional settlers into the area, Armijo's give-away land grant policies attracted new immigrants into New Mexico. Between 1821, New Mexico's population was estimated to be approximately 42,000, and by 1845, the number had virtually reached 65,000 inhabitants. Aside from maurading Texans and other Anglo-American, warring tribes continuously attacked Indian Pueblos and Hispanic villages. For defensive purposes, New Mexican frontiersmen

---

lection in Rich Collection. no. 94. Folder no. 3. New Mexico State Records Center and Archives. Santa Fe.

104 In 1889, Hubert Howe Bancroft wrote "There can be no doubt that Governor Armijo was fully justified in seizing the Texas invaders. disarming them, confiscating their property, and sending them to Mexico as prisoners of war. He and his officers are accused, however, of having induced their victims to surrender by false assurances of friendship and false promises of welcome as traders, the giving-up of their arms being represented as a mere formality imposed on all visitors to Santa Fé." Bancroft. Arizona and New Mexico. XVII:324.

were encouraged to settle river valleys on the northeastern and eastern plains facing Texas.[105]

The Mexican Period was a time of change, mainly administrative, that demonstrated the adaptability of New Mexicans to a new political system. In the short interval of twenty-seven years of Mexican rule, New Mexicans participated in the political system imposed by Mexico. Their novitiate in Mexican politics prepared them for the next cycle of change.

Great changes were in the wind by the middle 1840s. Between 1846 and 1848, New Mexicans watched the outcome of the war between Mexico and the United States with disquieting interest. As the Army of the West under General Stephen Watts Kearney occupied New Mexico, a new order was at hand. On September 18, 1846, Kearney addressed the people of New Mexico, but his words were no match to those of acting Governor Juan Baustista Vigil y Alarid. His words of acquiesence echoed with a certain *tristeza* throughout New Mexico.

Standing in the *Plaza de Santa Fe,* the terminus of the Camino Real, Vigil y Alarid looked at Kearney and said, "Do not find it strange if there has been no manifestation of joy and enthusiasm in seeing this city occupied by your military forces. To us the power of the Mexican Republic is dead. No matter what her condition, she was our mother. What child will not shed abundant tears at the tomb of his parents?…Today we belong to a great and powerful nation….we know that we belong to the Republic that owes its origin to the immortal Washington, whom all civilized nations admire and respect."[106] With those poignant words, New Mexico and the northern portion of *El Camino Real de Tierra Adentro* slipped into the hands of the United States.

---

105 Ralph Emerson Twitchell, The Leading Facts of New Mexican History, (1911), II:196-197. Also see Alan Ward Minge, "Frontier Problems in New Mexico Preceding the Mexican War, 1840-1846" (Ph.D. Diss., University of New Mexico, 1965), 306.
106 Translation quoted is from Twitchell. The original text in Spanish is in William G. Ritch Papers (R1241),. Huntington Library. See also, Robert J. Torres, "Juan Bautista Vigil y Alarid and the Occupation of New Mexico," 1846, *Genealogical Society of Hispanic America,* Spring 2010, Vol. 22, Number 1, pp3-7.

El Camino Real

# The Historical Significance of *El Camino Real de Tierra Adentro*

The significance of the *Camino Real* is based on its historic use and the resulting demographic pattern that evolved in the history of two countries as well as the evolution of the *Camino Real* as an interconnecting network of modern roads and railroads that are international in scope and character. In the broad facets of U.S. history and Mexican history, the *Camino Real* played a role in trade and commerce, settlement patterns, war, and transmission of culture.

The prehistory of the route which would become the *Camino Real* crosses many indigenous cultures. Especially since the formation of the Aztec kingdom in the Valley of Mexico, routes emanated in all directions from there. One route ran northward as a great trade trunk trail through the *meseta central*, the central corridor between the Sierra Madre Occidental and the Sierra Madre Oriental. The Aztec *pochteca* trade route led as far north as *Paquimé* and *Casas Grandes*, tribes that had trade relations with the Indian Pueblos of the Río Grande. This trade route paralleled the *Camino Real* as it developed in historic times. The location of this route was not accidental, for Spanish colonial frontiersmen tended to follow indigenous routes in their explorations as well as in their trading enterprises.

Historically, the *Camino Real* which ran from Mexico City to Santa Fe in New Mexico played a role in the Spanish empire as the main thoroughfare in the interior of the Mexican Viceroyalty. The *Camino Real* was more than an emigrant route; it was at once a 1200 mile-long linear frontier of settlements, a mining frontier, a missionary frontier, a commercial frontier, a military frontier, and an indigenous frontier. It was complemented by other *caminos reales* that traversed the viceroyalty, for all roads led to Mexico City. Its long history intersected with that of the United States, which today owns 400 miles of the *Camino Real* and shares in its history and heritage. The *Camino Real* became part of the national story of the United States long before the War with Mexico in 1846. By 1821, the Santa Fe Trail, established by William Becknell, became a significant emigrant route from the United States to the Mexican territory of New Mexico. In 1846, the established route of the Santa Fe Trail was used by General Stephan Watts Kearney in leading the Army of the

West during the Mexican War. The Chihuahua Trail portion of the Santa Fe-Chihuahua Trail was used by Alexander W. Doniphan in his march to capture Chihuahua during the Mexican War. Like the Hispanic settlement pattern along the *Camino Real* in New Mexico, Anglo-American settlement patterns followed the route between Santa Fe and El Paso. The broad themes of war and the settlement of the West are imbedded in the history of the *Camino Real* as part of the national story of the United States. The development of cities in the United States inclusive of Santa Fe, Albuquerque, Bernalillo, Socorro, Las Cruces, Alamogordo, and El Paso owe their existence to the *Camino Real*, for the Royal Road as an immigration route served the development of the United States as well as that of Mexico. Internationally, the NAFTA agreement has opened up a new phase in the international use of the route traversed by highways and railroads between both countries.

One of the most famous historical personages associated with blazing portions of the *Camino Real* is Juan Pérez de Oñate who founded Spanish New Mexico in 1598. Indeed, Oñate's settlement of New Mexico at the confluence of the Río Chama and the Río Grande predated Jamestown by nine full years. Later, in 1610, the settlement and its town council (*cabildo*) moved to Santa Fe. During the American Revolution, Spanish colonial soldiers at the presidio of Santa Fe contributed money to aid George Washington defeat the British at Yorktown. Santa Fe, the northernmost terminus of the *Camino Real*, remains the capital of New Mexico.

Other famous people associated with the *Camino Real* include Father Juan Agustín Morfí, who in 1777, visited New Mexico via the *Camino Real*, and who wrote extensive reports on the missions along the Río San Antonio in Texas which today are commemorated by the National Park Service at San Antonio Missions National Historic Park. Morfí's descriptions of his travels on *El Camino Real de Tierra Adentro* are important, for similarly they have played a role in establishing the significance of the San Antonio Missions.

In 1779, Governor Juan Bautista de Anza, who had led the 1776 expedition to settle San Francisco in California, came to live in New Mexico for nearly a decade. Anza, who came from an old family in Sonora, served as captain of the Tubac Presidio south of Tucson, Arizona. In 1779, he traveled through New Mexico on the *Camino Real* and played a role in pacifying New Mexico, thereby paving the way to the eventual settlement of southern Colorado.

Near the end of the Spanish colonial period, in 1807, Zebulon Montgomary Pike, captured by Spanish troops in 1807, was taken to Santa Fe. Pike and his men were next escorted to Ciudad Chihuahua so that officials could determine whether to punish Pike and his men for trespassing on Spanish soil, or release him. In the end, Pike was released by way of San Antonio in Texas, but not before he was inadvertently given a tour along *El Camino Real de Tierra Adentro* and the colonial road to Saltillo, thence north to San Antonio. His journals were subsequently published, revealing, to the outside world, one of the first outsiders' view of the *Camino Real* and the Spanish frontiers of New Mexico, Chihuahua, Coahuila, and Texas.

Between 1821 and 1846, Anglo-American traders engaged in trade with Santa Fe. Notable among them was Josiah Gregg whose account *Commerce of the Prairies: The Journal of a Santa Fé Trader* described New Mexico during the 1830s and 1840s. Gregg traveled on the *Camino Real* as a trader.

In the Anglo-American period following 1846, General Stephen Watts Kearney, commander of the Army of the West, led his force to New Mexico during the Mexican War. His second in command, Alexander W. Doniphan led troops southward along the *Camino Real* to capture Chihuahua.

*El Camino Real de Tierra Adentro* transcends time and place, for its contribution to history of two nations cuts across cultures as Indian, Spaniard, Mexican and Anglo-American have all left their trace on this ancient road. The *Camino Real* is a transmitter of culture. Historic, ethnic, and folk cultural traditions were transmitted through the *Camino Real*. Aside from Western Civilization cultural values, Hispanic folklore in the form of music, folktales, folk medicine, folk sayings, architecture, geographic place names, language, Catholic religion, land grants, irrigation systems, governing institutions, and Spanish law were transmitted through the *Camino Real*. Additionally, foodstuffs were transmitted through the *Camino Real*, one of which was the red chili pepper, introduced into New Mexico, ironically, by Spanish settlers from Mexico another product was the apple, which together with chili, is important in today's economy. The *Camino Real* was also a transhumance route through which cattle, oxen, horses, mules, sheep, and goats were transported as far north as New Mexico. Among the legal concepts presently utilized in the American legal system and governance which were transmitted through the *Camino Real* are community property laws, first priority in terms of water usage, mining claims, and the idea of sovereignty especially as applied to Native American land claims.

The *Camino Real* as a transportation network supported spur roads that led to Sonora and from there to southern Arizona as far as Tucson, which was founded in 1776. Another colonial spur led from the *Camino Real* to Monterrey and Saltillo and connected to San Antonio, Texas. The *Camino Real* intersected with the Santa Fe Trail running from Missouri to New Mexico. At Santa Fe, the *Camino Real* and the Santa Fe Trail joined the Old Spanish Trail that led to southern Utah, thence westward to Las Vegas, Nevada, and finally to Los Angeles, California. All of these trails were used for trade and immigration.

The United States shares in the ownership of the *Camino Real* as well as in its history and common heritage with Mexico. Born from prehistoric indigenous trade routes, the *Camino Real* in turn spawned the development of the Greater Southwest of the United States and the central corridor of Mexico.

MAP 2: ROUTE FROM MEXICO CITY TO SAN MIGUEL ALLENDE

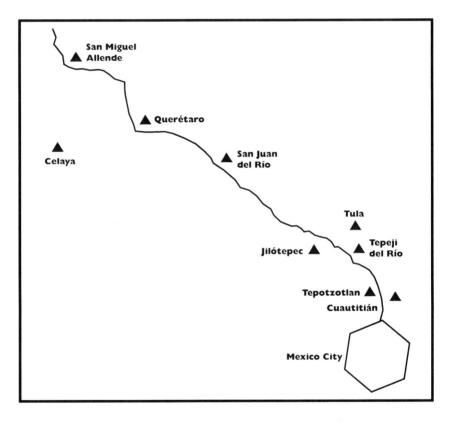

# Historical Dictionary of Place Names Associated with the *Camino Real de Tierra Adentro*

A word about maps. The number of place names recorded in this volume make it impractical to develop a master map showing every site discussed for each succeeding century in which the Camino Real de Tierra Adentro was used by traders and travelers. The maps in this volumes are meant to orient the the reader to the segments between Mexico City and certain places for example; from Guanajuato to Zacatecas; and, from Zacatecas to Durango, etc. Similarly, place names cited between El Paso del Norte and San Juan de los Caballeros can also be recognized by readers in the geographical sequence in which they occur. Thus, it is important to note that the latitudinal and longtitudinal readings that accompany each place name should assist the reader to locate a particular place on more detailed modern maps.

**Atzcapotzalco** [19 29N  99 09W]: In August 1777, Father Agustín Morfí briefly mentioned passing through Atzcapotzalco on the way out of México City in (Alessio Robles 1935:26).

**La Villa de Guadalupe** [≈19 29N  99 07W]: Pedro de Rivera wrote that on 21 November 1724, he left Mexico City and came to the Santuario de Guadalupe, where he stayed the night (Alessio Robles 1946:26). Morfí spoke at this shrine as his party was leaving the Valley of México to begin their expedition in August 1777 (Alessio Robles 1935:26).

EL CAMINO REAL

**El Paraje de Casas Blancas:** Morfí described this place as being at the entrance to the Cuesta de Barrientos. His party passed through there while leaving México City at the start of their journey in August 1777 (Alessio Robles 1935:26).

**Cuesta de Barrientos** [≈19 35N 99 11W]: Rivera wrote that on 22 November 1724, he left the Santuario de Guadalupe and traveled west northwest then northeast five leagues and passed the Cuesta de Barrientos (Alessio Robles 1946:26). Morfí described La Hacienda de la Lechería as lying north northwest of México City on a beautiful plain atop an elevation called "Barrientos" (Alessio Robles 1935:26-27).

**La Hacienda de la Lechería** [19 36N 99 11W]: Morfí described this hacienda as located north northwest of México City on a beautiful plain atop an elevation called "Barrientos." His party stayed there after passing through Atzcapotzalco, Guadalupe and a *paraje* called Casas Blancas at the entrance to "Barrientos." He noted in his journal that they left La Hacienda de la Lechería on 7 August 1777 (Alessio Robles 1935:26-27).

**Cuautitlán** [19 40N 99 11W]: Rivera wrote that on 22 November 1724, he passed Cuesta de Barrientos and came to the pueblo of Cuautitlán (Alessio Robles 1946:26). Morfí described this pueblo on 7 August 1777 as an *Alcaldia Mayor* and *Cabeza de Partido* as well as the source of much of New Spain's pottery (Alessio Robles 1935:27). This principal settlement was a stopping place on the road already established between the capital and Querétaro before the Zacatecas silver strike of 1546 (Powell 1952:17).

**Coyotepec** [19 46N 99 12W]: Rivera wrote that on 23 November 1724, he left Cuatitlán and traveled 10 leagues northwest west through land which he described as flat but that had some hills, both there and in view. He stated that he passed through the pueblos of Coyotepec and "Guegotoca," which can presently be identified as Huehuetoca (Alessio Robles 1946:26).

**Huehuetoca** [19 50N 99 12W]: Rivera stated that on 23 November 1724 he had left Cuatitlán and traveled 10 leagues northwest west through land which he described as flat. It had some hills, both there and in view. He wrote that he passed through the pueblos of Coyotepec and "Guegotoca," identified presently as Huehuetoca (Alessio Robles 1946:26). Morfí stayed here 7-8 August 1777 while going between México City and Tula. He described it as lying four leagues northwest of La Lechería and one and a half from the *desague*, making it the residence of officials who visited that project (Alessio Robles 1935:27). From Huehuetoca Morfí went to Tula. [See **TULA**]

**Tepotzotlán** [19 43N  99 13W]: Rivera passed the road to "Tepozotlán;" he wrote that on 23 November 1724, after passing through Coyotepec and "Guegotoca," he could see "Tepozotlán" to the west (Alessio Robles 1946:26). Lafora passed through on 18 March 1766, placing "Tepozotlán" seven leagues north northwest of Mexico City. The population was composed of Spanish, Indians, mulattoes, and mestizos, and the town contained a Jesuit seminary. It is now Tepotzotlán, México state. The name means *lugar del jorobado*, which can be "the place of the hunchback" (Alessio Robles 1939:35). From Tepozotlán Lafora went to Tepexe del Río. [See **TEPEXE DEL RIO**]

**Santa Bárbara**: Rivera wrote that on 23 November 1724, after passing through Coyotepec and "Guegotoca," he could see the pueblo of Santa Bárbara to the east. However, he did not go to this pueblo (Alessio Robles 1946:26).

**Theoloyuca (or Teoloyucan)** [19 45N  99 10W]: Rivera stated that on 23 November 1724, after passing through Coyotepec and "Guegotoca," he could see the pueblo of Theoloyuca to the east. It can be presently identified as Teoloyucan (Alessio Robles 1946:26).

**Santiago** [19 56N  99 08W]: Rivera wrote that on 23 November 1724, he could see the pueblo of Santiago to the east, although he did not go there. He had just passed through Coyotepec and "Guegotoca" (Alessio Robles 1946:26). After passing through Coyotepec and "Guegotoca" Rivera went to Tula. [See **TULA**]

**Tepexe del Río** [19 54N  99 21W]: Lafora visited Tepexe del Río on 19 March 1766, going east from Mexico City on a rugged, rocky road. He described the setting as in a peaceful valley alongside of the stream of the same name. The majority of the population was described as Indian. It is now called Tepezji (or Tepeji) del Río, Hidalgo state. The name means rocky place in Nahuatl (Alessio Robles 1939:36).

**Río de Tepeji**: Lafora passed this tributary to the Río Tula, in Hidalgo state, on 19 March 1766, by the town of the same name (Alessio Robles 1939:36). Tepejí was a principal settlement and stopping place on the road already established between the capital and Querétaro before the Zacatecas silver strike of 1546. In 1550, Viceroy Antonio de Mendoza ordered verification that a bridge was being constructed there (Powell 1952:17-18). In 1555, Viceroy Luis de Velasco took steps to increase the available supply of meat to travelers going there (Powell 1952:27).

**Tula (or Tula de Allende)** [20 03N  99 21W]: On 21 November 1724, Rivera began his long journey, spending that night in the *villa* of Guadalupe, and proceeding to San Juan del Río by way of Cuautitlán and Tula (Alessio Robles 1946:17). Rivera wrote that on 23 November 1724, after passing through Coyotepec and "Guegotoca," he spent the night in Tula (Alessio Robles 1946:26). Morfí also went there, on 9 August 1777. He described the road from Huehuetoca as rough and full of brush. His party entered the town after passing over a river on a wooden bridge; upon leaving they crossed again, this time by ford, and climbed a crest which was also named Tula (Alessio Robles 1935:27-28). In 1555, one of Viceroy Velasco's regulations allowed an increase in the food supply for those traveling to Tula (Powell 1952:27).

**Pueblo de San Francisco** [19 59N  99 30W]: Nicolas de Lafora passed through this Otomite village on 20 March 1766. It is now San Francisco Soyaniquilpan, México state (Alessio Robles 1939:36).

**Clauda and Cuesta de Clauda**: On 20 March 1766 Lafora described this hill and Otomite pueblo, two leagues from San Francisco Soyaniquilpan, México state, as being in a malpais (Alessio Robles 1939:37). From Clauda

EL CAMINO REAL

Lafora went to Arroyo Zarco. [See **ARROYO ZARCO**]

**Jilotepec** [19 58N   99 32W]: Jilotepec appears to be both the province directly to the north of México City and a principal settlement and stopping place on the road already established between the capital and Querétaro before the Zacatecas silver strike of 1546. It was located on the alternate road to the west of Tula (Powell 1952:17). A regulation in 1555 by Viceroy Velasco took steps to increase the available supply of meat to travelers going to Jilotepec (Powell 1952:27).

**Capulalpa** [20 04N   99 38W]: On 24 November 1724, after leaving Tula, Rivera traveled west and walked nine leagues through land which he described sometimes as flat and other times as having hills and ravines. He wrote that he then passed the hill named Capulalpa. (Alessio Robles 1946:26). Lafora passed by this small pueblo and a rocky hill of the same name on 21 March 1766. In 1939, it was known as Capulalpa San Miguel, in México state (Alessio Robles 1939:37).

**La Hacienda de San Antonio**: Morfí stayed at this hacienda, just north northwest of Tula, on 9 August 1777 and commented on the black and red coloration of the terrain (Alessio Robles 1935:28).

**Arroyo Zarco** [20 07N   99 44W]: Rivera wrote that on 24 November 1724, after passing Capulalpa, he stayed at a hacienda called Arroyo Zarco (Alessio Robles 1946:26). Lafora referred to this as "Hacienda de Arroyo Zarco" and the described the livestock there as belonging to the Jesuits. He was there on 21 March 1766. Presently, it can be identified as "Arroyozarco," an *estancia* in modern México state (Alessio Robles 1939:37). This hacienda, which formerly belonged to the Jesuits, was visited by Morfí on 10 August 1777. He located it on the bank of the arroyo from which it took its name in a range of gentle hills with many fields and pastures. Besides the house, chapel, and other hacienda buildings, Morfí noted the existence of an inn for the use of travelers (Alessio Robles 1935:28-29).

**El Ranchito de las Encinillas** [20 09N   99 45W]: Lafora described the maize fields and pastures as he saw them on 21 March 1766. It is now Encinillas Tenatzat, a *ranchería* in México state (Alessio Robles 1939:37).

**Ruano**: On 21 March 1766, Lafora went through this "Pueblito de Oto-mítes," which was made up of huts covered with straw in México state. There various streams joined to form the San Juan River. Next to the road was a small lake formed by a spring which supplied drinking water for most of the year (Alessio Robles 1939:37).

**Llano del Cazadero** [20 19N  99 52W]: Rivera wrote that on 25 November 1724, after leaving Arroyo Zarco, he traveled five leagues west southwest through plains, which had no mountains, and followed the extension of the plain called Llano del Cazadero (Alessio Robles 1946:26). Lafora, on 22 March 1766, described this plain northwest of Ruano, Mexico state. It was named for a hunt held in honor of Viceroy don Antonio de Mendoza in 1540. He noted that the road split there (Alessio Robles 1939:38). Morfi, on 11 August 1777, described leaving Arroyo Zarco, passing a stream which ran only after rains, climbing a small hill, and sighting a lagoon, then entering this plain which was five leagues in diameter. He also noted that its name commemorated a hunt in the early days of the conquest (Alessio Robles 1935:29-30).

**Venta del Cuervo**: Lafora described the Venta del Cuervo as being on the other fork of the road from that which he took from Llano del Cazadero to Palmillas (22 March 1766). (See also Alessio Robles 1939:38).

**Palmillas** [20 19N  99 55W]: Rivera wrote that on 25 November 1724, after leaving Arroyo Zarco, he followed the extension of the Llano del Cazadero to the "Rancho de las Palmillas" (Alessio Robles 1946:26). On the road taken by Lafora between Llano del Cazadero, México state and San Juan del Río, Querétaro, he described a ruined house with this name. Although not identifiable at present, it was located one league from San Juan del Río, Querétaro (Alessio Robles 1939:39).

**San Juan del Río** [20 23N  100 00W]: Rivera wrote that on 25 November 1724, he headed west southwest through land which he described as difficult because of rocks and because of the slope of the hill between Rancho de las Palmillas and the pueblo of San Juan del Río. He spent the night at this pueblo (Alessio Robles 1946:26). Lafora was at this city in Querétaro state alongside the Río de San Juan on 22 March 1766. San Juan del Río was founded in 1531 and named as a pueblo in 1557. Lafora reached it after crossing a small hill covered with loose rock and found a bridge with five arches (Alessio Robles 1939:39).

Morfí, on 11 August 1777, was quite impressed with the agricultural produce of this town, but not with the construction of its 400 houses. He described the population as being of all races and generally employed as muleteers; they also maintained a company of cavalry for the regiment of Querétaro. Its church was staffed by clerics of the archbishopric of México, and there was a Dominican convent and a hospital (Alessio Robles 1935:30). It was a principal settlement and stopping place on the road already established between the capital and Querétaro before the Zacatecas silver strike of 1546 (Powell 1952:17). As late as the 1580s, this town was in danger of depopulation due to Chichimeca raids (Powell 1952:173-175). From San Juan del Río Rivera went to Amascala. [See **AMASCALA**]

**Guichiapa** [20 23N   99 39W]: Lafora passed Guichiapa, ten leagues from San Juan del Río, on 22 March 1766. It was peopled by "*indios mecos*" (non-sedentary natives) who were used as soldiers for the colony of Nuevo Santander. This town is now called Huichapan, Querétaro. Lafora located it in the Sierra Gorda, but it is likely that he was mistaken. The name means Río Grande de la Chía or "sage seed" in Nahuatl (Alessio Robles 1939:39).

**Tolimanejo**: Lafora went there on 22 March 1766. He reported that it was populated by "*indios mecos*" (non-sedentary natives) and by a small squadron of soldiers of the colony of Nuevo Santander. Located in the Sierra Gorda near San Juan del Río, it is now called Tolimanejo San Francisco, Querétaro (Alessio Robles 1939:39).

**Estancia Grande** [20 25N  100 04W]: On 23 March 1766, Lafora passed by this area, which is simply labeled Estancia, Querétaro on modern maps. He observed horses, some small livestock, and cultivated fields in a dry region of prickly pear cactus and mesquite (Alessio Robles 1939:40). On

12 August 1777, Morfí noted that this hacienda was on his right and north of San Juan del Río (Alessio Robles 1935:30).

**El Paraje de Arroyo Seco**: Morfí passed by there on 12 August 1777 just north of San Juan del Río on a flat road, which was surrounded by mesquite and cactus (Alessio Robles 1935:30).

**Lira** [20 28N  100 09W]: Lafora called this place "La Lira" when he was there on 23 March 1766. It was in a dry area of cactus and mesquite two leagues south of Querétaro (Alessio Robles 1939:40). This hacienda was noted by Morfí on 12 August 1777 as being between San Juan del Río and Querétaro (Alessio Robles 1935:30-31).

**Noria**: Lafora called this place Noria on 23 March 1766. In was an *estancia* in the gully of Querétaro, located two leagues from the city over various hills and rocks (Alessio Robles 1939:40). Two leagues southeast of Querétaro, Morfí passed Noria on 12 August 1777 and commented on the irrigation works. The road in this area, which was bad because of loose rock, passed through a canyon in the hills toward the city of Querétaro (Alessio Robles 1935:31).

**Querétaro** [20 36N  100 23W]: Lafora stayed at Querétaro from 23 to 26 March 1766. He described it as setting beside a river which carried little water in the dry season, in a plain at the edge of a range of mountains. He noted that much food was produced nearby and that ample water was delivered by means of an arched aqueduct, which was constructed shortly before 1735. Both the religious and secular governments were subject to the jurisdiction of México. Five companies of calvary were stationed there, along with ten convents of priests and three of nuns, and many churches. The name is the Tarascan word for "place of the ball game." It is the capital of the state of the same name. Conquered on 25 July 1531 by don Fernando de Tapia, who named it Santiago de Querétaro, it gained title of *ciudad* in 1655 (Alessio Robles 1939:40-41).

Morfí conducted his *visita*, or inspection of the mission, there from 12-29 August 1777. He was most interested in some excavations of pre-Spanish sites outside of the city and described them in great detail. According to

Morfí, the city lay in a beautiful plain capable of producing all of its needs. The population amounted to 43,000 people spread along both sides of a river, which was spanned by a well-built stone bridge. He described the many churches, noting especially the Convent of San Francisco in the heart of the city, the large and ornate Santuario de Guadalupe, and the richly adorned Convent of Santa Clara (Alessio Robles 1935:31-41). This quickly became a center for wagon transport with the Zacatecas strike and the introduction of the new heavier covered wagon (Powell 1950:239). The route from México to here was already well-established before the strike at Zacatecas (Powell 1952:17). From Querétaro Lafora went to Apaseo. [See **APASEO**]

**Santa Rosa** [20 44N  100 27W]: Located just outside of the city of Querétaro, Morfí described Santa Rosa as an "unfortunate village" (*pueblito infeliz*) on 29 August 1777 (Alessio Robles 1935:41).

**La Hacienda de Buenavista** [20 49N  100 28W]: Morfí's party stayed at La Hacienda de Buenavista, six leagues north of Querétaro, from 29 August to 1 September 1777. He described it as deserving of its name, occupying a large fertile valley surrounded by mountains. Water was supplied by a dam and reservoir, and a poor inn cared for travelers. Upon leaving, Morfí's party climbed a small hill called Puerto Nieto on a stretch of bad road and then entered a large plain of good land filled with mesquite, cactus, and huizache (Alessio Robles 1935:42). From La Hacienda de Buenavista Morfí went to Puerto de Nieto. [See **PUERTO DE NIETO**]

**Hacienda de Amascala** [20 42N  100 16W]: Rivera wrote that on 26 November 1724, after leaving San Juan del Río, he traveled northwest 11 leagues through land which he described as flat but with hills, which were full of mesquite, *huisapoches* and prickly pear growth. He stated that he could see some hills in the distance two or more leagues from the road. He stopped that day at a hacienda called Amascala (Alessio Robles 1946:26).

**Puerto de Pinto (or El Pinto)** [20 48N  100 25W]: On 27 November 1724, Rivera left Amascala and traveled west through land which he described as flat and with dense hills. He could see some hills to the north and south. He then passed the Puertos de Pinto and Nieto (Alessio Robles 1946:27).

**El Portezuelo de Jofre** [20 51N  100 26W]: The 1550s eastern road from Querétaro to Zacatecas by way of San Felipe passed east of Nieto Pass then went across this pass near the later San Luis de Paz (Powell 1952:17). A *presidio* was established there in the 1580s (Powell 1952:144).

**Puerto de Nieto** [20 53N  100 32W]: On 27 November 1724, Rivera left Amascala and traveled west through land which he described as flat and with dense hills. He could see some hills to the north and south. He then passed the Puertos de Pinto and Nieto (Alessio Robles 1946:27). Upon leaving Buenavista, Morfi's party climbed a small hill called Puerto Nieto on a stretch of bad road and then entered a large plain of good land filled with mesquite, cactus, and huizache (Alessio Robles 1935:42). Puerto de Nieto was probably the first landmark on one of two 1550s roads between Querétaro and San Felipe, leading toward Zacatecas. The road went directly north and passed just to the east of Puerto de Nieto. There another road spurred off to San Miguel (Powell 1952:17).

**Palmar de Vega**: Palmar de Vega can be identified with present-day Pozos. Mines were opened there, just north of the Portezuelo de Jofre on the Jofre River in 1575-1576, and a *presidio* was in operation before 1582. The eastern route was the main branch of the Querétaro to Zacatecas road at that time (Powell 1952:144).

**Llano de la Mohina**: The 1550s road from Querétaro to Zacatecas by way of San Felipe passed east of Nieto Pass, then went across Jofre pass near the later San Luis de Paz and then through this plain. It joined the other road between Río de los Sauces and San Felipe (Powell 1952:17).

**San Miguel (el Grande)** [20 55N  100 45W]: Rivera wrote that on 27 November 1724 he passed the mountain passes of Pinto and Nieto and found the *villa* of San Miguel el Grande. He described it as consisting of Spaniards, mestizos and mulattoes, and Otomite Indians. It is now known as San Miguel de Allende, in the state of Guanajuato (Alessio Robles 1946:28).

Morfi described this *villa* on 1 September 1777, placing it on the slope of a large gorge. According to Morfi, the view was impressive but the streets, plaza, and architecture were poor. Two parish churches, one new and one old, occupied the central plaza, and the town also boasted of a Franciscan convent along with a large and beautiful house occupied by Los Padres del Oratorio and a convent of Santa Clara. Despite the profusion of religious institutions, Morfí criticized the morality of the population as well as their industry. The region produced both fruits and livestock (Alessio Robles 1935:42-45).

There was more than one San Miguel, one of which is known as simply "El Grande" and was established in or near 1542 with the involvement of a Franciscan named Fray Juan de San Miguel. A church and convent were soon constructed by a French Franciscan, Bernardo Cossín (Powell 1952:7-8). San Miguel was largely abandoned in 1551 as a result of Indian raids. On 15 December 1555, Viceroy Luis de Velasco ordered its official founding as a defensive site due to the frequency of raids in the area and its being the most important center of highway traffic from both México and Michoacán. Viceroy Velasco himself was on his way to supervise it but took ill in Apaseo and commissioned Angel de Villafañe. Numerous grants were made there through the 1560s (Powell 1952:67-68).

Between Querétaro and the later site of San Felipe there were two main roads leading toward Zacatecas in the 1550s. One went directly northwest to San Miguel and followed the east bank of the river of that name to San Felipe. The two joined between Río de los Sauces and San Felipe. This was also an entry point for a road from Michoacán which carried supplies north and silver south. After the mineral strikes at Guanajuato in the mid-1550s, a road connected that city directly to San Miguel and the *Camino Real* (Powell 1952:17-19).

## Map 3: Route from San Miguel Allende to Ojuelos de Jalisco

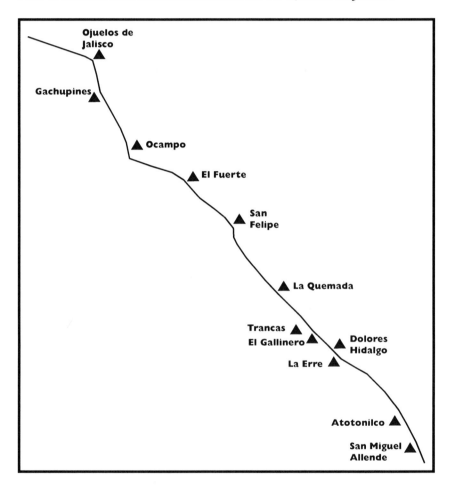

**Pequeño Río de San Miguel**: Rivera wrote that on 29 November 1724 he left San Miguel el Grande and headed west northwest through land which he described as flat but with some hills and mounts of mesquite. He stated that at the beginning of this day's travels he passed the small river of San Miguel (Alessio Robles 1946:28). One road north from Querétaro went northwest to San Miguel and followed the river of the same name to San Felipe (Powell 1952:17-19).

**El Santuario de Atotonilco** [Estación de Atotonilco 21 01N 100 47W]: Encountered one hour out of "La Villa de San Miguel el Grande" over good land and reasonable road by Morfí on 3 September 1777, this was described as a collection of curiously adorned chapels (Alessio Robles 1935:45-46). There was a *presidio* there, just a few leagues north of San Miguel el Grande on the western branch road to Zacatecas. It was built between 1590 and 1595 by order of Viceroy Velasco II and abandoned before 1607 (Powell 1952:147).

**Hacienda de la R (or Hacienda de la Erre)** [21 06N 100 54W]: Rivera wrote that on 29 November 1724, he left San Miguel el Grande and passed the small river of San Miguel and stayed at the Hacienda de la R (Alessio Robles 1946:28). Morfí passed by there on 3 September 1777 on a road covered with brush a half day out of San Miguel el Grande, after crossing a river at a good ford. He described it as having a grand house with a plaza where bullfights were held on special occasions and irrigated gardens which grew all manner of produce. An alternative name is that of "La Erre," which is located in the modern Municipalidad of Dolores Hidalgo (Alessio Robles 1935:46).

**Dolores** [Dolores Hidalgo 21 09N 100 57W]: This was described by Morfí as a "*pequeño pueblo*" just north of La Hacienda de la R on 4 September 1777. He went on to write that it was situated on the bank of a river in a beautiful land. According to Morfí, it had all the conditions for making its inhabitants happy if only the land wasn't all taken up by the local haciendas (Alessio Robles 1935:47).

**Hacienda del Gallinero**: Rivera wrote that on 30 November 1724 he left the Hacienda de la R and headed northwest through land which he described as flat, with very little mounts, and with hills to the west of the road. He then passed the Hacienda del Gallinero (Alessio Robles 1946:28). Morfí passed there, northwest of La Hacienda de la R, on 4 September 1777 (Alessio Robles 1935:48).

**Hacienda de las Trancas** [21 15N  101 01W]: Rivera wrote that on 30 November 1724, after leaving the Hacienda de la R, he headed northwest through land which he described as flat, with very few mounts, and with hills to the west of the road. He then also passed the Hacienda de las Trancas (Alessio Robles 1946:28). This was one of a series of haciendas passed by Morfí on 4 September 1777 northwest of La Hacienda de la R. He described it as lying on a small hill next to which was an arroyo with water. The road was good, and other arroyos and small lagoons also dotted the area (Alessio Robles 1935:48).

**Hacienda de la Quemada** [21 19N  101 07W]: On 30 November 1724, after passing the Haciendas del Gallinero and las Trancas, Rivera stopped at the Hacienda de la Quemada (Alessio Robles 1946:28). This was one of a series of haciendas passed by Morfí on 4 September 1777 northwest of La Hacienda de la R. The road was good, and arroyos and small lagoons dotted the area. It sat next to an arroyo which ran very fast after a rain. It was dedicated to the raising of small livestock; Morfí saw a fine house, a chapel, and an inn for travelers (Alessio Robles 1935:48).

**Hacienda de la Huerta**  [21 25N  101 11W]: On 5 September 1777, Morfí passed this hacienda shortly after leaving La Hacienda de la Quemada. The road was generally good to there, and he described the land as pretty but uncultivated. He considered the hacienda as very miserable because it possessed little land. Beyond this spot the road entered some mountains and the road became poor and rocky; the land was also arid between rainfalls (Alessio Robles 1935:48-49).

**San Felipe** [21 29N  101 13W]: On 1 December 1724, Rivera wrote that he left the Hacienda de la Quemada and headed north northwest through land which he described as good pasture land that did not have any mounts worth mentioning, and found the Villa de San Felipe, which he stated was populated by settlers similar to those at San Miguel. Presently it can be identified as Ciudad González, Guanajuato (Alessio Robles 1946:28).

Viceroy Velasco gave the title and privilege for this town on 1 January 1562 as a defensive outpost. Francisco Velasco was commissioned for the task of "re-foundation." It was placed near Tunal Grande and the San Francisco valley, both Chichimeca population centers, and close to the pass called Portezuelo, a favorite target for attacks. It was also a base for northward expansion and for the cochineal trade from San Luis Potosí (Powell 1952:68-69). It was also the entry point for a road from Guanajuato to the *Camino Real* and Zacatecas (Powell 1952:19). San Felipe was awarded the title of *villa* for its efforts in the Chichimeca campaign of 1570 (Mecham 1927:100).

**La Hacienda de Santa Bárbara** [21 32N  101 22W]: This hacienda was passed by Morfí after leaving the mountains north of the Hacienda de la Huerta on 5 September 1777. He described its setting as "delightful," being in a valley surrounded by mountains and beside a dry arroyo; it was watered by an abundant spring. It was dedicated to the raising of small livestock. Morfí gave a very unflattering description of the house and the care given it by its owners (Alessio Robles 1935:49).

**La Cuesta de San Felipe** [Ocampo 21 39N  101 30W]: Rivera wrote that on 3 December 1724, after stopping at San Felipe, he headed northwest through land he described as flat and passed La Cuesta de San Felipe (Alessio Robles 1946:28). This pass, near the town of the same name, was a point on the road north to Zacatecas in the 1550s (Powell 1952:17-18). A *presidio* was established there, ca. 1570. It lay between the sierras of San Pedro and Pájaro at or near the present town of Ocampo (Powell 1952:143).

**Hacienda de los Gachupines** [21 46N  101 34W]: Rivera wrote that on 3 December 1724, after passing the Cuesta de San Felipe, he stopped at the Hacienda de los Gachupines (Alessio Robles 1946:28).

**El Rancho Santa Efigia**: This rancho was found by Morfí beside a flat road in good land on 6 September 1777. He gave it as the boundary between the bishoprics of Michoacán and Guadalajara and at the beginning of Nueva Galicia as well as at the start of an immense plain. He described the road as flat and good (Alessio Robles 1935:49).

**Los Ojuelos (Ojuelos de Jalisco)** [21 52N  101 35W]: On 4 December 1724, after leaving the Hacienda de los Gachupines, Rivera headed west northwest through plains which he described as having some mounts of oak trees, mesquite and prickly pear cactus, and passed the hacienda called "los Ojuelos" on the east side (Alessio Robles 1946:28).

On 6 September 1777, Morfí described this hacienda in detailed and glowing terms. Beside the large house was an inn and across from them a chapel; along with the habitations of the priest and others, these formed a great plaza. Morfí also noted a sizable garden and store in this central area. The hacienda was set in pleasant hills of good pasture (Alessio Robles 1935:50-51).

Ojuelos was established early as a stop along the road from Querétaro to Zacatecas. It was north of the Portezuelo de San Felipe and south of Encinillas (Powell 1952:18). In 1554, this was the site of a disastrous defeat for the Spanish at the hands of the Chichimeca (Powell 1952:61). It was probably established as a *presidio* in 1570 by Capitán Pedro Carrillo Dávila. It is now known as Ojuelos de Jalisco (Powell 1952:143).

## Map 4: Route from Ojuelos de Jalisco to Zacatecas

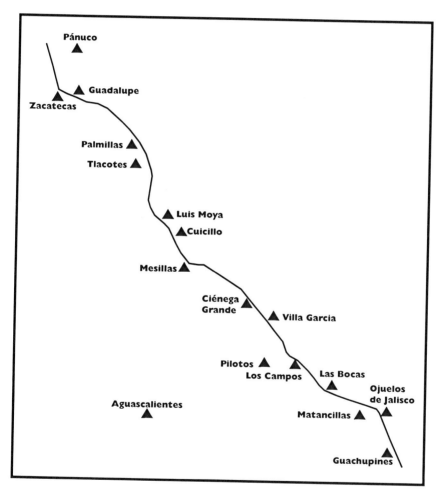

**Matancillas** [21 53N  101 38W]: Rivera wrote that after passing Los Ojuelos, he passed Matancillas, a hill or incline full of rocks, on his way west northwest on 4 December 1724 (Alessio Robles 1946:28). From Matancillas Rivera went to Bocas de Gallardo. [See **BOCAS DE GALLARDO**]

**Las Letras**: Morfí described this collection of ranchos set in a canyon in some damp hills on 7 September 1777. It was between the haciendas of Los Ojuelos and Ciénega Grande (Alessio Robles 1935:51).

**El Rancho de Encinillas** [Encinillas 21 58N  101 44W]: On 7 September 1777 Morfí passed El Rancho de Encinillas, which was part of a group of ranchos located between the haciendas of Los Ojuelos and Ciénega Grande (Alessio Robles 1935:51). Encinillas, north of Ojuelos and San Felipe, was the dividing line between the Audiencias of México and Nueva Galicia in the 1550s (Powell 1952:18).

**El Rancho de Los Pilolos**: On 7 September 1777 Morfí passed El Rancho de los Pilolos, which was part of a group of ranchos between the haciendas of Los Ojuelos and Ciénega Grande, (Alessio Robles 1935:51).

**El Rancho de Borunda**: El Rancho de Borunda was one of the ranchos passed by Morfí on 7 September 1777, which were located between the haciendas of Los Ojuelos and Ciénega Grande (Alessio Robles 1935:51).

**El Rancho de Agua Gorda** [22 07N  101 55W]: This was one of a group of ranchos passed by Morfí on 7 September 1777 between the haciendas of Los Ojuelos and Ciénega Grande (Alessio Robles 1935:51).

**Bocas de Gallardo**: Rivera wrote that on 4 December 1724, after passing Matancillas, he stopped in the small hacienda called Bocas de Gallardo (Alessio Robles 1946:28). "Las Bocas" was a stop on the Querétaro to Zacatecas road between Encinillas and Ciénega Grande in the 1550s (Powell 1952:18). This was the site of a disastrous Spanish loss to the Chichimeca in the middle 1580s (Powell 1952:139). A *presidio* was established there around that time. It is possible that modern Bocas de Gallardo occupies this site (Powell 1952:143).

**Ciénaga de Larrañaga** [Los Asientos 22 14N  102 06W]: On 5 December 1724, after stopping at the hacienda called Bocas de Gallardo, Rivera came to Ciénaga de Larrañaga, a hacienda where Rivera stated that the metal produced by the mines in the "*real de los Asientos*" was processed (Alessio Robles 1946:29).

**La Hacienda de Ciénega Grande** [22 12N  102 01W]: Morfí judged this the best hacienda that he had seen up to this point, despite its not being cared for properly. It had many fields for cultivation, good pasture, and an arroyo which carried water more than sufficient to its needs.  Along with its agricultural uses, this hacienda processed the products of Las Minas de Ibarra in its *patio*. It had a grand house, a chapel, and extensive gardens. Morfí stayed there on 7 September 1777 (Alessio Robles 1935:51-52). By the 1550s, this was already a well-known place on the *Camino Real*, just south of Zacatecas and to the north of Las Bocas (Powell 1952:18). A *presidio* was established there around the 1580s. Modern Tepezala may be near its site (Powell 1952:143). From Cíenega Grande Morfí went to La Hacienda del Pabellón. [See **LA HACIENDA DEL PABELLON**]

**Paraje de Mesillas** [22 19N  102 10W]: On 6 December 1724, after leaving Ciénaga de Larrañaga, Rivera headed northwest through land which he described as marked with hills and rocks. He went through some hills with dense terrain, and then passed the uninhabited Paraje de Mesillas (Alessio Robles 1946:29).

**La Hacienda de San Agustín de Buena Vista**: The fertile lands and abundant water, delivered by pipeline as well as held by a dam, were wasted, according to Morfí, by the poor care given to this site by its owners. On 8 September 1777 he noted the ruins of a mill on this almost abandoned hacienda, located some distance south of Zacatecas (Alessio robles 1935:52).

**Hacienda de San Diego (Hacienda de Los Diegos)**: Rivera wrote that on 6 December 1724, after passing the Paraje de Mesillas, he could see the Hacienda de San Dicgo to the east (Alessio Robles 1946:29). On 8 September 1777, Morfí passed by the "Hacienda de Los Diegos" south of Zacatecas, noting the good quality of the road and the red coloration of the soil. He commented on how well-managed the estate was, its field and livestock, and the good care and use of its chapel (Alessio Robles 1935: 52-53). From Hacienda de Los Diegos Rivera went to Tlacotes and Morfí went to El Colegio Apostólico de Guadalupe. [See TLACOTES and EL COLEGIO APOSTOLICO DE GUADALUPE]

**Apaseo** [20 33N 100 37W]: Lafora called this place "San Juan Bautista de Apaseo" and describes it as a small adobe Indian town on flat ground. He arrived traveling west from Querétaro over level land covered with mesquite and other brush on 26 March 1766. One small hill was visible in the distance. Apaseo is Tarascan for "place of weasels" (Alessio Robles 1939:41-42). Before the end of 1542 Hernán Pérez de Bocanegra y Córdoba had been given land grants for mills and an inn at Apaseo, which was the "nucleus of settlement on the very edge of the Chichimeca tribes." He and the settlement were military mainstays of the province for at least a decade (Powell 1952:5).

**Celaya (or Zelaya)** [20 31N 100 48W]: Lafora called this town "Celaya" when he passed through on 26 March 1766 and described it as a small Indian pueblo. Lafora mentioned that there was little water there. There were, however, many olives which gave much oil (Alessio Robles 1939:42). It was founded as a defensive settlement in 1570 by Lieutenant Captain-General Francisco de Sande on the authorization of Viceroy Enríquez. A *presidio* was established within the first decade of Spanish occupation (Powell 1952:116,152-153).

**Río de la Laja**: Lafora crossed this small but permanent stream at La Venta del Guaje, Guanajuato on 27 March 1766. He then followed this to Salamanca, where it joined the Río Grande de Lerma (Alessio Robles 1939:42).

**La venta del Guaje**: On 27 March 1766 Lafora crossed the Río de la Laja, where the road was flat and good and the area well-cultivated (Alessio Robles 1939:42).

**Salamanca** [20 34N 101 12W]: Lafora visited this *villa* in the state of

Guanajuato on 27 March 1766. It was founded in 1603. The Río de la Laja joins the Río Grande de Lerma in Salamanca. The road into this city was mostly flat, through country unsuited to cultivation because of a profusion of thistles and swampiness in the rainy season (Alessio Robles 1939:42).

**Río Grande (Río Grande de Lerma):** Lafora referred to this as the Río Grande de Lerma when he encountered it in the *villa* of Salamanca on 27 March 1766 and traced its route in his *Relación*. Variations of Río Lerma include Río Grande and Río Santiago (Alessio Robles 1939:42).

**Temascatío** [San José Temascatío 20 41N  101 16W]: Lafora approached Temascatío, described as a small pueblo, heading north from Salamanca on 28 March 1766. The name is an Azteco-Tarascan hybrid meaning "steambath." Four place names in the state of Guanajuato contain this word. San José Temascatío best fits into Lafora's route (Alessio Robles 1939:43).

**Puerto Blanco** [Guadalupe de Paseo Blanco 20 45N  101 24W]: Lafora passed through this area of gentle rocky hills on 28 March 1766 heading north into Guanajuato (Alessio Robles 1939:43).

**El Rancho de Sierra:** On 28 March 1766 Lafora described this rancho located in the Puerto Blanco area of Guanajuato. He also described the arroyo which passed through the rancho and which formed various pools. Just west of there the road split, with one branch going into the city of Guanajuato and the other toward Silao (Alessio Robles 1939:43).

**Troje Blanca** [Troje 20 56N  101 22W; Trejo 20 49N  101 25W]: Lafora wrote of this rancho on 28 March 1766. It was a quarter league from the fork in the roads near Rancho de Sierra, Guanajuato (Alessio Robles 1939:43). Modern maps show a Troje and a Trejo, both in the same area. Trejo features a permanent arroyo which could supply water year around as described by Lafora at Caleras, one quarter league distant. Troje reflects Lafora's spelling.

**Caleras:** Lafora went through this rancho in Guanajuato, 6 leagues southwest of Silao, Guanajuato on 28 March 1766 and one quarter league from

Troje Blanca. There was a river bed with various pools which supplied water to the local inhabitants (Alessio Robles 1939:43).

**Silao** [20 56N 101 26W]: Lafora described the area of Silao, Guanajuato as being flat and well-cultivated, providing staple crops and pasture for animals. He passed through on 28 March 1766. The population was Indian and *gentes de razón*. It was founded by the year 1553 (Alessio Robles 1939:44).

**Guanajuato** [21 01N 101 15W]: Lafora called it by the more formal "Real de Minas de Guanajuato" when he passed nearby on 28 March 1766. He followed the other fork when the road split near Rancho de Sierra. It is the capital of the state of the same name. The name is Tarascan for "frog hill" (Alessio Robles 1939:43).

The minerals of Guanajuato were discovered by a convoy en route to Zacatecas, shortly after the founding of those great mines. A succession of finds culminated in the discovery of La Veta Grande in 1558. In 1554 it was named Real de Minas de Santa Fe de Guanajuato; it became a *villa* in 1619, and a ciudad in 1741 (Mecham 1927:50).

**Rancho de los Sauces** [21 01N 101 32W]: Lafora went there on a flat road over gentle hills surrounded by pasture and cultivated fields between Silao, Guanajuato and León on 29 March 1766 (Alessio Robles 1939:44).

**Villa de León** [21 07N 101 40W]: On 29 March 1766 Lafora described 3000 houses, some of stone, and ten churches, containing both Jesuits and Franciscans. Villa de León can be presently identified as León de los Aldamas (Alessio Robles 1939:44). León was founded in 1575-1576 under orders of Viceroy Enriquez, mainly to provide protection for mines in the area and pacify local Indians (Powell 1952:153).

**Hacienda de Lagunillas** [21 12N 101 46W]: Now in Guanajuato, Lafora noted this hacienda, three leagues northwest of León over hills of loose rock, as the beginning of the jurisdiction of Nueva Galicia. He was there on 30 March 1766. The road divided there (Alessio Robles 1939:44).

**El Saucillo**: Lafora encountered El Saucillo one half league from the divide in the road at Hacienda de Lagunillas, Guanajuato down a rocky road. He described it as consisting of Indian huts on 30 March 1766. There is a rancho in Guanajuato with the same name but it appears to be in a different location (Alessio Robles 1939:44).

**Lagos** [Lagos de Moreno 21 21N  101 55W]: Bishop Mota y Escobar, writing between 1602 and 1605, gave the founding date of the "Villa de los Lagos" as 1561. The reasons for building there were defense against Indians and the agricultural potential of the area. He noted that Lagos was situated on the *Camino Real* that went from Nueva Galicia to México and from México to Zacatecas, one of the most often used roads of the time (Ramirez Cabañas 1940:122). The town still retained its defensive character with the adobe house set far apart and resembling small forts. Bishop Mota y Escobar described the setting as the best in the kingdom, with two rivers and a large lake watering a flat, fertile landscape. The only drawback was that firewood was scarce due to the distance of the nearest mountains (Ramirez Cabañas 1940:121-123).

Lafora entered Lagos, now Lagos de Moreno, a city in the state of Jalisco, on 30 March 1766. He described it as being made up of rocky hills and ravines which made for difficult passage. In the *villa* itself the Río de San Juan de Lagos split into two arms, between which the ground was very sandy. There were 400 adobe houses and countless huts, a church and convents for both Capuchins and Mercedarians. This mountainous terrain was dedicated to the breeding of horses and mules. The founding date given here, 1563, differs from that given by Bishop Mota y Escobar (Alessio Robles 1939:45).

**Lugar de Buenavista**: Lafora went through there on 1 April 1766, one league north northwest of Lagos, Jalisco. He passed an unnamed lake half way between the two points (Alessio Robles 1939:47).

**Cuesta de Portezuelo**: This unidentified hill north northwest of Lagos, Jalisco, was passed by Lafora on 1 April 1766 (Alessio Robles 1939:47).

**Hacienda de Doña María Guerra**: This unidentified hacienda at the foot of the Cuesta de Portezuelo, north northwest of Lagos, Jalisco, was passed by Lafora on 1 April 1766 (Alessio Robles 1939:47).

**El Cauce del Río de Mariquita**: This unknown arroyo north northwest of Lagos, Jalisco was mentioned by Lafora on 1 April 1766 (Alessio Robles 1939:47).

**Hacienda de Los Sauces** [≈21 35N  102 07W]: Lafora passed the Hacienda de Los Sauces on 1 April 1766; it was located beside an arroyo eight leagues north northwest of Lagos, Jalisco. A 1925 Rand McNally map shows the place name "Sauces" (Alessio Robles 1939:48).

**Ciénaga de Matas** [Ciénega de Mata 21 44N  101 49W]: On 1 April 1766 Lafora described this as the source of the arroyo beside which was found the Hacienda de Los Sauces, Jalisco and six leagues above it. It is now called Ciénega de Mata (Alessio Robles 1939:48).

**Hacienda de San Bartolomé** [≈21 44N  102 10W]: Now San Bartolo, Lafora found this hacienda five leagues south southeast of Aguascalientes on 2 April 1766. It had a brook with a pool which held enough water to supply animals during the dry season. (Alessio Robles 1939:48).

**Aguascalientes** [21 53N  102 18W]: Bishop Mota y Escobar described this town briefly in the early years of the seventeenth century. He noted adobe houses laid out in a disorderly manner and a parish church. Its name stems from the presence of hot springs whose water supported the mostly poor and mestizo population. The main local industry was the raising of livestock (Ramirez Cabañas 1940:124).

Lafora described "La Villa de Aguascalientes" as he saw it on 2 April 1766. He saw 2000 houses plus numerous huts spread on a fertile wooded plain which produced an abundance of chile plants, maize, beans and some wheat. As his party entered from the south southeast they passed a canyon with a stream which ran only after rains. One league to the east was a hot spring whose water carved an arroyo through the *villa*. A spring to the west, at a *paraje* called Morcinique, supplied drinking water. Of the six churches found there, three belonged to the convents of the Merced, San Juan de

Dios, and San Diego. Lafora also commented on the presence of the European merchants who served the population (Alessio Robles 1939:48).

Josiah Gregg visited Aguascalientes in 1835 and mentioned its beautiful setting in a level plain. He guessed its population at 20,000 and noted that the area produced textiles. He went to visit some famous nearby hot springs but found them too crowded (Gregg 1933:274).

Aguascalientes was founded in 1575, declared a *villa* in 1611, a *ciudad* in 1824 and the capital of the state of Aguascalientes on 23 May 1835 (Alessio Robles 1939:48). Even before that date there were already settlers in the region. The specific reason for its founding was the protection of travelers to and from mines. A *presidio* was established soon thereafter but even that was almost insufficient to save the town in the face of native hostilities (Powell 1952:154-155). Josiah Gregg had come south to Aguascalientes from Refugio. [See **REFUGIO**]

**Morcinique**: Lafora described this *paraje* one league to the west of the *villa* of Aguascalientes as the location of a spring which provided drinking water (2 April 1766) (Alessio Robles 1939:48).

**Río de San Pedro**: Lafora crossed this as a dry riverbed twice just outside of Aguascalientes to the north on 3 April 1766 (Alessio Robles 1939:49).

**Río de Santiago**: Lafora crossed this river, low on water, just north of the city of Aguascalientes on 3 April 1766. The road divided near there, where Lafora took the left fork (Alessio Robles 1939:49).

**Hacienda de Pozo Bravo**: Lafora went through this hacienda one league north of the city of Aguascalientes on 3 April 1766. This area contained some cultivated fields but more cactus and pasture land dedicated to the raising of horses and mules (Alessio Robles 1939:49).

**Chicolote**: Lafora called this a "*rancho de indios*" when he was there on 3 April 1766. It was located two leagues north of the city of Aguascalientes. This area contained some cultivated fields but more cactus and pasture land dedicated to the raising of horses and mules. It is now a hacienda with a railroad station (Alessio Robles 1939:49).

**La Hacienda del Pabellón** [El Pabellón 22 10N 102 21W]: Lafora saw some cultivated fields there on 3 April 1766 but wrote that the hacienda, on which were raised horses and mules, contained much pasture and cactus. It was located just north of the city of Aguascalientes and is now in the state of the same name. On 24 January 1811, Generalissimo Miguel Hidalgo was removed from power while at this hacienda (Alessio Robles 1939:49). On 8 September 1777, five leagues north of the Hacienda de Ciénega Grande over good road, Morfí passed this hacienda on the slopes of a hill of the same name. He commented on its beauty and fertility and on the red and black coloration of the land (Alessio Robles 1935:52). From Pabellón Morfí went to La Hacienda de San Agustín de Buena Vista. [See LA HACIENDA DE SAN AGUSTIN DE BUENA VISTA]

**Tepezala** [22 13N 102 10W]: Founded by royal order in 1573 as a defensive towns, it had difficulty surviving its first years due to the danger to potential settlers (Powell 1952:154).

**El Rancho del Saucillo**: Lafora described cactus and pasture in this region two leagues north northeast of Hacienda del Pabellón, now in the state of Aguascalientes on 4 April 1766 (Alessio Robles 1939:50).

**Rancho de la Punta** [≈22 18N 102 12W]: Now a hacienda in the state of Aguascalientes, Lafora described it as four leagues north northeast from Hacienda del Pabellón in a region of pasture and cactus. He passed by on 4 April 1766. The road divided just north of this point (Alessio Robles 1939:50).

**Paraje del Cuicillo** [Cuisillo 22 23 N 102 15W]: This was the last stop along the road to Zacatecas in the 1550s, nine leagues south of that city. There, a major road north from Michoacán joined the *Camino Real* as well as one from San Luis Potosí to the north (Powell 1952:18).

**Hacienda de San Pedro** [San Pedro Piedra Gorda or Ciudad Cuauhtémoc 22 27N 102 21W]: Lafora said that this hacienda was just west of the fork in the road at Rancho de la Punta in Aguascalientes and was irrigated using water from a stream which originated in the mountains near Zacatecas. He passed near there on 4 April 1766. It is now a pueblo in the state of Zacatecas (Alessio Robles 1939:50).

**El Rancho de Tlacotes** [*Población* 22 34N 102 19W, Rail Station 22 34N 102 21W]: On 6 December 1724, after passing the Paraje de Mesillas and the Hacienda de San Diego, Rivera stopped at the rancho of Tlacotes (Alessio Robles 1946:29). Lafora described this as being on the north fork of the road from Rancho de la Punta in Aguascalientes (4 April 1766). The name derives from the Nahuatl word for a shrub of the arum family (Alessio Robles 1939:50). From El Rancho de Tlacotes Rivera went to Zacatecas. [See **ZACATECAS**]

**Las Palmillas** [22 39N 102 21W]: Lafora, on 5 April 1766, located Las Palmillas six leagues to the east southeast of the city of Zacatecas in an area of rugged hills. It is now a rancho in the same state (Alessio Robles 1939:50). A *presidio* was placed there, between Zacatecas and Cuicillo, in the 1580s to defend the road against the Chichimeca (Powell 1952:143).

**El Colegio Apostólico de Guadalupe** [Guadalupe 22 45N 102 37W]: Within one league of the city of Zacatecas, Morfí passed by El Colegio Apostólico de Guadalupe on 9 September 1777. He described a plain but neat church and wrote that it had been founded in 1702 (Alessio Robles 1935:53). In 1681, this *santuario* was built one league from the city of Zacatecas (Bargellini 1991:268).

**Refugio**: In 1835, Josiah Gregg turned southwest from Cuencamé and went to Durango. When his group left for Aguascalientes he wrote that it was a few days before they were again on "the *camino real* that led from Chihuahua to Zacatecas." Another road was shown which went more directly south from Cuencamé toward Fresnillo. Just north of Fresnillo, in the town of Salado, this road split, with one branch going through Fresnillo, where it met the road from Durango, and Zacatecas. The other branch bypassed both. The two met at Refugio, just south of Zacatecas. Gregg later inferred that the *Camino Real* did not go into Zacatecas. (Gregg 1933:270-273,277).

**La Bufa** [Cerro la Bufa 22 46.5N 102 33.8W]: Lafora, on 5 April 1766, described this notable brown bluff in the neighborhood of Zacatecas (Alessio Robles 1939:51). Morfí and his party approached the city of Zacatecas, on 9 September 1777, from the south. They were on a good road which passed over a red landscape in a fertile area dotted with pastures. As they neared, the city they climbed hills and then entered a canyon formed by this prominence and other hills which they followed into Zacatecas (Alessio Robles 1935:53).

**Zacatecas** [22 47N 102 35W]: In 1554 it was calculated that there were around 300 *vecinos* or *jefes de casa*, some 1,000 Spaniards, and also 1,500 Indians in Zacatecas (Lebrón Quiñonez oidor de la Nueva Galicia al príncipe, 1554). In another census of 1584 there were around 1,300 Spaniards in the *real* (El obispo Alzola a la corona, 1584). Zacatecas was given the title of *ciudad* and given a *corregidor* in 1586 (Noticias de Zacatecas). That year, 1586, differs from the one given by Lafora of 1585. It was awarded a coat of arms and the title "muy noble y leal" on 20 July 1588 (Mecham 1927:46).

On 6 June 1596 Viceroy Martín López de Gauna ordered Don Lope de Ulloa, captain of the guard, to go to the mines of Zacatecas to examine and ascertain what Don Juan de Oñate and his people were taking on the expedition to New Mexico. The inspection was to determine whether or not Oñate was fulfilling the terms of his contract. Many of the people in the expedition were recruited at the mines of Zacatecas (Hammond and Rey 1953:Vol. I.95-96).

Soon after 1600, Bishop Mota y Escobar described Zacatecas. He began by noting that the area's arroyos had originally contained large groves of trees. Now that they were gone, firewood was brought in by *carro or cart* and sold at as premium. Some 300 houses, which he thought should be called hovels (*tugurios*), were scattered and temporary in appearance. Most were of adobe with only a few larger stone houses scattered along seven streets, four plazas, and one main road. Along with the parish church were convents of the Franciscans, Agustinians, Dominicans and Jesuits. Among the population, Mota y Escobar numbered some 1500 Indian laborers and 800 black and mulatto slaves. He provided a short history and description of the mines and summarized the city's politics (Ramirez Cabañas 1940:139-155). In 1623 there were 300 Spanish *vecinos*, as well as others not specified, dispersed in 20 or more bordering haciendas (Arregui 1980:163).

On 7 December 1724, Rivera traveled north northwest passed a small slope, descended a small hill and traveled through flat land to reach "Nuestra Señora de Zacatecas," a settlement of Spaniards, mestizos and mulattoes, some principal mines, and more than 24,000 souls. Rivera stayed in this city until 21 January 1725. He described the city as located between hills that ran the length of the city, northeast, south, and southwest. A ditch that ran through the middle of the city flooded part of the city in 1722. It is probable that this flooding occurred June 14, 1723 (Alessio Robles 1946:29-30). Rivera began his return trip to "Nuestra Señora de los Zacatecas" on 4 April 1725 and arrived there on 13 April 1725, where he stayed until 20 May 1725 (Alessio Robles 1946:34).

Lafora located Zacatecas on the four slopes of two canyons in rocky hills on bad road when he stayed there from 5-8 April 1766. He noted one parish church and five convents belonging to the orders of San Francisco, Santo Domingo, San Agustín, and San Juan de Dios as well as one Jesuit seminary. Despite this, he noted the presence of few priests, which he blamed on the decline of the region's mines. He gave the same reason for the decrease of the population, which he places at 6,778 "souls of communion" and 4,300 "innocents," made up of Spanish, Indians, mestizos and mulattoes. Five hundred people were said to live on the adjoining haciendas. Silver was discovered 8 September 1546 and it was declared a city on 17 April 1585. It was named for the local indigenous people, Zacatlán meaning the "place of grass or hay" (Alessio Robles 1939:50).

Morfí stayed in this city from 9 to 12 September 1777. He described it as sitting at the junction of two canyons, one of which traversed the city from the Franciscan convent to the foot of La Bufa. His depictions of the main buildings in Zacatecas are critical to the point of cruelty. From the *Cajas Reales* to the churches, Morfí paints a picture of shabby architecture and ornate bad taste. He gives the population as amounting to 15,000 souls of all castes. Most of the houses were small and of adobe, while others were of stone and lime. For Morfí, the most notable feature of Zacatecas, outside of the ugly grand architecture, was the red coloration of the adobes and stones of the houses and of the streets themselves (Alessio Robles 1935:53-59).

In 1835, Josiah Gregg wrote that "the *camino real*... led from Chihuahua to Zacatecas." A spur did turn southwest from Cuencamé toward Durango but the main road went directly south from Cuencamé toward Fresnillo. Gregg implied that the *Camino Real* did not go into Zacatecas but passed nearby. He guessed that the population of Zacatecas was 30,000 (Gregg 1933:270-273,277-279).

The following information offers a summary of the development and growth of Zacatecas. By 1550 there were 34 miners established there, as well as 100 Spanish *vecinos* that were not proprietors of mines, and 80 metal mills (*ingenios de metales*–generally mills for crushing metals). At this time, there were also 235 houses for slaves found here (Secosse 1975:4). After the silver strike, the *Camino Real* between Zacatecas and Mexico City became the main regional artery. It was surveyed and improved in 1550-1551 in order to equip it to handle the new, heavy-duty covered carros (Powell 1950:238-239). By 1555 it became "one of the great roads of America." Between 1550 and 1560 numerous inns were licensed by the government; prices were controlled and specific quantities of beds, blankets, sheets, and pillows were mandated. Food supplies and armaments on caravans were increased and regulated (Powell 1950:241).

From this point on, two routes, the first from Guadalajara, which gave "birth" to Zacatecas, and the second from México City, ensured that Zacatecas would remain a stable and flourishing mining center. But its demographic growth appeared to have slowed down; in 1572 it was calculated that there were around 300 *vecinos* living here (Gerhard 1993:158;AGI, Guadalajara 55, exp. 5) and in a brief re-count in 1581, there appeared to be a total of around 500 Spaniards living in Zacatecas (Zavala 1987:301;Paso y Troncoso 1940:50-54). Zacatecas could then have been described as a dispersed group of Spanish plots, clustered around the *haciendas de minas* and the Indian *barrios*, who were of different origins: *mexicanos and tlaxcaltecas, cazcanes, zacatecos*, etc. (Alvarez 1989:111-112).

Bishop Mota y Escobar described a long road that traversed the city from one end to the other, which was called the "Calle de Tacuba." In 1575 a wooden bridge was built over the arroyo next to the principal plaza in order to facilitate the passage of carts and merchandise from this road to the principal plaza. A stone bridge was then built in 1622 over the same arroyo for the same reason (Bargellini 1991:265). From this point the road continued across the city north, until it came to the Franciscan convent, where it then separated to head to the mines (Bargellini 1991:379;Bakewell 1976:353). The "Calle de Tacuba," the main road for merchants, was one of the few roads given names in this time (Bakewell 1976:85). By 1640 the population had reached 500 *vecinos* (Gerhard 1993:159), and in 1732 it was calculated that the population was at 40,000 inhabitants (Bakewell 1976:159). But its population did see a decline due to epidemics and death; in 1739 the figures had dropped to 24,000 inhabitants and in 1754 there were only 21,250 people. The population figures for the next few years are as follows: 25,000 in 1760; 16,260 in 1770 and 19,840 in 1772. Then the figures begin to go up during the last third of the 18th century: 32,720 people in 1798 and, in 1805, there were around 33,000 inhabitants (Gerhard 1993:159).

## MAP 5: ROUTE FROM ZACATECAS TO PARRAL & CIUDAD JIMÉNEZ

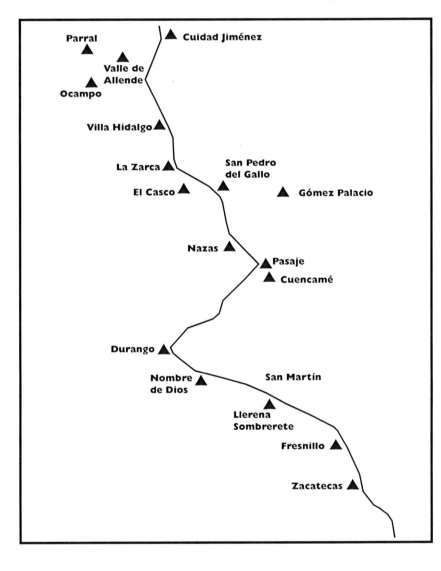

**La Calera** [22 57N  102 42W]: Lafora passed through La Calera, located five leagues northwest of the city of Zacatecas, on 8 April 1766. It was in flat land with much pasture and cactus and some small hills. It is now a rancho in Zacatecas state with a railroad station (Alessio Robles 1939:51). Morfí, on 12 September 1777, noted that he left Zacatecas by the old road over steep hills and gullies, then entered a plain covered with mesquite, huizache and cactus. There he encountered this hacienda at the banks of a permanent arroyo (Alessio Robles 1935:59).

**El Rancho de Los Cerritos**: Morfí passed here, some seven leagues north of Zacatecas, on 12 September 1777. He noted that it enjoyed a good water supply from an arroyo (Alessio Robles 1935:59).

**Las Tapias**: Lafora went through Las Tapias, located eight leagues northwest of Zacatecas, on 8 April 1766, on his way to Fresnillo. Las Tapias was located in the hills called the Portezuelo de La Estanzuela. It is now a rancho in the municipality of Fresnillo, Zacatecas (Alessio Robles 1939:51). This *paraje* was found by Morfí on his first day out of Zacatecas, on 12 September 1777. He noted that it took its name from one of two friars killed by Guachichile Indians in 1557. It was located on a good road next to an arroyo (Alessio Robles 1935:59-60).

**Fresnillo** [23 10N  102 53W]: Shortly after 1600, Bishop Mota y Escobar went from Zacatecas to Fresnillo and noted that it was quite small by comparison. Nevertheless, he saw twelve mills and five stores that carried goods from Spain and China as well as fruits of the region. He described two roads going west toward Nueva Vizcaya, their fork being at a hacienda called Medina seven league west of Fresnillo (Ramirez Cabañas 1940:172-174).

On 22 January 1725 Rivera left Zacatecas for the Nuevo Reino de Toledo, Provincia de San José del Nayarit, heading northwest north through flat land covered with hay. He arrived at the *real y minas* of Fresnillo, a small settlement made up of Spaniards, mestizos and mulattoes; at the time he was there the flow of its metals had declined (Alessio Robles 1946:30). After returning to Zacatecas on 13 April 1725 Rivera left there on 21 May 1725 and again stopped at the *real de minas* of Fresnillo (Alessio Robles 1946:35).

On 8 April 1766 Lafora described Fresnillo as sitting on hills covered with loose rock (Alessio Robles 1939:51). After leaving Zacatecas heading north on 12 September 1777, Morfi crossed some steep hills and a large beautiful plain. After leaving this plain, he crossed into gentle hills of loose stone and dry arroyos and then entered Fresnillo. He described its setting as between some low hills and a large plain in an area so dry that not one tree existed outside of the irrigated gardens. The landscape remained remarkably red (Alessio Robles 1935:60-62). Josiah Gregg turned southwest from Cuencamé and went to Durango in 1835. There was another road which went more directly south from Cuencamé toward Fresnillo. Just north of Fresnillo, in the town of Salado, this road split, with one branch going through Fresnillo, where it met the road from Durango, and Zacatecas. The other branch bypassed both. The two met at Refugio, just south of Zacatecas (Gregg 1933:270-273,277).

This region of Fresnillo, located 63 km northwest of Zacatecas was first explored in 1554 by Francisco de Ibarra, who, nevertheless, did not establish a permanent settlement. Even in 1561, when there was a great rebellion of the Zacatecos and Guachichiles, there was no evidence of a Spanish settlement. At that time, Fresnillo, who derived its name from the fact that a small *fresno*, or ash tree, grew there, served as a resting stop on the road that went from Zacatecas to the mines of Sombrerete. On 16 September 1566, the *real de minas*, San Demetrio (later known as Real de Plateros), became the first permanent mine established in this area. Soon after that, the pueblo of Fresnillo was founded (Kenaston 1978:268-270).

A *presidio* was located there, perhaps as early as 1568 and at least as late as 1585 (Powell 1952:145). In 1569 there were around 40 *vecinos* in the two settlements, most of them poor miners (Bargellini 1991:197, Gerhard 1993:85). In 1582 there were more than 100 *vecinos* in the area, and in 1586 there was mention of six large *haciendas de minas* and a parish church (Bargellini 1991:197). Large farms with livestock and extensive agricultural areas could be found in that zone, especially on the banks of the Río Aguanaval. After this time, Fresnillo, along with Jerez, became one of the principal providers of supplies for Zacatecas (Kenaston 1978:270-271).

During the years following 1601, the mine production suffered but the agricultural farms and livestock holdings became more productive and grew in importance (Visita del oidor Gaspar de la Fuente, 1608-1610). In 1609 there were only about 28 *vecinos* left in the mines. In 1621 there was mention of the existence of nine or ten *haciendas de minas* and the population was calculated to be around 70 *vecinos* (Arregui 1980). During the second half of the 17th century, the population of Fresnillo increased bit by bit, and by 1684 construction of a new church was begun (Bargellini 1991:199). In 1709 there were nine haciendas and 47 smaller residences in the Fresnillo parish (Gerhard 1993:85). In 1760 the population was at 14,260 settlers, and at 21,587 in 1798. From the decade of 1630 and onward, the local population was mostly made up of Indians, mestizos and mulattoes (Kenaston 1979:224). From Fresnillo, Lafora went to El Portezuelo de la Estanzuela, Rivera went to Río de Medina, the road described by Mota y Escobar went to La Hacienda de Medina, and Morfí went to El Rancho de Tolosa. [See also **EL PORTEZUELO DE LA ESTANZUELA, RIO DE MEDINA, LA HACIENDA DE MEDINA,** and **EL RANCHO DE TOLOSA**]

**Salado** [Loma Salado 23 25N  102 53W]: In 1835, when Josiah Gregg turned southwest from Cuencamé toward Durango he considered it a side trip from "the camino real that led from Chihuahua to Zacatecas." He also showed the road which went more directly south from Cuencamé toward Fresnillo (where Gregg rejoined it), passing through or just west of a settlement marked Juan Pérez, then a little east of Saucillo and Carboneras, and through La Fonda, Río Grande, and Salado. Two roads are shown going south from Salado, one through Fresnillo and Zacatecas, and the other passing east of both (Gregg 1933:270-273,277).

**Río Grande:** In 1835, Gregg went to Durango from Cuencamé but thought that he was off the *Camino Real* at that time. In connection with his side trip to Salado, he showed another road which went directly south from Cuencamé toward Fresnillo (where Gregg rejoined it) passing through or near Juan Pérez,  and as he had indicated leading to and through Río Grande and La Fonda. (Gregg 1933:270-273).

**La Fonda**: As indicated Gregg turned southwest from Cuencamé and went to Durango. He showed a road which went directly south from Cuencamé toward Fresnillo, which Gregg considered the *Camino Real*. It passed  Saucillo and Carboneras and through La Fonda, Rio Grande, and Salado (Gregg 1933:270-273).

**Carboneras**: Similarly, as he had said, he passed through or near Juan Pérez, then a little east of Saucillo and Carboneras on its way to Fresnillo and points south (Gregg 1933:270-273).

**Saucillo**: In 1835,Gregg passed just east of Saucillo between Juan Perez and Carboneras while going from Cuencamé to Fresnillo (Gregg 1933:270-273).

**Juan Pérez**: In 1835, Gregg went directly south from Cuencamé to Fresnillo, avoiding Durango. Juan Pérez was on this road just south of Cuencamé (Gregg 1933:270-273). [See also **CUENCAME**]

**El Portezuelo de La Estanzuela**: Lafora mentioned this as the range of hills in which Fresnillo is located on 8 April 1766 (Alessio Robles 1939:51).

**Río de Tolosa or Río de Medina**: On 24 May 1725 Rivera traveled north northwest of Fresnillo through flat lands that had some hills and came to a hacienda located on the northern bank of the Río de Medina (Alessio Robles 1946:35). Lafora crossed this river six leagues north of Fresnillo, Zacatecas on 9 April 1766, near where the huts of a dozen mestizos were located along the bank. It is also known as Río Grande in its middle and Río Aguanaval at its lower course (Alessio Robles 1939:52). Morfí also gave the name of "Río Zanja" when he crossed there on 13 September 1777. It was located six leagues northwest of Fresnillo, over good road and red land (Alessio Robles 1935: 62).

**La Hacienda de Medina** [23 30N  103 01W]: Shortly after 1600, Bishop Mota y Escobar found a fork in the road from Zacatecas to Nueva Vizcaya at this hacienda on what he called the Río Grande (also the Aguanaval). He described cultivated fields, livestock, and mills for processing silver from nearby mountains (Ramirez Cabañas 1940:174). Mota y Escobar's second route to El Asiento del Capitan Loiz began from here. [See **EL ASIENTO DEL CAPITAN LOIZ**]

**Rancho de la Escondida** [23 07N  103 07W]: Lafora mentioned this rancho, ten leagues southeast of the Hacienda de Atotonilco, on 9 April 1766. This may be the modern rancho of the same name in the state of Zacatecas (Alessio Robles 1939:52). This rancho was in ruins when Morfí passed by on 13 September 1777, just beyond his crossing of the Río Tolosa (Alessio Robles 1935:62).

**Los Sauces** [23 34.1N  103 19.2W]: On 25 May 1725, after stopping at a hacienda on the northern bank of the Río de Medina, Rivera headed west northwest first through flat land and then through land marked with hills and ravines, and passed an arroyo called Los Sauces (Alesseio Robles 1946:35).  From Los Sauces, Rivera went to Sain. [See also **SAIN**]

**El Rancho de Tolosa**: Morfí passed this "miserable" and uncultivated rancho near his crossing of the river of the same name on 13 September 1777. He noted, nonetheless, its pleasant setting beside the bank of the river (Alessio Robles 1935:62).

**La Hacienda de la Torrecilla**: This hacienda took its name from a feature of its chapel, according to Morfí. He stayed there on the night of 13 September 1777, in an area of huizache, mesquite, nopal cactus, and rough road. The hacienda sat near a dry arroyo which the road passed through and at the foot of a hill called Chapultepeque. Morfí noticed an abundance of cultivation and livestock of all kinds (Alessio Robles 1935:62).

**Pueblo de Sain** [Sain Alto 23 34.6N  103 15.3W; Sain Baja 23 36.9N  103 10.4W]: Bishop Mota y Escobar came across this settlement five leagues to the west of the fork at Medina early in the seventeenth century. He found two water-run mills for processing ore and some livestock in the area (Ramirez Cabañas 1940:175).

On 25 May 1725, Rivera passed the arroyo he called Los Sauces and stayed at a hacienda called Sayn (Alessio Robles 1946:35). In 1759, while at the Real de Sombrerete, Bishop Pedro Tamarón visited the pueblo of Sain, located 12 leagues north of that *real*. He counted 101 families of both Indian and mixed origin, which totaled 889 people (Alessio Robles 1937:192). Sain can presently be identified as Sain Alto (Alessio Robles 1937:195). From there Bishop Tamarón visited El Real de Nuestra Señora de las Nieves, the pueblo of Río Grande, San Juan del Mezquital, and San Miguel del Mezquital (Alessio Robles 1937:192-193).

Morfi's party came to this Indian pueblo located in a pleasant plain atop a range of hills north of the Hacienda de la Torrecilla on 14 September 1777. It was divided into two parts, named Alto and Baja, both of which sat alongside a river from which they cultivated their fields. Morfi designated this place as the dividing line between the bishoprics of Guadalajara and Durango or Nueva Vizcaya. He gave a good description of the road in this vicinity. Between the two parts of the pueblo it was tortuously difficult. Then it crossed the river at a good ford, climbed a long hill of good pasture and passed a small lagoon. At the bottom of the hill was a pleasant valley with a perennial arroyo which was used for cultivation. It continued through beautiful hills filled with white, yellow, and purple flowers atop green foliage and red earth. Beyond these hills lay the Hacienda de Calahorra (Alessio Robles 1935:62-63).

The Ginés Vázquez de Mercado expedition of 1552 was attacked by the residents of this *ranchería* somewhere near the later site of Sombrerete, contributing to the failure of the "first attempt to penetrate the northern hinterland" (Mecham 1927:56-57). Francisco de Ibarra and Juan de Tolosa crossed the Río de Nieves, or Río Grande as it was called, nearby and then passed through there in 1554 (Mecham 1927:61). From Pueblo de Sain Rivera went to Sombrerete. [See also **SOMBRERETE**]

**El Baptismo**: After crossing the Río Nieves and passing Sain, Ibarra and Tolosa, in their 1554 expedition, came to a pueblo from which the inhabitants fled. They pursued them and brought them back to the pueblo and then baptized them, thus the name (Mecham 1927:61-62).

**Hacienda de Atotonilco** [23 33.1N  103 15.8W]: In 1759 Bishop Tamarón visited this pueblo located nine leagues south of the *villa* of Nombre de Dios. He counted 24 Indian families, which totaled 120 people (Alessio Robles 1937:184). Lafora stayed at this present rancho in the state of Zacatecas 10 April 1766. He described the setting as a small, rocky cultivated valley with much pasture and many cactus. Its name means "place of the warm water" (Alessio Robles 1939:52).

**San Miguel** [San Miguel de la Herradura 23 47.1N 103 35.4W]: Ibarra and Tolosa arrived there on September 29, 1554, or on "Michaelmas," and named the Zacateco pueblo accordingly. They had come north from Sain and El Baptismo. At San Miguel they first heard about the mineral deposits which were later exploited under the name of San Martín and traveled to them to take samples before returning there and resuming their journey (Mecham 1927:66).

**Hacienda de Calahorra**: On 10 April 1766 Lafora placed this hacienda with cultivated fields four leagues southeast of Sombrerete. A source published in 1888-1891 located Hacienda de Calahorra 21 km east of Sombrerete but it cannot be identified presently as a current place name (Alessio Robles 1939:52).

Morfí gave a vivid description of the road leading to this hacienda from the south on 14 September 1777 (see Pueblo de Sain). This hacienda lay so directly beneath a hill that Morfí commented that one was in it before one saw it. Next to the large house was a chapel, partially in ruins, some shacks, and a reservoir which provided water for the inhabitants and their livestock. The lands were small but excellent and most were dedicated to raising animals. Just beyond there was the hill which gave its name to Sombrerete (Alessio Robles 1935:63-64).

**Sombrerete** [23 45N 103 50W]: According to Oñate, his father-in-law, Juanes de Tolosa, discovered, conquered and settled the mines of Sombrerete, San Martín and Aviño. Oñate also stated that these mines had added greatly to the royal treasury and that an infinite number of souls had been baptized (Hammond and Rey 1953:II.1146).

In 1579 Sombrerete became the principal town of the district. Sombrerete was also the last important settlement in Nueva Galicia on the road to Durango, and a place everyone had to pass to trade with both Nueva Galicia and Nueva Vizcaya (Visita del oidor Gaspar de la Fuente, 1608-1610). Bishop Mota y Escobar called this both "La Villa de Llerena" and "El Real de Minas de Sombrerete" when he was there early in the 17th century. Already the richest ores had been exhausted, although five or six haciendas were still in operation. He also noted a Franciscan convent (Ramirez Cabañas 1940:176-177). On 26 May 1725, after leaving "Sayn," Rivera came to the Villa of Llerena and to the site and mines of Sombrerete; this settlement of Spaniards, mestizos and mulattoes, which was quite important in the past, was then destitute due to the decline of its mines (Alessio Robles 1946:35). In 1759 Bishop Tamarón described this *real* and the Villa de Llerena as the capital of this area of Nueva Galicia. It was located 30 leagues east of the city of Durango and 16 leagues from the *villa* of Nombre de Dios. This parish consisted of Spanish inhabitants in the *villa* as well as in the outskirts. He counted 748 families, which totaled 6,184 people. Tamarón also described an Indian pueblo called San Matheo, which was located right next to the *real*; there he counted 35 Indian families totaling 151 people. He described several beautiful churches in this *real* as well as the holy imagery found there (Alessio Robles 1937:191).

On 11 April 1766 Lafora called this "Villa de Llerena" and "Real de Minas de Sombrerete" and noted that mineral production had declined, taking the town with it. Lafora located it high up in rough, rocky hills. He described the road leaving the city toward the west northwest as climbing a steep rocky hill for a fourth of a league and then becoming flat. The orders of San Francisco and Santo Domingo maintained convents in Sombrerete, and there was one parish church and several smaller churches. Plentiful water of good quality was delivered via a wooden aqueduct. Ore was discovered by Juan de Tolosa in 1555. It was also known in the colonial period as "San Juan Bautista de Llerena" (Alessio Robles 1939:52).

Morfí arrived there on 15 September 1777. He wrote that it lay in the middle of a range of mountains on red terrain beside a hill, which really did look like a hat. The land was sufficiently fertile to support the population, given its plentiful water. Morfí described a large parish church with plenty of light, a Dominican and a Franciscan convent, and a small building housing the *Casas Reales*. Across from the church, on a hillside, was a beautiful and ornate sanctuary chapel of Nuestra Señora de la Soledad. Sombrerete also contained the best and most well-constructed hacienda that he had yet seen, with spacious rooms and baths and many archways (Alessio Robles 1935:64-66).

In 1835, Josiah Gregg turned southwest from Cuencamé and went to Durango. When his group left for Aguascalientes he wrote that it was a few days before they were again on "the *camino real* that led from Chihuahua to Zacatecas." He went through Nombre de Dios and Sombrerete before joining the other road south from Cuencamé at Fresnillo (Gregg 1933:270-273).

The Ginés Vázquez de Mercado expedition of 1552 was attacked by the residents of the *ranchería* of Sain somewhere near the later site of Sombrerete, contributing to the failure of the "first attempt to penetrate the northern hinterland." Later, Francisco de Ibarra and Juan de Tolosa discovered the mineral deposits there during their entrada of 1554. They were later explored and settled by Martín Pérez. There is also an account which explains that the silver veins of Sombrerete were discovered by a group from San Martín that was looking for water. This party was led by a Juan Bautista de Llerena and was named in his honor: San Juan Bautista de Llerena, Real y Minas de Sombrerete. The Convent of San Mateo was erected in 1567 and the title of *villa* bestowed in 1570 (Mecham 1927:56,69,73,89-90). A garrison of soldiers was probably stationed at Llerena during the 1580s due to the Chichimeca wars (Powell 1952:148). Lic. Pedro de Otalora set limits for the new bishopric on 4 February 1622, with the Río de Medina marking the boundary between the two as far as the haciendas of Nieves, belonging to the heirs of Juan Bautista de Lomas. These consisted of the jurisdiction of the Villa of Llerena, the mines of Sombrerete in the kingdom of New Galicia and the *villa* of Nombre de Dios and its district in New Spain (Adams 1953:82).

The following information gives a summary of the growth and development of Sombrerete. In 1555 the mines of Sombrerete were founded, as well as those of nearby San Martín. In 1559 an *alcalde mayor* was named for both settlements (Gerhard 1993:130). In 1572 the population reached 40 Spanish *vecinos*, with around 500 Indians (Gerhard 1993:130). There was also a strong indication that by 1576 the Franciscans were already established there). In 1582 Sombrerete's population had reached more than 200 *vecinos* (Gerhard 1993:131). Soon after, however, the settlers began to disperse to other nearby areas, and in 1587 the lack of inhabitants forewarned of its abandonment (Bargellini 1991:249). In 1621 there were about 40 or 50 Spanish *vecinos* divided among 12 *haciendas de minas* (Arregui 1980:166). By 1645 or 1646 there was a mining boom that lasted for the rest of that century, thanks in great part to the opening of the famous Pavellón (or Pabellón) mine in 1675 (Bargellini 1991:250).

A Dominican convent was founded in 1682 and, a year later, a *Caja Real* was also founded (TePasque and Klein 1988:15). By the 1730s Sombrerete was beginning to be an important settlement, and by the 1750s some of the more powerful *hacendados* began to rival those of Zacatecas (Alvarez 1990:128-168). In 1761 the population was at 8,052 and in 1777 it reached a total of 11,086. By the year 1804 it had reached 22,946 people (Gerhard 1993:131). From Sombrerete Rivera and Lafora went to the Hacienda del Calabazal. [See also **HACIENDA DEL CALABAZAL**]

**El Real de Minas de San Martín** [23 40N 103 42W]: Bishop Mota y Escobar found this almost abandoned mine two leagues west of Sombrerete just after 1600. He stated that it had once been prosperous but by the time of his *visita* the five or six Spanish residents were sustained by groves of apple trees, which were in great demand. The terrain was mountainous and cold (Ramirez Cabañas 1940:177). Francisco de Ibarra and Juan de Tolosa were in the pueblo of San Miguel at the end of September 1554, when they were told about nearby mineral deposits. Tolosa and five others were guided to the area and took some samples, which they brought back to San Miguel. Because four of the six soldiers had the name of Martín, the mines were named Las Minas de San Martín. Ibarra later described this as the discovery of these mines (Mecham 1927:66). Two or three years later these mines were settled by a group from Zacatecas, probably led by one Martín Pérez. Various authorities place the official founding date anywhere from 1556-1558 (Mecham 1927:71, n. 28).

By around 1560, already existing mines there were in danger of closing due to Chichimeca pressure (Powell 1952:74,78). A *presidio* was established there, between Sombrerete (Llerena) and Nombre de Dios, in 1584 (Powell 1952:148).

**Rancho del Alamo** [23 44.3N 103 45.9W]: On 16 September 1777, Morfi left Sombrerete and crossed over some rugged hills and onto a large, beautiful plain surrounded by mountains and containing gentle hills. His vivid description of this region is of red earth with patches of white, covered with flowers of many colors. Small trees dotted the white areas but none grew in the red lands. At the end of these meadows and the beginning of a rough climb over a small hill lay this tiny rancho. Beyond the hill was the hacienda which he called El Calabazal (Alessio Robles 1935:66-67).

**Chalchihuites** [23 28.4N  103 52.9W]: While in San Bartolomé, in the province of Santa Bárbara, on 7 December 1597, Francisco de Sosa Peñalosa, captain and *alférez real* of the army going to New Mexico with Oñate, made a declaration in which he stated that he originally left the mines of "Chalcheutes" to serve His Majesty on this expedition. He was accompanied by his wife, children, servants, arms, horses, mules, mares, carts, 100 oxen, 400 quintals of flour, two pipes of wine and other possessions. At the time of his statement, he had already served two years in this post and most of his provisions and supplies had either been used up, stolen or lost (Hammond and Rey 1953, I:246).

These mines were described by Bishop Mota y Escobar between 1602 and 1605. They were some six leagues southwest of Sombrerete and contained four ore-processing haciendas, one run by water and the others by mules. Fifteen to twenty Spaniards and more than one hundred Indians described as Tlaxcateco and Chichimeca were administered by Franciscans. Mota y Escobar was particularly complimentary of the water, land, and local produce (Ramirez Cabañas 1940:177-178).

In 1759, Bishop Tamarón visited this "Real de Chalchiguites" located ten leagues east of Nombre de Dios. He wrote that this parish used to be divided into two but could not maintain two separate priests. He counted 236 Spanish families and *gente de razón*, which totaled 1,050 people (Alessio Robles 1937:184). From there he visited Tonalá, Tlaxcala and San Andrés (Alessio Robles 1937:184). Presently, Chalchiguites is a *villa* in Zacatecas; this name is the Spanish plural derived from the Aztec noun chalchihuitl, which means "precious stone" (*esmeralda sin labrar—emerald in the rough*). Of the places Tamarón visited from this *real*, only San Andrés can be presently identified as San Andrés del Teúl (Alessio Robles 1937:187).

**Hacienda del Calabazal** [23 45N  103 50W]: In the late 1550s, Fray Jerónimo de Mendoza, Viceroy Antonio de Mendoza's nephew, preached to great numbers of Zacateco Indians who lived in this area, especially along the banks of the Río Súchil (Mecham 1927:74).

On 28 May 1725, after leaving Sombrerete, Rivera traveled northwest west through flat land with some hills covered with hay and small mounts of palms and passed an arroyo called El Calabazal, where there is an *hacienda de labor* or farm (Alessio Robles 1946:35-36).

On 11 April 1766, Lafora called this hacienda "Calabazar." It lay in the valley below the steep hills of Sombrerete. Its population of two hundred were employed growing corn and caring for herds of animals. A source published in 1888-1891 gives the location of a rancho called Calabazal in the municipality of Fresnillo (Alessio Robles 1939:53).

Morfí passed through there on 16 September 1777, after leaving the hills of Sombrerete for the north. It lay at the head of a valley surrounded by high mountains. The hacienda lands itself were split by an arroyo that provided water for the 200 people who lived there as well as for their crops and animals. The earth was black and cut by many rocky arroyos. As they left this valley through the mountains on their left side, they came to a valley called "Las Poanas," at the middle of which were two sugarloaf shaped elevations (Alessio Robles 1935:67).

**Hacienda de Muleros** [23 45N  103 59W]: On 28 May 1725, Rivera stopped at the Hacienda de Muleros, located near the El Calabazal arroyo (Alessio Robles 1946:36). Lafora was there on 12 April 1766. He described the road as generally good in this area and the population as mulattoes who raised horses. According to Alessio Robles, it is now called Pueblo Vicente Guerrero, Durango (Alessio Robles 1939:53).

After Morfí's party left the Hacienda del Calabazal, on 16 September 1777, they passed through a thick stand of mesquite, left behind the valley of Las Poanas and entered the Hacienda de Muleros. This hacienda, to the north of Sombrerete, marked the beginning of the Jurisdicción Real de la Vizcaya. It lay in a broad valley beside an arroyo whose many springs provided water and was rich in both livestock and cultivated fields. The house was large and comfortable and the chapel spacious but plain. Upon leaving, on 18 September 1777, the party retraced its steps to the entrance of the hacienda and mesquite grove, and turned north. They followed a flat road through good pasture dotted with mesquite and reentered the valley of Las Poanas (Alessio Robles 1935:67-70). From Hacienda de Muleros Morfí went to Hacienda de San Diego. [See also **HACIENDA DE SAN DIEGO**]

**San Quintín**: On 29 May 1725, after leaving Hacienda de Muleros, Rivera traveled through flat land with dense mounts of palm groves, mesquite and huizaches and stopped at a hacienda called San Quintín (Alessio Robles

1946:36). From San Quintín Rivera went to Río de la Santiago. [See **RIO DE LA SANTIAGO**]

**Hacienda de Juana Guerra (or Amado Nervo)** [23 50N 104 10W]: Lafora visited on 12 April 1766, traveling west northwest from Sombrerete. He described the area as containing pastures and groves and no more than forty people. In the twentieth century it is a hacienda in the municipality of Nombre de Dios, Durango. (Alessio Robles 1939:53).

**El Río de Graseros**: Lafora followed this tributary of the Río Mezquital for one league into Nombre de Dios, now in the state of Durango on 12 April 1766 (Alessio Robles 1939:53).

**El Valle de Suchil** [23 38N 103 55W]: During the Zaldivar inquiry of 1602, Vicente de Zaldivar, captain and *sargento mayor*, stated that he went from the mines of Casco to the valleys of Suchil and Las Poanas and other places in order to inspect the soldiers and colonists of the Oñate expedition and to get them ready for the inspection by Francisco de Esquivel (Hammond and Rey 1953:II.811). Bishop Mota y Escobar was most impressed by the fertility of the eight estates in this small valley between Sombrerete and Nombre de Dios. He turned north from Chalchihuites to get there and then west toward Nombre de Dios (Ramirez Cabañas 1940:178-179). In 1759, while visiting Nombre de Dios, Bishop Tamarón described this *valle* as having one large church that was frequented often by the faithful because it held a miraculous statue of Our Lady (Alessio Robles 1937:183).

**Nombre de Dios (Durango)** [23 51N 104 14W]: Bishop Mota y Escobar noted shortly after 1600 that Nombre de Dios had been founded for security of the road because the *paraje* there had suffered greatly from Chichimeca attacks. It was located in a hot and humid basin alongside an arroyo which carried water year around. Fifteen or twenty Spaniards lived in small adobe houses. Many of them also owned estates in the region so that they did not always reside in town. A pueblo of some 50-70 Indians lived nearby, and all were served by a Franciscan convent. Mota y Escobar identified this town as being at the far edge of Nueva Galicia although under the jurisdiction of Nueva España (Ramirez Cabañas 1940:179-180).

In 1759 Bishop Tamarón visited this *villa* located 14 leagues east of Durango. In this *villa* and the two valleys of Las Poanas and Suchil he counted 936 Spanish families and *gente de razón*, which totaled 6,024 people. While there he also described the pueblo of Nombre de Dios, which was administered by the priest in the *villa*. There he counted 170 Indian families, which totaled 809 people (Alessio Robles 1937:183). One year given as the founding of Nombre de Dios by Francisco de Ibarra and Fray Pedro de Espinareda is 1563 (Alessio Robles 1937:185). Lafora entered by way of the Río de Graseros on 12 April 1766. He saw some Spaniards, a few more mulattoes and 800 Mexican Indians ("*indios mexicanos*") whose pueblo was divided by a canal. The road was generally flat through this entire valley (Alessio Robles 1939:53).

In 1835, Gregg went through Nombre de Dios and Sombrerete between Durango and Fresnillo. He wrote that he had left the *Camino Real* when he turned southwest from Cuencamé toward Durango (Gregg 1933:270-273). Another founding date given is that of 1561; it was organized during the subsequent two years as a defense against Chichimeca raids (Powell 1952:69).

The following is a more involved and controversial history of the founding of Nombre de Díos. In summary, Fray Mendoza founded a pueblo of resettled Zacatecos at a place which he named Nombre de Díos sometime before 1558. This settlement failed, but its name survived in a *villa* founded in 1558 by three priests with the help of Francisco de Ibarra. One of these, Fray Espinareda, was given a license to found this *villa*, already in existence, in 1663. Ibarra officially registered the *villa* and named its first officials. It later became a bone of contention between Nueva Galicia and Nueva Vizcaya, and was ruled first by Nueva Galicia, then directly by the Viceroy, and was finally transferred to Nueva Vizcaya in 1611 (Mecham 1927:74,81,121-123,198-201). Bishop Mota y Escobar's first route to La Punta began from here. [See also **LA PUNTA**]

**Ranchito de los Berros**: Lafora passed this ranchito on 13 April 1766 and met a stream which he followed through the woods, almost into La Punta. It is located in the present municipalidad El Oro, Durango (Alessio Robles 1939:54). "Ojo de Agua de los Berros" was identified as the location of a *ranchería* of great numbers of Zacatecos which served as an outpost against the Tepehuanos in the late 1550s (Mecham 1927:74). From Ranchito de los Berros Lafora went to La Punta. [See also **LA PUNTA**]

**El Asiento del Capitán Loiz**: Leaving Medina for the northwest, Bishop Mota y Escobar delineated the second of two routes to La Punta and Nueva Vizcaya. There, five leagues from Medina, he found four water-driven mills for processing ores from the area and some for grinding wheat. He also commented on the livestock operations in the area and its richness in wildlife (Ramirez Cabañas 1940:182).

**Real de Minas de las Nieves**: Bishop Mota y Escobar found this *real* some eight leagues northwest of Medina on his second road to Nueva Vizcaya. He was impressed by its abundant water and the fields and livestock to the north. There were four or five quicksilver processors for ore and a mule-driven flour mill (Ramirez Cabañas 1940:183).

**Estancia del Comendador Rodrigo del Río**: In the 1598 itinerary of the Oñate expedition two routes are described in detail to reach "Caxco." One of them, the better route, began at the "Estancia de Rodrigo de Rio." On the way to "Caxco," one passes Las Peñuelas, which was five leagues from the estancia (Pacheco, Cárdenas, y Torres 1871:XVI.229). This *estancia* was west of Nieves and before Joachín on Bishop Mota y Escobar's second road from Medina to La Punta and Nueva Vizcaya at the beginning of the seventeenth century. It had a large population of slaves and free Indians and mulattoes who worked as stock herders and field hands and in the local carretería (Ramirez Cabañas 1940:183).

**El Real de Joachín**: Beyond Nieves and the Estancia del Comendador Rodrigo del Río on Bishop Mota y Escobar's second road to Nueva Vizcaya, he came to this small *real*, on which livestock was also raised (Ramirez Cabañas 1940:183-184).

**San Juan de Mezquital**: On Bishop Mota y Escobar's second road to Nueva Vizcaya, he came to this small Chichimeca pueblo of some 100 inhabitants beyond Nieves, the Estancia del Comendador Rodrigo del

Río, and El Real de Joachín  (Ramirez Cabañas 1940:184).

**Gracián**: Beyond the Estancia del Comendador Rodrigo del Río, and El Real de Joachín on Bishop Mota y Escobar's second road to Nueva Vizcaya, he came to this collection of coal mines which served the local mines (Ramirez Cabañas 1940:184).

**El Valle de la Poana** [Las Poanas 23 54N  104 07W]: During the Zaldivar inquiry of 1602, Vicente de Zaldivar, captain and *sargento mayor* of the Oñate expedition, stated that he went from the mines of Casco to the valleys of Suchil and Las Poanas and other places in order to inspect the soldiers and colonists of the Oñate expedition and to get them ready for the inspection by Francisco de Esquivel (Hammond and Rey 1953:II.811). Years later, Bishop Mota y Escobar went through there, four leagues northeast of Nombre de Dios, while going between Gracián and La Punta on his second road from Medina to La Punta and Nueva Vizcaya. It contained several estates and an arroyo which carried a permanent water-course. From here, he went directly into La Punta, where the two roads met (Ramirez Cabañas 1940:184). In 1759, while visiting Nombre de Dios, Bishop Tamarón wrote that there were large haciendas in this *valle* in which all type of *grano* were grown. There were also some churches and chapels (Alessio Robles 1937:183).

**La Punta** [La Punta de los Padres 24 03N  104 21W]: Bishop Mota y Escobar cited this as the beginning and entry to Nueva Vizcaya at the start of the 17th century. At La Punta his two routes from Medina rejoined. He also noted crossing a sizable current of water called Los Berros (Ramirez Cabañas 1940:180,185). Lafora was at this hacienda on 13 April 1766 and described it as belonging to the Jesuits and dedicated to raising horses. It was located on the banks of the river of the same name, which they crossed upon leaving. Lafora mentioned the *Camino Real* when he wrote, "...y rodeando por una lomita con algunos pedazos de mal país, se sale al *camino real* todo bueno." It can be presently identified as a hacienda in the municipalidad de Durango (Alessio Robles 1939:54). From La Punta Bishop Mota y Escobar went to Durango. [See also **DURANGO**]

**Río de Santiago**: Right before the city of Durango, on 30 May 1725, Rivera passed the rivers Santiago, La Sauceda and "El Tunar" (El Tunal.) Rivera stated that this last one separated and extended two leagues past the city (Alessio Robles 1946:36). During his *visita* of 1759, Bishop Tamarón stated that this river, running south, was half a league from the Río del Tunal, and contained less water than the Tunal river (Alessio Robles 1937:29). When Lafora crossed this river two leagues northwest of La Punta, Durango on 14 April 1766, it had very little water. Lafora said that it later joined the Río La Punta. It is now presently identified as a tributary of the Tepehuanes (Alessio Robles 1939:54).

**Pueblo de Santiago**: In 1759 Bishop Tamarón described this as the third Indian pueblo located three leagues south of Durango, and to the southeast was the "stream" called Santiago. This pueblo was made up of Tepehuanos Indians, which he counted as 48 families totaling 221 people. Tamarón commented that the Indians of Santiago, Tunal and Analco are poor and unhappy, and content to plant very little (Alessio Robles 1937:37).

**Río de la Calera**: Morfí crossed this small creek near its confluence with the Río de la Sauceda, then swollen with water, on 20 September 1777 (Alessio Robles 1935:71).

**Río de la Sauceda**: Right before the city of Durango, on 30 May 1725, Rivera passed the rivers Santiago, La Sauceda and "El Tunar" (El Tunal.) During his *visita* of 1759, Bishop Tamarón described this river as running from west to east and turning southward. It was about three leagues from the city of Durango, for which it provided irrigation waters (Alessio Robles 1937:29). Lafora crossed the dry channel of this stream southeast of Durango on 14 April 1766 (Alessio Robles 1939:54). Morfí crossed this and its tributary, Río de la Calera, on 20 September 1777 and then headed into the Hacienda de Navacoyán over good road bordered by abundant marigolds (Alessio Robles 1935:71).

**La Hacienda de Navacoyán** [Also Francisco Montes de Oca 24 03N 104 33W]: Morfí described this large and beautiful hacienda in the valley of Durango on 20 September 1777. It was two leagues south of that city, had just completed a dam for providing water and raised mules and horses. The house and chapel excited less comment than the setting and value of the hacienda (Alessio Robles 1935:71-72).

**Río del Tunal**: On 30 May 1725, right before the city of Durango, Rivera passed the "Río del Tunar," or El Tunal, which separated and extended two leagues past the city (Alessio Robles 1946:36). In 1759 Bishop Tamarón stated that this river was found one league from Durango; its water was abundant and potable and used for watering crops, especially the wheat-fields (Alessio Robles 1937:28). Lafora crossed this stream three leagues southeast of the city of Durango on 14 April 1766 (Alessio Robles 1939:54).

**Hacienda de San Miguel**: Lafora passed through this hacienda on the banks of the Río Tunal on 14 April 1766, three leagues southeast of the city of Durango. It is now a rancho in the municipalidad of Durango (Alessio Robles 1939:54).

**Durango** [24 02N  104 40W]: When Bishop Mota y Escobar passed through here, shortly after 1600, he found 500 Spaniards living in moderately sized adobe houses. The *villa Casas Reales* were similar to the houses but larger, although they were meant to handle all of the quicksilver and silver of the realm. There were four major streets running east and west and others going north and south. A nearby arroyo provided good drinking water and fish all year around.  In addition to a parish church, there was a church for Indians which was dedicated to San Juan, a Franciscan convent, and a Jesuit convent (Ramirez Cabañas 1940:190-193).

On 30 May 1725 Rivera reached Durango. Some called this capital of the reign and province of Nueva Vizcaya "Guadiana;" it was populated by Spaniards, mestizos and mulattoes, and its population was much smaller than that of Zacatecas. Rivera mentioned the following towns found around Durango: to the south was Analco, to the southwest was the "Pueblo del Tunar" (or El Tunal) and Santiago, all inhabited by Tepehuanos Indians. Rivera stayed there until 7 October 1725 (Alessio Robles 1946:36-37). Rivera also described a flying company (*compañía volante*) of 15 soldiers, previously of the Valle de San Bartolomé, stationed in Durango. Rivera stated that the squadron was in poor shape, with no one in command and the soldiers spending the funds as they pleased. At this point each one was receiving 450 pesos, totaling 6,750 pesos per year (Alessio Robles 1946:102).

During his *visita* of 1759, Bishop Tamarón also mentioned that Durango was called "Guadiana." He wrote that in Durango one could find the episcopal seat and the governor and general capitan of this kingdom. There were also two councils there, one secular and one ecclesiastical, and the royal treasuries with treasurer and bookkeeper was also located here. The land was flat and extended several leagues to the east, and to the west it extended two leagues to the foot of the Sierra Madre. To the south it extended almost 500 leagues until the end of the Sonora [desert]. Bishop Tamarón described the roads as being very open, flat, extended and clear, and stated that carriages and carts could travel without encountering obstacles. One could also find hares and ducks in abundance around the city (Alessio Robles 1937:28-29).

Tamarón also described four convents in Durango. San Francisco consisted of 10 or 12 clergy; San Agustín consisted of four; the Colegio de la Compañía de Jesús had 10 or 12 clergy along with 70 or 80 collegiates in its seminary; and the San Juan de Dios convent, which consisted of eight or nine clergy, also had a hospital for both men and women. In Durango there was also a chapel dedicated to San Miguel, another dedicated to Santa Ana and two large chapels dedicated to Nuestra Señora de Guadalupe and to Nuestra Señora de los Remedios (Alessio Robles 1937:32-33). According to Bishop Tamarón, the population consisted of 1,311 Spanish families totaling 8,937 *gente de razón*, the majority of which lived within the city and of which less than half lived in the haciendas on the outskirts of the city (Alessio Robles 1937:35).

Lafora came to the Ciudad de Durango on 14 April 1766 and stayed until the 26th of the same month. He said that it was the capital of Nueva Vizcaya and the residence of its governor. It was located in a beautiful plain which was not cultivated due to lack of water. It had a cathedral with a bishop and canons, three convents representing the orders of San Francisco, San Agustín and San Juan de Dios, a Jesuit seminary and various smaller churches. Here, the quinta was taken from silver mined in Chihuahua and Sonora. Lafora gave the population at 1,311 families of Spaniards, mestizos and mulattoes or 1,937 "*almas de comunión*." In addition, 610 Indians in ninety-five families lived in the section known as Analco. Durango was founded in 1563 by Capitan Alonso de Pacheco by order of Francisco de Ibarra (Alessio Robles 1939:55-56;Mecham 1927:123).

Morfí and his party worked out of Durango from 22 September to 15 October 1777, venturing out for inspection tours throughout the region. He described the city in some detail, mentioning a spacious plaza and a large cathedral with three domes and a tower that, like the rest of the city, had been allowed to deteriorate in the recent past. The former Jesuit seminary and the Franciscan convent were virtually in ruins. Morfí noted a hill called Mercado beside which sat the Santuario de Guadalupe and another, Los Remedios, which held a chapel dedicated to *La Madre de Dios* (Alessio Robles 1935:72-82).

In 1835, Josiah Gregg estimated that Durango contained a population of 20,000. He also commented on the beauty of its squares and buildings. Gregg noted that water was supplied to the city by open aqueducts whose water was polluted enough that those who could afford to bought drinking water. When his group left for Aguascalientes he wrote that it was a few days before they were again on "the *camino real* that led from Chihuahua to Zacatecas." He later mentioned that the main wagon road did not go through Durango but continued south from Cuencamé to Fresnillo (Gregg 1933:270-273,281).

The following information provides a synthesized history of the development and growth of Durango. The first expedition clearly documented in the Durango region was that of Ginés Vázquez de Mercado, who left Guadalajara in 1552 (Gallegos 1982:12). In 1563, Francisco de Ibarra chose this site to be the capital of the newly founded province of Nueva Vizcaya (Mecham 1968:123). Despite its status, at that time, there were only 13 *vecinos* present (Gerhard 1993:202). By 1572 there were 26 *vecinos*, all of them *encomenderos*. The convent of San Antonio de Durango was founded in 1573, but it wasn't until the 1580s that Durango began to prosper, thanks to the success of the mines of Chiametle (Alvarez 1992:17). By 1604, according to the census of Governor Urdiñola, Durango had stores, a public mill and several mining haciendas (Censo del gobernador Francisco de Urdiñola, 1604). By the time of the Tepehuanos rebellion of 1616-1618 there were 150 *vecinos* in Durango (Gerhard 1993:204), and in 1645 there were about 120 (Gerhard 1993:20). But, by 1663, the population had declined to 30 due to the establishment of a more direct route to Parral that interrupted the commercial traffic to Durango (Porras Muñoz 1980b:68). But it still remained the seat of the only *Caja Real* of the province, and, little by little, its population increased. In 1674 its population was at 40 (Porras Muñoz 1980b:65). By 1707 there were 84 *vecinos* (Gerhard 1993:204) and in 1723 Benito Crespo became bishop of Durango and issued a title as vicar and ecclesiastical judge to Fray Salvador López, the vice-custos at El Paso (Adams 1953:94-95). According to the census of 1806 there were 22,401 people living in the district, but only 8,919 of them lived in the actual city of Durango (Gerhard 1993:204). From Durango, Rivera went to Canatán, Lafora went to El Chorro, and Morfí went to Guadalupe. [See also **CANATAN, EL CHORRO, GUADELUPE**]

**Analco**: On 30 May 1725 Rivera mentioned that Analco was one of the towns located south of Durango (Alessio Robles 1946:36-37). During his *visita* of 1759, Bishop Tamarón described this as an Indian pueblo which received water from an arroyo that also reached Durango (Alessio Robles 1937:28). Tamarón called this pueblo "San Juan de Analco" and placed it the environs south of Durango. Their church, dedicated to San Juan Bautista, was antiquated, and when Tamarón visited, they already had the foundation ready for a bigger and better church. The priest who oversaw this and two other Indian pueblos resided primarily in Analco. The population of Analco was made up of Tlaxcalteca Indians--95 families totaling 610 people (Alessio Robles 1937:36-37). In 1766, Lafora reported this same population for what he called the section of Durango known as Analco (Alessio Robles 1939:55-56).

**Tunal** [23 57N  104 43W]: When Bishop Mota y Escobar was visiting Durango in the early 1600s, he described Tunal as a pueblo of peaceful Chichimecos located two leagues south of Durango and subject to the Franciscan convent there. It was located along the same arroyo as Durango and used its water to produce crops in abundance for the Spanish (Ramirez Cabañas 1940:193). In 1759, Bishop Tamarón described this as an Indian pueblo near Durango located two leagues southwest of the cathedral in Durango on the other bank of the Río del Tunal. Tunal had a small church and house for the priest, and was made up of Tepehuanos

Indians, which Tamarón counted as 74 families totaling 328 people (Alessio Robles 1937:37).

**Cañón del Mezquital**: The pueblo of Mezquital is located in some hills and mountain ranges that form the first part of the Cañón del Mezquital (Alessio Robles 1937:69).

**Río del Mezquital**: This river originates in the Altos de Cuevecillas y Culebras, in the main point of the Sierra Madre, municipality of Durango. It was first known as the Río de la Casita and then as the Río de Tunal or the Río de Durango (Alessio Robles 1937:69).

**Santa Elena**: During his visit of 1759 Bishop Tamarón located this hacienda four leagues west of Durango; 53 families totaling 193 people resided here. In November and December 1763, while at Santa Elena, he visited six other pueblos (Alessio Robles 1937:57).

**La Hacienda de San Diego** [San Diego de Alcalá 24 00N 103 58W]: This was one of eight haciendas of the large, fertile, and well-watered valley of Las Poanas, mentioned by Morfí on 18 September 1777 after leaving Muleros (Alessio Robles 1935:70).

**La Hacienda de San Nicolás**: This hacienda, in the large, fertile, and well-watered valley of Las Poanas, was mentioned by Morfí on 18 September 1777. It featured a large house and chapel and well-cultivated fields. After leaving there, Morfí passed through some good road and beautiful country and then came upon a stretch of malpais (Alessio Robles 1935:70).

**La Hacienda del Ojo** [24 10N 104 03W]: On 18 September 1777, Morfí reported passing through a stretch of malpais in the valley of Las Poanas and then entering this hacienda. He then described it as being in the middle of a malpais which he reentered upon leaving. El Ojo was immense and contained some water, It raised crops and livestock and had an opulent house and a chapel which served the whole area. It presently remains as a populous hacienda in the Municipio de Poanas, Durango (Alessio Robles 1935:70).

**La Hacienda del Saucillo** [Also Antonio Amaro 24 16N  104 00W]: Leaving the badlands in the area of the haciendas of San Nicolás and El Ojo on 19 September 1777, Morfí headed toward the city of Durango. He soon passed this hacienda, which he described as not as opulent as the preceding haciendas (Alessio Robles 1935:70-71).

**Hacienda de Guadalupe**: After Morfí's stay in Durango he crossed the Río de Guadalupe and visited the Llano de Guadalupe, describing some of the haciendas there on 16 October 1777. He passed this one first and thought it the grandest, with a great house and expansive gardens (Alessio Robles 1935:82).

**Hacienda de la Laguna**: On 16 October 1777, after staying in Durango, Morfí crossed the Río de Guadalupe and visited the Llano de Guadalupe, describing some of the haciendas there on 16 October 1777, including this one, which sat at the foot of a mountain (Alessio Robles 1935:82).

**Hacienda de San Salvador**: On 16 October 1777, Morfí left Durango and visited several haciendas, this among them. He noted ducks, geese, and cranes in great numbers in its vicinity as well as flowers of many colors and good pasture. He went by there after the Hacienda de la Laguna; then the road climbed a small hill of loose rock, after which it descended to the Hacienda del Chorro (Alessio Robles 1935:82-83).

**Hacienda del Chorro** [24 16N  104 27W]: On 9 October 1725, after leaving Batres and heading northeast, Rivera traveled through flat land flooded with swamp water and mudholes, with hills clear of mesquite and huizache, and came to Hacienda del Chorro. (Alessio Robles 1946:37). Lafora came to the Hacienda del Chorro, ten leagues northeast of the city of Durango, on 26 April 1766, after traveling over a plain made up of pasture, mesquite, and other brush. As he left it heading north, he passed a small marsh. It can be found as a hacienda in the *municipalidad* de Durango (Alessio Robles 1939:57).

Morfí passed by here during his entrance to the city of Durango after passing La Boca de Santo Domingo. It lay in the valley of Durango amid pastures with many flowers near a mesquite grove which was marshy from rain and difficult to cross (Alessio Robles 1935:71). After Morfí's stay in Durango, he crossed the Río de Guadalupe and visited the Llano de Guadalupe, describing some of the haciendas there on 16 October 1777, including this one. He passed it between the Hacienda de San Salvador and La Boca de Santo Domingo (Alessio Robles 1935:82). From Chorro Rivera went to Los Ojos Azules. [See also **LOS OJOS AZULES**]

**Hacienda de Santo Domingo de la Boca**: This hacienda was described by Lafora on 26 April 1766 as being at the entrance of a gap between two mountains one league south of Avino, Durango. It is now called Boca de Avino on modern maps (Alessio Robles 1939:57). Morfí went by there on 20 September 1777, describing it as a miserable little rancho. It was in a region of mountains and canyons just before the valleys of Durango (Alessio Robles 1935:71). After going to Durango, Morfí did a tour through the Llano de Guadalupe and described the haciendas there. He passed back this way through the Hacienda del Chorro on 16 October and went on to "Avinito" (Alessio Robles 1935:83).

**Avino** [24 31N  104 18W]: In the Oñate itinerary of 1598 two routes to "Caxco" are described; the one considered the worse one was described as beginning at "Aviño" (Pacheco, Cárdenas, y Torres 1871:XVI.228). Shortly after 1600, Bishop Mota y Escobar stated that he was impressed by the silver produced there and processed with quicksilver. Avino was on the border between Nueva Galicia and Nueva Vizcaya and eleven leagues of virtually unpopulated terrain northeast of Durango. There were six mills powered by mules and a large number of Indian and African workers (Ramirez Cabañas 1940:194).

In 1759 Bishop Tamarón visited this *real*; he described the silver mines as old but as always producing well. The church there had a decent "*adorno*" and was administered by an assistant priest from San Juan del Río. He counted 186 families in the area, which totaled 1,230 people, and located this *real* 10 leagues northwest of San José del Río and 18 leagues north of Durango (Alessio Robles 1937:95).

Lafora went by there going due north 18 leagues north northeast of the city of Durango on 26 April 1766. It was a silver mining complex (*hacienda de plata*) in a mountain basin which contained some 2000 people of a mix of Spaniard, mestizo and mulatto. It was also known as Aviño and Avinito. Silver was discovered by Francisco de Ibarra in 1563 in a part of Cerro Avino called Veta Grande (Alessio Robles 1939:57).

Morfi referred to this as "Las Minas de Avinito." The area was entered and exited by winding canyons formed by large mountains where the road passed close to dangerous precipices. Morfi stayed there on the night of 19 September 1777 and then went into Durango (Alessio Robles 1935:71). He came back from Durango on 16 October after going through the Llano de Guadalupe and La Boca de Santo Domingo and stayed until the 31st. This time he visited the mine itself and took several other side trips (Alessio Robles 1935:83-84). Ibarra and Tolosa went there from the area of San Miguel and San Martín on their 1554 expedition. They baptized over 200 natives, discovered the mineral deposits located there, and obtained the services of an Indian woman ("a 'Doña Marina'") who served as a guide and interpreter. Within a few years, Ibarra planted a settlement there and maintained it at his own expense. Later, Aviño "arbitrarily" transferred its allegiance from Nueva Galicia to Ibarra and Nueva Vizcaya (Mecham 1927:67-68,87-88).

**Pánuco**: In 1759 Bishop Tamarón visited this *real de minas* whose patron saint was San Fermín. He described it as having a decent church with an assistant priest and silver mines, the same as "Avinito" (Avino). He counted 231 families, which totaled 1,479 people. Tamarón located this *real* a quarter of a league from "Avinito" (Alessio Robles 1937:95). This *real* can presently be identified as Pánuco de Coronado (Alessio Robles 1937:104).

**Cieneguilla de Santa Gertrudis or de Avino**: This was passed by Lafora on 28 April 1766 two leagues north of Avino on steep rocky road. From there two roads ran to Santa Catarina, only one of which was passable for wagons over some low hills (Alessio Robles 1939:58).

Approaching Durango, Morfi passed by there on 19 September 1777. He noted that he had passed from gentle hills with good pasture into flowered valleys and now mountains began as well as bad roads. Leaving there they entered a canyon with little water and headed into the Minas de Avinito (Alessio Robles 1935:71). Morfi came through El Rancho de Santa Gertrudis on 31 October 1777, after leaving Avinito for the second time, heading north. He identified the road as the same one that he had entered on, although he had not mentioned it at that time. This time he went around a hill and past two *parajes*, named El Fresno and El Durazno and went north into a plain called La Bermeja (Alessio Robles 1935:93).

**El Paraje del Fresno**: On 31 October 1777, Morfí passed by there going north from Avinito into the plain which he called La Bermeja (Alessio Robles 1935:93).

**El Paraje del Durazno** [24 32N  104 13W]: On 31 October 1777, Morfí passed by there going north from Avinito into the plain which he called La Bermeja; this was after passing El Paraje del Fresno (Alessio Robles 1935:93).

**Hacienda de Santa Catarina**: Located five leagues by wagon road, or three direct, beyond Avino, Durango, Lafora passed there on 28 April 1766. The main purpose of this hacienda was as a place for the yearly shearing of sheep. The population numbered 2,000. There were two springs for drinking water and two ranks or pools (*tanques*) with water for the livestock. It is called Ignacio Allende on modern maps (Alessio Robles 1939:58).

Morfí encountered this hacienda on 31 October 1777 shortly after entering the plain of La Bermeja. He noted that the color of the earth changed from red to brown and it was covered by good pasture. Morfí gave an account of a large number of livestock but noted that little beans and maize were grown for the 2000 inhabitants. The large house and chapel were located adjacent to a central plaza as were tanks for watering the stock (Alessio Robles 1935:93).

**Peñol Blanco (El Peñol or Peñón Blanco)** [Peñón Blanco 24 47N  104 02W]: Bishop Mota y Escobar identified mines there, six leagues to the northeast of Avino, in the early seventeenth century. Much of the minerals from Avino were also processed there in two water-driven mills (Ramirez Cabañas 1940:194). In 1759, Bishop Tamarón located this Indian town, whose patron saint was San Diego, 10 leagues west of Cuencamé. A new church was being built there, and one of the *tenientes* of the clergy resided there. There were 89 families totaling 447 people here, and nine families *de vecinos* totaling 61 people. The Indians maintained a rich *cofradía* of the Purísima Concepción (Alessio Robles 1937:97). El Peñol is presently identified as Peñón Blanco (Alessio Robles 1937:105). On 1 November 1777, Morfí left La Hacienda de Santa Catarina on horseback and headed north over smooth hills with good pasture to this landmark and adjacent pueblo. Before arriving there they entered an area of deep gorges containing extensive meadows. There the road forked with the coach road going off to the right. They went to the left into the sierra which he called Gaitán (Alessio Robles 1935:94).

**Ciénega de Jaques:** This *paraje* was encountered by Morfí on 1 November 1777, after he followed a road fit for horses but not coaches north from La Hacienda de Santa Catarina and Peñol Blanco through a Sierra Gaitán. It held a spring of sparse but pure water. From there, they climbed some hills and entered a plain some three leagues in diameter (Alessio Robles 1935:94).

**Rancho de Las Tortuguillas:** This rancho was passed by Lafora on 29 April 1766, three leagues north of La Hacienda de Santa Catarina in an area of gentle hills with much pasture and mesquite on the hillsides. It is now a rancho of the same name in the municipalidad of El Oro in Durango state (Alessio Robles 1939:58-59).

**El Alamo:** On 11 October 1725, after leaving Los Ojos Azules and heading northeast, Rivera spent the night at an uninhabited ranch called El Alamo (Alessio Robles 1946:38). On 30 June 1727, Rivera headed east northeast and passed a canyon formed by two elevated sierras. He came to an *aguaje* called El Alamo. Alessio Robles identified El Alamo as Alamo de Parras, and, in 1731, after Rivera's trip, a settlement called San José y Santiago del Alamo was founded (Alessio Robles 1946:71).

In 1759, Bishop Tamarón located this town 20 leagues west of Parras. Its patron saints were San José and Santiago. The population consisted of *vecinos de razón* and Tlaxcalteca Indians. The *vecindario* is composed of 51 families totaling 270 people, and there were 83 Indian families totaling 455 people. Alamo was not too far from a lagoon, and  described it as a very pleasant place, with many vineyards and orchards as well as wheat, corn and beans. He also explained that due to their disputes the Indians did not plant nor do they allow others to plant, which Tamarón identified as a common problem in this bishopric between the Indians and the *vecinos*. Tamarón wrote that he had done what he could in order to separate the *vecinos* from the Indians so that they could have two separate towns, each with its own church and lands and both sharing the water available. In this way neither would be dependent upon the other (Alessio Robles 1937:111-112).

Alamo was founded by the mayor of Parras, D. Prudencio Basterra, on July 24, 1731. He was accompanied by the priest D. Manuel Valdés and by 45 Tlaxcalteca families. They named it San José y Santiago del Alamo but on September 21, 1830, by decree of the Coahuila government, it was renamed San José de Viesca y Bustamante. It is generally known by the name Viesca (Alessio Robles 1937:116).

Lafora called this the "Hacienda del Alamo" when he passed it on 29 April 1766, going north six leagues out of Hacienda de Santa Catarina. It was located along an almost dry stream of the same name which begins near Las Tortuguillas and runs into the Río Nasas. The ninety families who lived there were employed in raising livestock (Alessio Robles 1939:59). From El Alamo Rivera went to Presidio del Pasage. [See also **PRESIDIO DEL PASAGE**]

**La Peña**: In 1759, Bishop Tamarón placed this hacienda six leagues east of Alamo. There was a large chapel located there which was administered by the assistant priest of Alamo (Alessio Robles 1937:112). Modern maps show two places, La Peña and Las Peñas, in the same region; either could be the one visited by Tamarón.

**Paraje de las Tapias** [24 49N 103 51W]: Lafora mentioned this, on 29 April 1766, as being near Rancho de las Tortuguillas, in Durango, and the source of the Riachuelo del Alamo (Alessio Robles 1939:59). Morfí, on 1 November 1777, also mentioned it as the source of the water in the Arroyo de San Pedro (Alessio Robles 1935:94).

**El Arroyo de San Pedro**: Morfí made mention of this and its small supply of good water on 1 November 1777. He arrived after crossing a plain in the region of the Sierra Gaitán and following a rough, rocky road. According to his account, during rains this arroyo flooded water down from the area of Las Tapias and Las Tortuguillas, which eventually emptied into the Río de las Nasas (Alessio Robles 1935:94).

**La Estancia de San Pedro de Alamo**: Morfí stayed there on 1 November 1777. He came six leagues north by the most direct road from La Hacienda de Santa Catarina and noted that it was nine leagues by the coach road. This hacienda was known for its horses and cheese. It lay near the northern end of the Sierra Gaitán among mesquite, huizache, and various types of cactus. Some ninety families lived in poor houses, and the chapel was described as an unadorned hut (Alessio Robles 1935:95).

**Ranchito de Chupaderos** [24 50N  103 49W]: Lafora passed by there on 30 April 1766. He headed northeast out of Las Tortuguillas over brushy hills with little pasture, turned to the north northwest and found this ranchito in a steep-sloped canyon that extended four leagues to the Presidio de la Limpia Concepción del Pasaje (Alessio Robles 1939:60). When Morfí visited there on 2 November 1777, it was abandoned due to the attacks of Apache Indians. It lay in a plain crossed by numerous rain-cut arroyos south of Los Llanos de Pasaje across from another rancho called Guadalupe (Alessio Robles 1935:96).

**Cañón de Culantrillo**: Lafora mentioned this as being on a short horse trail into the Presidio de la Limpia Concepción del Pasaje in Durango on 30 April 1766 (Alessio Robles 1939: 60). On 2 November 1777, Morfí followed this canyon from La Estancia de San Pedro de Alamo through La Sierra Acatita del Oro, or El Orito. He described the road as being on a steep slope, of poor quality, and so little used that there was more than one path in many places. These mountains were sixteen leagues long by one and a half wide, made up of white limestone, and covered with mesquite, cactus, and palmilla (Alessio Robles 1935:95-96).

**El Rancho de Guadalupe**: When Morfí visited there on 2 November 1777, it was abandoned due to the attacks of Apache Indians. It lay in a plain crossed by numerous rain-cut arroyos south of Los Llanos de Pasaje across from another rancho called Chupaderos (Alessio Robles 1935:96).

**Rancho de las Burras**: Lafora mentioned this as being on a short horse trail into the Presidio de la Limpia Concepción del Pasaje in Durango on 30 April 1766 (Alessio Robles 1939:60). Traveling north from two ranchos called Guadalupe and Chupaderos on 2 November 1777, Morfí entered Los Llanos de Pasaje and encountered this rancho. It was almost deserted due to conflicts with Indians but still defended by an old man and his family. It held a good spring, and Morfí noted that the landscape was covered by good pasture (Alessio Robles 1935:96).

**Cuencamé** [24 53N  103 42W]: The mines there were in their infancy when Bishop Mota y Escobar wrote sometime shortly after 1600. He gave the date of their discovery and settlement as 1601. One large mountain contained many mines whose product was processed both there and elsewhere. There was a parish church for the hundred or more Spanish residents and a Franciscan convent which served the Chichimeca Indians for whom the town was named (Ramirez Cabañas 1940:195).

On 26 June 1727, Pedro de Rivera, returning from New Mexico, went from the presidio of Pasaje to the "Real y minas de San Antonio de Cuencamé." The population was a mixture of Spanish, mestizo, and mulatto with an attached Indian pueblo. The next day he continued on to the northeast (Alessio Robles 1946:70). In 1759 Bishop Tamarón described this as a *real de minas* whose patron saint was San Antonio. This head pueblo had an extensive group of clergy. In this *real* and in its outskirts (*campos*) there were 321 families totaling 2,148 people. There was a beautiful church of stone and lime with a vault and a cross-vault. Tamarón described a statue of Christ on the left wall of the church and the sick people who come to pray for the miracles that many had reported (Alessio Robles 1937:96).

On 30 April 1766, Lafora did not go to Cuencamé on his way north but pointed out the road leading to it from the Presidio de la Limpia Concepción del Pasaje. The founding date for this convent is probably 1589 (Alessio Robles 1939:60). When Lafora returned from New Mexico by way of Sonora he crossed the road which he had followed to the north at the *presidio* of Cerro Gordo and continued southeast into Cuencamé. He described it on 27 May 1767 as the "*realito* de Cuencamé" and commented that small amounts of both silver and gold were slowly taken from mines in the area (Alessio Robles 1939:165-166).

Josiah Gregg, in 1841, showed the road going from La Zarca to Gallo and Cuencamé. Gregg noticed an abundance of churches in Cuencamé. From there he proceeded directly to Durango. He showed another route, which he considered the *Camino Real*, leading southeast toward Fresnillo (Gregg 1933:270).

**La Noria**: In 1835, Gregg passed through a mining village called La Noria on the road between the Río Nazas and Cuencamé. To his surprise, he and his party had to buy water at La Noria. Gregg noted that hacienda owners also charged travelers for pasturage (Gregg 1933:269-270). Gregg came to La Noria from the Río Nazas [See also **RIO NAZAS**]

**Santiago** [24 53N 103 42W]: In 1759, Bishop Tamarón described this as a town of Indians of San Pedro Alcántara. It was located almost directly next to Cuencamé. The Indians had to rely on a ravine containing some water; when this dried up they had to go far to look for water. There were 14 families totaling 100 people residing there who maintained a church and a chapel (Alessio Robles 1937:96).

**Oquila**: In 1759, Bishop Tamarón located this Indian town one and a half leagues west of Cuencamé. There were 26 families totaling 166 people residing there, all of whom knew the Christian doctrine (Alessio Robles 1937:96).

**Los Cinco Señores** [24 53N 103 42W]: In 1759, Bishop Tamarón located this Indian town 15 leagues north of Cuencamé; its patron saint was *Los Cinco Señores*. There were eight families totaling 22 people here, and in the neighboring area there were 139 families totaling 898 people. The church there was almost useless when Tamarón visited; he laid the first stone for its rebuilding. After it was abandoned by the Jesuits in 1753, it was joined with Cuencamé (Alessio Robles 1937:97).

**Presidio del Pasage** [Pasaje 24 56N 103 51W]: On 12 October 1725, after leaving El Alamo, Rivera headed northwest through hilly land, ravines and dense mounts of huizaches and cat's claw. Rivera then stopped at the "Presidio Concepción del Pasaje." On 13 October he sent Barreiro to mark the confines of Nueva Vizcaya, Nuevo de Leon and Nuevo de Extremadura or Coahuila (Alessio Robles 1946:38). At this *presidio* there was a company of 40 soldiers and one captain. According to Rivera they were so idle that they spent their time escorting the passengers to the next *presidio*, which wasted seven days each time. They also extorted payment from these travelers and weren't fulfilling their duties of maintaining order in the *presidio*. The salary was 450 pesos for each soldier and 600 for the captain, totaling 18,600 pesos per year (Alessio Robles 1946:102).

In 1759, Bishop Tamarón described this as "El Real Presidio del Pasaje," located three leagues northwest of Cuencamé. There was a chapel there and a *presidio* made up of 35 soldiers; its location was on the *Camino Real* that goes from Durango and Mexico to Chihuahua. The *presidio* was important because the soldiers acted as escorts for the conducts of gold and silver that passed through this *camino* every year. They also observed the actions of the Indians of the Tepehuanes, guarded the borders of Cuencamé, and defended the boundaries of Parras, which had been invaded by enemy Indians. There were 83 Indian families totaling 59 people residing there (Alessio Robles 1937:97).

Lafora called this *presidio* "La Limpia Concepción del Pasaje" when he passed it on 30 April 1766. He was traveling northeast ten leagues out of El Alamo over brushy hills and discussed two roads, the shorter of which he referred to as a *"camino de herradura."* It was surrounded on all sides by high mountains except to the northeast where the road to Cuencamé ran over low hills (Alessio Robles 1939:59-60).

In his entry of 2 November 1777, Morfí mentioned a "Hacienda del Pasaje," three leagues from Cuencamé. It had good pastures which remained virtually unexploited because of the danger from hostile Indians. Nonetheless, Morfí described it enthusiastically as being in the large plain named Pasaje and surrounded by mountains. The house was new, the chapel sufficient, and the owner was required to maintain a *presidio*. A plentiful arroyo supplied water for some 35 families (Alessio Robles 1935:96-97). From Presidio del Pasaje Rivera went to Tinaja. [See also **La TINAJA**]

**Las Peñuelas**: In the Oñate itinerary of 1598 two routes to "Caxco" are described; the one that began at the Hacienda de Rodrígo de Río, was considered the better one. Traveling this route, one passed Las Peñuelas on the way from the *estancia* to "Caxco" (Pacheco, Cárdenas, y Torres 1871:XVI.229).

**Titiritero or Fuente del Sacramento**: As described in the Oñate itinerary of 1598, traveling the better route from the Hacienda de Rodrígo de Río to "Caxco," Titiritero or Fuente del Sacramento was located five leagues from Las Peñuelas. The Aguaje de la Vieja was described as being three leagues from Titiritero (Pacheco, Cárdenas, y Torres 1871:XVI.229).

**Arroyo or Aguaje de la Vieja** [Agua Vieja 25 01N 103 51W]: In the 1598 itinerary of the Oñate expedition, this *aguaje* was described as being three leagues from Titiritero or Fuente del Sacramento (Pacheco, Cárdenas, y Torres 1871:XVI.229). Lafora passed by there, four leagues northwest of the Presidio de la Limpia Concepción del Pasaje, on 14 May 1766. This was the only *aguaje* that they had seen that day (Alessio Robles 1939: 61).

On 3 November 1777, Morfí passed by this abandoned rancho called "El Rancho de Agua de la Vieja" and spring on the right side of the road four leagues north of the Hacienda del Pasaje at the foot of the Sierra de Pasaje along a dry arroyo. There, they turned away from the Sierra de Pasaje and toward Cerro Gordo (Alessio Robles 1935:97). From Aguaje de la Vieja, Lafora went to Tinaja. [See also **La TINAJA**]

**Las Huertecillas**: On 3 November 1777, Morfí left La Hacienda de Pasaje and went north for four leagues before turning away from the Sierra de Pasaje and toward Cerro Gordo. He described the view as he entered this "unhappy" country. Ahead in the distance was a mountain called Santa María and to the east of it one called San Isidro, where Morfí located the mines of San Antonio de Cuencamé. Near these was a peak named Alacrán. They followed a mountain some distance to their left called San Miguelito and passed Cerro Gordo (Alessio Robles 1935:97-98).

**Cerro Gordo**: On 3 November 1777, Morfí passed Cerro Gordo north of La Hacienda del Pasaje and heading into La Tinaja (Alessio Robles 1935:98).

**El Paraje de la Cruz del Sargento**: Morfí mentioned this *paraje* on 3 November 1777, in the vicinity of the Sierra de las Vueltas between Cerro Gordo and la Tinaja. He said that its name referred to a squad of soldiers and their leader who were killed there by Indians (Alessio Robles 1935:98).

**Paso de Renteria (The Ford at the Río de las Nasas)** [Nazas 25 14N 104 08W]: In the 1598 itinerary of the Oñate expedition, two routes to Caxco are described. The better one began from the Hacienda de Rodrígo de Río, proceeded to Las Peñuelas, then to Titiritero or Fuente del Sacramento, and then to Aguaje de la Vieja. From Aguaje de la Vieja to this ford it was a distance of eight leagues (Pacheco, Cárdenas, y Torres 1871:XVI.229).

**Río Grande de las Nazas (or Nassas)**: On 2 November 1725, Rivera left La Tinaja, traveled northwest and stayed on the south side of the Río Grande de las Nassas, in the *población* of San Antonio (Alessio Robles 1946:38-39). Morfí described this river on 3 and 4 November 1777 at La Hacienda de San Antonio and then at a *paraje* just north of it called La Plazuela de los Arrieros. He noted a profusion of trees and discussed its potential for irrigation. At the *paraje* the river cut a large channel through which there were several streambeds which changed course each year (Alessio Robles 1935:99-100). In 1835, Josiah Gregg crossed the Río Nazas, seemingly near a settlement called San Antonio, and called its valley beautiful and fertile. He noted that much cotton was grown there (Gregg 1933:269). Gregg approached the Río Nazas from San Antonio to the north and headed south to La Noria. [See also **SAN ANTONIO**]

**La Tinaja** [25 32N  104 10W]: On 1 November 1725, Rivera left the Presidio del Pasaje and traveled west northwest through flat land with some mounts of huizache and uñas de gato and stopped at an uninhabited place with no water called La Tinaja (Alessio Robles 1946:38). Lafora (14 May 1766) described this as a *puertecito* (small pass) eight leagues from the Presidio de la Limpia Concepción del Pasaje (Alessio Robles 1939: 61). When, on 3 November 1777, Morfí's party arrived at this *aguajito*, they greatly appreciated the water, despite its poor quality, due to the extreme heat. It was located between the haciendas of Pasaje and San Antonio (Alessio Robles 1935:98).

**Mesa del Puerto**: On 3 November 1777, between the "Aguaje de la Tinaja" and La Hacienda de San Antonio, Morfí described a group of mesas along the Río Nasas which gave the appearance of a fortification. This was the most notable of the group and was given as the true beginning of the Bolsón de Mapimí (Alessio Robles 1935:98).

**Presidio del Gallo (Ojo del Gallo)** [25 33N  104 18W]: Following the better route to Caxco from the Hacienda de Rodrígo de Río as described in the 1598 itinerary of the Oñate expedition, Ojo del Gallo was a distance of seven leagues from the Renteria ford of the Río de las Nasas (Pacheco, Cárdenas, y Torres 1871:XVI.229). Oñate's "Ojo del Gallo" seems to match the location of the Presidio del Gallo. On 4 November 1725, Rivera left Las Manos, traveled west northwest and passed a small mountain pass and came to the Presidio del Gallo. Right next to this *presidio* was a hot spring that Rivera described as medicinal. (Alessio Robles 1946:39). The company was made up of 39 soldiers and one captain, whom Rivera felt had them well trained not because they excelled above others but because they still maintained their excursions as well as escorted travelers without extorting payment from them. The soldiers received 450 pesos each and the captain 600, totaling 18,150 pesos per year (Alessio Robles 1946:102-103).

In 1759, Bishop Tamarón wrote that this *presidio* was abolished in 1751. There was still a priest there and 84 families *de vecinos* totaling 546 people. It was located 20 leagues northwest of Mapimí and 58 leagues north of Durango (Alessio Robles 1937:119).

Lafora visited there on 15 May 1766 and located it twelve leagues north northwest of San Antonio. It was located in a plain surrounded by high mountains and cliffs next to a small hill from which Lafora described the town and *presidio*. Eight hundred people lived there in small adobe houses built around an old square plaza whose shape could still be discerned. Two round towers stood at opposite corners connected by four walls. Three of these were in use as parts of houses, and the fourth contained the main entrance and its guard houses. The modern name is San Pedro del Gallo in the municipalidad of the same name in Durango state (Alessio Robles 1939:61-62).

Morfí noted that this had been a *presidio* but was then only a pueblo. He was there on 4 November 1777 and described it as sitting in a small plain surrounded by hills. Some 800 people raised crops and livestock, using the small amount of water available. The old *presidio* was in ruins, the church poorly built and ill-maintained, and the plaza large and empty. Most of the population lived in small adobe houses, the exception being the large house of the priest. Just north of Gallo, Morfí noted the road from La Zarca that led to Chihuahua (Alessio Robles 1935:101-102).

In 1841 Josiah Gregg showed the road going from La Zarca to Gallo and Cuencamé (Gregg 1933:269). From Presidio del Gallo Rivera went to Sierra de la Cadena, Lafora went to Carrizal, Morfí went to La Loma de la Larga, and Gregg went to San Antonio. [See also **SIERRA DE LA CADENA, CARRIZAL, LA LOMA DE LA LARGA, SAN ANTONIO**]

**La Cieneguilla** [25 39N  104 39W]: In the 1598 itinerary of the Oñate expedition, La Cieneguilla was described as being located a distance of two leagues from Ojo del Gallo; this was following the better route to Caxco, which began at the Estancia de Rodrigo de Río (Pacheco, Cárdenas, y Torres 1871:XVI.229).

**Aguaje de Brondate**: Following the better route from Hacienda de Rodrígo de Río to Caxco as described in the 1598 itinerary of the Oñate expedition, this *aguaje* was located a distance of half a league from La Cieneguilla. From there to Caxco it was another two and a half leagues (Pacheco, Cárdenas, y Torres 1871:XVI.229).

**Caxco (Casco)** [El Casco 25 34N  104 35W]: In the 1598 itinerary of the Oñate expedition, two routes are described for reaching the mines of Caxco. The worse route began at Avino. From there one headed to Caxco by way of San Juan del Río, Ontiveros, Arroyo de Coneto de las Nasas, and the Cacapa ford of the Río de las Nasas (Pacheco, Cárdenas, y Torres 1871:XVI.228). The other route for reaching Caxco began from the Hacienda de Rodrígio de Río. From the *hacienda* it continued to Las Peñuelas, Titiritero or Fuente del Sacramento, Aguaje de la Vieja, Rentería ford of the Río de las Nasas, Ojo del Gallo, La Cieneguilla, and then Aguaje de Brondate. Following this route, it was a total of 30 leagues from the Hacienda de Rodrígo de Río to Caxco, and the road was very good for carts (Pacheco, Cárdenas, y Torres 1871:XVI.229). Marcelo Espinosa testified that the members of the Oñate expedition were detained at Casco until December 1597, and in 1602, Mexico city, Captain Juan Gutiérrez Bocanegra testified that when Oñate reached the mines of Casco, located 150 leagues from Mexico City, he was ordered to stop there by order of the Count of Monterrey for an inspection (Hammond and Rey 1953: II. 632, 887). The Oñate expedition left Caxco for New Mexico on 1 November 1597, heading north north west to Carrizal (Pacheco, Cárdenas, y Torres 1871:XVI.229).

When Bishop Mota y Escobar described the route leaving Durango for the north in the early seventeenth century, it led through a San Juan del Río and Palmitos, and then the distances between towns grew. Caxco lay some 25 leagues almost directly north of San Juan del Río through country unpopulated except for some livestock *estancias*. The mines themselves were run by a few miners with their families. They also raised some livestock and crops for their subsistence (Ramirez Cabañas 1940:198).

**Canatán**: On 8 October 1725, after leaving Durango, Rivera came to the pueblo of Canatán. According to Rivera, it was a pueblo of the nation of Tepehuanos. There is a Canatlán located some 54 kilometers northwest of Durango but this does not seem to be on Rivera's route (Alessio Robles 1946:37).

**Batres** [24 12N  104 42W]:  On 8 October 1725, after leaving Canatán, Rivera came to the Río Sauceda and found it impassable. Rivera returned two leagues to Canatán and headed northeast and stopped at a hacienda next to Batres, which is a small lake or lagoon (Alessio Robles 1946:37). From Batres Rivera went to Hacienda del Chorro.[See also **HACIENDA DEL CHORRO**]

**Cacaria** [24 24N  104 45W]: Describing the road from Durango north to Santa Bárbara at the start of the seventeenth century, this was the first stop along the road for Bishop Mota y Escobar. This Chichimeca pueblo enjoyed plentiful fresh water from springs, lagoons, and marshes. The natives exploited fish and waterfowl, while the region also contained many Spanish estates with livestock and cultivated fields (Ramirez Cabañas 1940:196).

**Hacienda de Sauceda** [24 32N   104 32W]: This name was given to a *paraje*, a Chichimeca pueblo and *encomienda*, as well as some haciendas when Bishop Mota y Escobar described them shortly after 1600. All were located there because of the water from a perpetual arroyo. This area was north of Durango between Cacaria and San Juan del Río. The road split here, with one fork going west and the other east and then north (Ramirez Cabañas 1940:196).

**Los Ojos Azules** [24 34N   104 25W]: On 10 October 1725 Rivera left the Hacienda del Chorro and headed east northeast and stopped in Los Ojos Azules, which was uninhabited (Alessio Robles 1946:38).

**San Juan del Río** [24 47N   104 27W]: In the Oñate itinerary of 1598 two routes to Caxco are described. The worse route was the one described as beginning at Aviño; according to the description, one reaches Casco from Aviño by way of San Juan del Río ("Sant Joan del Río") (Pacheco, Cárdenas, y Torres 1871:XVI.228). Bishop Mota y Escobar described this San Juan del Río as a *pueblo de indios* northeast of Durango around 1600. It lay beside a river with the same name and impressed Mota y Escobar as having perfect land and water for Castilian fruits, especially grapes from which were made both wine and vinegar. The Franciscan convent, he wrote, had one of the best gardens in the kingdom (Ramirez Cabañas 1940:197).

The following is a brief history of San Juan del Río. In 1558 Ibarra's people began to work the nearby mines of Aviño, and it was at this time that the Indians of San Juan del Río were first placed in *encomienda* (Gerhard 1993:234). In 1562 Ibarra chose the fertile valley of San Juan del Río as his center of operations and named an *alcalde mayor* (Gerhard 1993:234). In 1575 there was a Franciscan church established and 300 Indian catechumens that cultivated the corn (Saravia 1980:10). At this time there were around 100 Spanish families in the area, and, after 1599, the Franciscan convent became one of the most important ones in that province. Because of the Tepehuanos rebellion of 1616-1618, many haciendas and farms were destroyed, and by 1622 there were only about 60 Indian families and some single individuals left (Saravia 1979:192-193). Nevertheless, during the 1620s, San Juan del Río did benefit from the success of nearby mines such as Coneto, Cuencamé and Papasquiaro, and, little by little, new Spaniards began to settle in (Cuentas de la Real Caja de Durango, 1624-1638). In 1761 the population reached 8,299 people, and in 1790 it had grown to 11,256. By then it was under the jurisdiction of Durango (Gerhard 1993:234).

**Ontiveros**: In the 1598 itinerary of the Oñate expedition, two routes to Caxco are described; on the one considered the worse one, heading from Avino, Ontiveros was described as being six leagues from San Juan del Río (Pacheco, Cárdenas, y Torres 1871:XVI.228).

**Palmitos** [25 03N  104 29W]: This hacienda, near San Juan del Río, Durango, produced maize, wheat, and livestock in the early 1600s. According to Bishop Mota y Escobar, the road to the mines of Coneto left the main route north at Palmitos (Ramirez Cabañas 1940:197).

**Coneto** [Coneto de Comonfort 24 59N  104 46W]: Bishop Mota y Escobar noted that from Palmitos, it was five leagues to the silver mines of Coneto, which he described as poor in both ores and people (Ramirez Cabañas 1940:197). Two roads from the Real de Minas de San Martín to the Nazas and then to Santa Bárbara have been described for the 1570s; one through Aviño and San Juan, and the other by way of Nombre de Dios, Durango and Coneto.  Coneto was established in about 1572; in 1574 some fifty Spanish families lived there (Mecham 1927:230-231).

**Cacapa ford of the Río de las Nasas, near Caxco**: In the 1598 itinerary of the Oñate expedition, two routes to Caxco are described; on the one considered the worse one, which began at Avino, the Cacapa ford of the Río de las Nasas was described as being six leagues from Ontiveros (Pacheco, Cárdenas, y Torres 1871:XVI.228).

**Arroyo de Coneto de las Nasas** [25 09N  104 33W]: There are two routes to Caxco described in the 1598 itinerary of the Oñate expedition. Following the worse one described heading from Avino, one crosses this arroyo half-way between the Cacapa ford and Caxco (Pacheco, Cárdenas, y Torres 1871:XVI.228). Just north of here was Caxco.

**San Antonio** [25 30N  103 40W]: On 2 November 1725 Rivera stayed in the *población* of San Antonio on the south side of the Río Grande de las Nassas. It was a small settlement of Spaniards, mestizos and mulattoes. He wrote that one league from this place there was a small pueblo inhabited by the Babos-Arigames Indians (Alessio Robles 1946:38-39).

Lafora referred to this as "La Hacienda de San Antonio" on 14 May 1766. It was situated on the bank of the Río Nasas fourteen leagues northeast of the Presidio de la Limpia Concepción del Pasaje in Durango. Between these two stops they rode through a valley in high mountains. The range on their right, to the east, was called Rosario. There is a modern rancho in the municipalidad of Cuencamé named San Antonio (Alessio Robles 1939:61).

Morfí stayed there on 3 November 1777 just after entering the Bolsón de Mapimí from the south. The area was described as very dry, rocky, and covered with thickets, although containing good pasture. It was near enough to the Río Nasas to allow some irrigation (Alessio Robles 1935:98-99). Josiah Gregg, in 1841, showed the road going from La Zarca to Gallo and Cuencamé. A settlement named San Antonio is shown between the last two, evidently near the Río Nazas (Gregg 1933:269).

**Sierra del Rosario** [25 36N  103 52W]: On 25 November 1725 Rivera, after camping at the foot of the Sierra de la Cadena, traveled east northeast through flat land which had some hills, leaving to the south the sierra called El Rosario (Alessio Robles 1946:39). This is the name given by Lafora to a mountain range which they followed northeast from Presidio de la Limpia Concepción del Pasaje to San Antonio in present Durango state (Alessio Robles 1939:61).

**La Plazuela de los Arrieros**: This was a *paraje* visited by Lafora on 15 May 1766 just north of San Antonio in modern Durango state. It was next to a small stream divided into several arms and just south of a circular plain which they traversed to the Presidio del Gallo (Alessio Robles 1939: 61). This is a *paraje* where Morfí encountered the Río Nasas, just north of La Hacienda de San Antonio, on 4 November 1777 (Alessio Robles 1935:100).

**La Vaquilla**: This was a narrow canyon midway between San Antonio and El Gallo in modern Durango used by Lafora to traverse an almost circular plain which he described on 15 May 1766. It was surrounded by high bare mountains with cliffs and extraordinary shapes (Alessio Robles 1939:61).

After leaving the Río Nasas at La Hacienda de San Antonio on 4 November 1777, Morfí climbed onto a plain surrounded by mountains and headed west northwest. The earth was brown and dry but the pasture was good. The road was flat and dusty. After going eleven leagues he climbed the "Puerto de la Vaquilla" between low hills which marked the halfway point between Nasas and Gallo. Morfí noted some caves which could be used to escape the wind and rain in the sandstone rock veined with quartz (Alessio Robles 1935:100). From La Vaquilla Lafora went to the Presidio del Gallo. [See also **PRESIDIO DEL GALLO**]

**Las Manos**: On 3 November 1725, Rivera left San Antonio, traveled northwest, and stayed at Las Manos, an unpopulated place without water; it was named after the Indians killed and nailed many of their victims' hands to mesquite trees (Alessio Robles 1946:39). Morfí entered this plain northwest of Puerto de la Vaquilla on 4 November 1777 and noticed, to his surprise, a well-kept milpa next to a roadside spring in this area of much hostility between the Spanish and Indians (Alessio Robles 1935:101).

**Paraje del Palo Blanco**: Morfí went there, in the midst of gentle hills, on 4 November 1777, after crossing the Puerto de la Vaquilla and the plain which he called Las Manos (Alessio Robles 1935:101).

**La Loma de La Larga**: On 6 November 1777, Morfí climbed this hill and then entered the Cañón de la Cueva, following La Sierra de Jacalco or Rosario. He had left Gallo that morning and went by the edge of some hills called Potrero, following on his right one called La Porta (Alessio Robles 1935:102).

**La Hacienda de Jacales o Rosario** [25 41N  103 48W]: Morfí passed this hacienda near the mountains of the same names on 6 November 1777 between Gallo and Cadena (Alessio Robles 1935:102).

**Presidio de Mapimí** [25 49N  103 51W]: Bishop Mota y Escobar labeled this a *paraje* when he was there in the early 1600s. He said that it had been deserted after its mineral wealth had been depleted. A Tepehuanos pueblo had been founded and produced all the "fruits of Castille" with the good water there. This place marked the end of Mota y Escobar's account of this route (Ramírez Cabañas 1940:196). On 25 November 1725, Rivera came to the Presidio de Mapimí. This *presidio* and others were supplied by a large hot spring that could very well supply a bigger population. It was a small *real de minas* whose metals were of good quality but which had declined due to the poor abilities of the miners. When the *presidio* was first established it housed 33 men from different presidios in la Vizcaya; nine of them were sent from a *presidio* previously known as Santa Catalina. Rivera wrote that because they were so far away from the *Camino Real* these soldiers did not provide escorts for anyone. They did, however, spend time going to Durango 70 leagues away to pick up the captain's correspondence as well as to pick up supplies. Twenty-four of the soldiers received 450 pesos each, the nine from Santa Catalina received 337 pesos each while the captain received 500, totaling 14,333 pesos per year (Alessio Robles 1946:104).

In 1759, Bishop Tamarón wrote that this abolished *presidio* was located 60 leagues west of Parras. It was a moderate place with some silver mines. There were 286 families totaling 1,260 people, who were *vecinos de razón* (Alessio Robles 1937:119). On 8 November 1777, Morfí left Cadena heading east toward the Sierra de Rosario or Cadena, crossing it at its northernmost pass. They continued east into Mapimí, which they recognized from a distance by the steam of its foundries. It was in a nearly circular plain cut by many dry arroyos and limited on the south and west by the Sierra del Rosario and to the north by its foothills, notably Cerro Colorado. To the east was the Sierra de Mapimí and an elevation called La Bufa. The road was good though filled with loose rock. Mapimí was first founded shortly after 1589, destroyed by Indians three times and finally abandoned in 1715. It was refounded as a *presidio*, but in 1752, the *presidio* was moved, leaving the town. From there, Morfí's party turned to the east toward Parras, Saltillo and Texas (Alessio Robles 1935:107-109).

Pike came to "Maupemie" on 11 May 1807, and described the mines of the area and their "wretched" workers. His route took him south from the Río Florido and around the Bolsón de Mapimí before heading him further east (Coues 1895:II.675).

On 9 May 1847, Wislizenus described Mapimí as being in the eastern corner of a valley, surrounded by mountains in which much silver was found. The town was somewhat empty, probably due to the war and the arrival of the army to which Wislizenus was attached. From there they continued east into the Bolsón de Mapimí (Wislizenus 1848:67).

**Bolsón de Mapimí**: Wislizenus approached the Bolsón de Mapimí through a canyon, from the town of the same name, on 10 May 1847. He described it as starting at the mouth of that canyon, some five miles east of Mapimí, and extending to the north. Wislizenus wrote that this large depression was often considered a desert and a swamp, neither of which was completely true. He thought that the soil was blacker and richer than the sand which he had been passing through (Wislizenus 1848:67-68).

**Los Peñoles**: On 9 December 1725, after leaving El Presidio de Mapimí, Rivera traveled west northwest through hilly land with mounts of mesquite and hills within sight, and stopped at an uninhabited place called Los Peñoles (Alessio Robles 1946:40). From Los Peñoles Rivera went to La Zarca. [See also **LA ZARCA**]

**Sierra de la Cadena** [25 54N  104 06W]: On 24 November 1725, Rivera camped at the foot of the Sierra de la Cadena (Alessio Robles 1946:39). Wislizenus and the United States Army crossed over these mountains by a pass, or *puerto*, of the same name on 9 May 1847. He thought the pass narrowed but was a good passage. He also commented on the limestone which he saw in these mountains (Wislizenus 1848:67).

**La Cañada de Agostadero**: On 6 November 1777, Morfí passed by there shortly before climbing La Cuesta del Corral de los Dueños and arriving at El Puerto de los Volantes, then going on to Cadena (Alessio Robles 1935:102).

**La Cuesta del Corral de los Dueños**: On 6 November 1777, Morfí climbed this after passing La Cañada de Agostadero and shortly before arriving at El Puerto de los Volantes and going on to Cadena (Alessio Robles 1935:102).

**El Puerto de los Volantes**: Morfí's party stopped at this *paraje* on 6 November 1777. It was within view of the mountains and hacienda of Jacales or Rosario, El Puerto de Cadena, and the hills of Pelayo and between Gallo and Cadena (Alessio Robles 1935:102-103).

**La Hacienda de la Cadena** [25 53N  104 12W]: Morfí's group went there on 6 November 1777. It was at the foot of a hill and the beginning of a large plain. To the east was a mountain range called Rosario or Cadena which ran from east to west, then turned to the northwest and to the north. It had three passes to the western part of the plain of Mapimí. The house was large and partially destroyed and good water ran in an arroyo nearby. A good maize field nearby had a guardhouse set in its middle for protection from Indians (Alessio Robles 1935:103-104).

Pike came to this "house built and occupied by a priest" on 10 May 1807. He situated it near a stream on a pass with the same name (Coues 1895:II.674). On 8 May 1847, Wislizenus and the U.S. Army left Pelayo and crossed over a mountainous road to another valley and this hacienda which, Wislizenus thought, belonged to the governor of Durango. Large mountains rose to the east and west, and a creek from the western chain, the Sierra de Mimbres, ran through the hacienda (Wislizenus 1848:67). Pike came to Cadena from Pelayo to the north.[See also **PELAYO**]

**El Llano de la Cadena**: Morfí rode northwest from La Hacienda de la Cadena on 7 November 1777, onto this large plain covered with mesquite, huizache, lechuguilla and cat's claw. They continued over hills, valleys, and dry arroyos and entered into a canyon filled with trees (Alessio Robles 1935:104).

**Cerro Blanco**: Morfí went by this hill on 7 November 1777, in the plain of La Cadena north of the hacienda of the same name (Alessio Robles 1935:104).

**El Aguaje de San Jose**: This waterhole was visited by Morfí on 7 November 1777, eight leagues north northwest of La Hacienda de la Cadena. The landscape was of hard clay and saltpeter, and nothing grew near the spring due to the trampling of wild horses and cattle. Elsewhere, this plain supported extensive pastures. Morfí guessed that the water of this spring originated in the larger spring at Pelayo and ran underground to there (Alessio Robles 1935:104-105).

**Oruilla**: Wislizenus described this deserted hacienda which he passed on 8 May 1847, about half-way between Pelayo and Cadena. It showed signs of past use as a copper smelter (Wislizenus 1848:67).

**Pelayo** [26 04N  104 20W]: This large spring was eight leagues north of La Hacienda de la Cadena at the foot of a rocky point. On 7 November 1777, Morfí explored this area with a patrol. To the east was a mountain range of the same name; to the north the continuation of the Sierra de la Cadena which ran to the south; to the west were gentle hills. The soil was black. On this day, Morfí and the patrol left Cadena and went to the north northwest as far as the Aguaje de San Jose, a distance of some eight leagues. They then worked their way toward Pelayo, less than a league distant, passing along the way the ruins of building and stone corral in a sand dune. From Pelayo, Morfí wrote, they entered the *Camino Real* that went back to Cadena (Alessio Robles 1935:105-107).

On 9 May 1807, Zebulon Pike described "Pelia" as a small outpost surrounded by copper mines (Coues 1895:II.673). After crossing some mountains between Santa Bernardo and Cerro Gordo Creek, Wislizenus and the U.S. Army crossed a broad plain for some 25 miles and reached "San José de Pelayo," which Wislizenus called a village or hacienda, on 7 May 1847. He commented on the many springs, some of them hot, in the area, and some stone fortifications set atop a steep hill. When the army left here they crossed some mountains and headed into Cadena (Wislizenus 1848:66-67). Pike came to Pelayo from Ojo San Bernarde and Wislizenus came south to

Pelayo from Cerro Gordo Creek. [See also **OJO SAN BERNARDE AND CERRO GORDO CREEK**]

**El Arroyuelo del Carrizal**: According to the Oñate itinerary of 1598 the Oñate expedition left Caxco on 1 November 1597 and headed north northwest to Carrizal (Pacheco, Cárdenas, y Torres 1871:XVI.229). On 16 May 1766 Lafora found the only water of the day there, fourteen leagues north northwest of El Gallo and two leagues before La Zarca. The landscape was very flat and dry with wild palms and a little pasture land (Alessio Robles 1939:62).

**La Zarca** [25 50N   104 44W]: On 2 November 1597, the Oñate expedition left Carrizal and went to "La Carca," a distance of three leagues, where they stayed for 11 days. They buried a child there (Pacheco, Cárdenas, y Torres 1871:XVI.230). On 10 December 1725, after leaving Los Peñoles and heading west northwest, Rivera stopped at a hacienda called La Zarca (Alessio Robles 1946:40).

Lafora, on 16 May 1766, described two haciendas there, called La Zarca de Arriba and La Zarca de Abajo, which together contained 250 people employed in the raising of all kinds of livestock. In the twentieth century, La Zarca can be found in the municipalidad of Villa Hidalgo, Durango (Alessio Robles 1939:62).

After his 1835 trip, Josiah Gregg described La Zarca as the center of one of the largest haciendas of the north, over 100 miles in length. He showed the road going from there to Gallo and Cuencamé (Gregg 1933:269). From La Zarca Rivera, Lafora, and Gregg went to Cerro Gordo. [See also **PRESIDIO DE SAN MIGUEL DE CERRO GORDO**]

**Los Patos**: On 14 November 1597, the Oñate expedition left La Zarca and went to Los Patos, a distance of four leagues. They buried a servant there who had been killed by a colt (Pacheco, Cárdenas, y Torres 1871:XVI.230).

**Indehe or Indé** [25 54N   105 13W]: Bishop Mota y Escobar placed this mine complex 26 uninhabited leagues northwest of Caxco in an area of mountains and plains. There were four or five miners and three mills for processing minerals. A little wheat and corn was raised here along with some assorted livestock (Ramirez Cabañas 1940:198). In 1759, Bishop Tamarón placed this *real* of "Yndeé," whose patron saint was San Juan Bautista, six leagues from El Oro. There were good gold mines there, and 108 families *de razón* totaling 866 people resided there (Alessio Robles 1937:120). Mecham postulated that these deposits at Indé were discovered in 1562 by Francisco de Ibarra and that the area was first settled by Rodrigo del Río in 1567. The mines were immediately productive but, due to trouble with the Tepehuanos Indians, by 1573 only ten Spaniards remained. They were reported closed before 1575 (Mecham 1927:126-127,188-189).

The following information provides a summary of the history of Indé. , This *villa* of San Juan Bautista de Indé was also called Indehé during the colonial period and was the first Spanish settlement north of the Río Nazas in the 16th century. In 1563, the troops of Francisco de Ibarra, on their journey to New Mexico, discovered a series of rich mining veins west of the Río Nazas, in the direction of the Sierra Madre, which they named Indé (Cramaussel 1990:18).

The *villa* was completely abandoned two years later. In 1567, Rodrígo del Río de Losa was ordered by Francisco de Ibarra to repopulate the town, but, in 1574, Indé was abandoned again because of Indian attacks and the leaving of some of the settlers. In 1583, Indé was repopulated due to the return of the Antonio de Espejo expedition; in 1586, the *villa* of Santa Bárbara was burned by the Indians, and both *villas* were temporarily abandoned (Cramaussel 1990:46;"Nombramiento a Juan de Sanabria como alcalde mayor de Indé," 1590); and again, in 1594, the Spaniards abandoned the mines, although they were repopulated a few years later. It wasn't until after the start of the 17th century that the Spanish presence became solidified.

Indé was located on the *Camino Real* that connected Durango with the province of Santa Bárbara. The *Camino Real* left the provincial capital, heading north by the Río Matalotes, passed through Indé and then went up the river basin of the Río Florido towards the *reales* of Santa Bárbara and Todos Santos and towards the San Bartolomé mission. During the Tepehuanos rebellion of 1616, the region of Indé as well as the rest of the province was burned by the Indians, and even in 1624, the majority of it was still in ruins (Hackett 1923-37:146). With the establishment of the Presidio de Cerro

Gordo in 1646, the short road from Zacatecas to Parral was opened, which meant that it no longer passed through Indé. This old road was used only in times of violence. It was also used by those going to Guanaceví and the famous hacienda of General Sextín de Cañas. In 1755, Indé lost its status as religious capital when the local priest moved his residence to the Real del Oro (Gerhard 1982:225).

**El Oro or Real de Oro or Real de Minas de Oro** [Santa María del Oro 25 56N 105 22W]: In 1759, Bishop Tamarón located this "Real de Minas de Oro" 41 leagues north of El Gallo. , Its patron saint was Nuestra Señora de la Merced and there were 229 families (*vecinos)* totaling 1,082 people. El Oro was considered the head pueblo of this jurisdiction, and Tamarón visited many villages in this jurisdiction (Alessio Robles 1937:119).

**Las Bocas**: In 1759, Bisop Tamarón placed this Indian town 19 leagues north of El Oro. Its patron saint was San Miguel de las Bocas, and there were 74 Indian families totaling 251 people. In the parish there were 74 families *de razón* totaling 296 people (Alessio Robles 1937:120-121). A town by this name is not evident on any modern map. Modern maps, however, show the following three places: La Boquilla, municipality of San Bernardo; Boquilla Colorado, municipality of El Oro; and Boquilla del Muerto, municipality of Indé (Alessio Robles 1937:125).

**San Gabriel**: In 1759, Bishop Tamarón placed this Indian town two leagues west of Las Bocas. It was composed of 30 Indian families totaling 102 people (Alessio Robles 1937:121).

**Hacienda de las Mimbreras** [26 04N 105 04W]: In 1759, Bishop Tamarón placed this hacienda seven leagues east northeast from "Yndeé." (Indé) The assistant priest who resided there oversaw the demolished Presidio de Cerro Gordo and other haciendas. All together there were 163 families totaling 1,032 people (Alessio Robles 1937:120).

**Presidio de San Miguel de Cerro Gordo**: On 15 November 1597, the Oñate expedition left Los Patos and headed to Cerro Gordo, a distance of four leagues (Pacheco, Cárdenas, y Torres 1871:XVI.230).

On 11 December 1725, after leaving La Zarca and heading west north-west, Rivera came to the "Presidio de Cerro Gordo." The *presidio* San Miguel de Cerro Gordo, identified presently as Villa Hidalgo, Durango, was situated south of a deep ditch that contained enough water to supply both the *presidio* and the farming hacienda on the other side of it (Alessio Robles 1946:40). The garrison consisted of 30 soldiers and one captain, and Rivera wrote that they generally did only what pleased them, failing to comply with all of their duties. He observed that they still escorted the herds and travelers to Valle de San Bartolomé but, based on the reputation of the soldiers, Rivera felt this only caused the people more harm than good (Alessio Robles 1946:104-105).

In 1759, Bishop Tamarón described this *presidio* as demolished. The population was made up of 51 families *de vecinos* of the former soldiers totaling 298 people. They asked Tamarón to send a priest there, but he told them that he could not promise anything (Alessio Robles 1937:120).

This *presidio* was visited by Lafora's party on 17 May 1766. It was located on the bank of a deep gorge in which flowed a stream, which was formed by two arroyos combining a little above the *presidio*. One of these streams flowed out of the Sierra de Tramojos six leagues to the southwest and the other from the Mimbrera four leagues to the west. Combined, they flowed past the *presidio* and toward the Sierra de Pozo Hediondo, twenty leagues to the north. Lafora named several dependents in the jurisdiction of this *Alcalde Mayor* and estimated their total population as one hundred, mostly mulatto (Alessio Robles 1939:62-63).

In 1835, Josiah Gregg passed through this town and described it as the northernmost in the state of Durango. He had come from Valle de San Bartolomé and left toward Gallo and Cuencamé (Gregg 1933:269).

The following information provides a few more details about this *presidio*. Around 1646, the governor of Nueva Vizcaya, Luis de Valdés, planned the building of a new *presidio* whose objectives would be to stop the attacks of the Salineros and the Tobosos as well as to open a road directly to Parral from Zacatecas, without having to go through Durango and Indé. This project was started in 1646, (Naylor and Polzer 1986:335) and in July of that year the *presidio* was officially founded. The first *presidio* captain was Juan de Barraza. The *presidio* continued to exist until 1751 when the King decided to eliminate it (Registros parroquiales de la Mimbrera). From Cerro Gordo

Gregg went to the Hacienda de la Concepción. [See also **HACIENDA DE LA CONCEPCION**]

**Cerro Gordo Creek (or El Andabazo)**: Wislizenus called this creek both Cerro Gordo and El Andabazo and referred to it as a "considerable creek." It was reached on 6 May 1847 after a crossing of the mountains near the spring named Santa Bernardo. A mile through a limestone canyon brought the army to the valley watered by this stream. Camp was made near an abandoned rancho (Wislizenus 1848:66).

**Ojo San Bernarde**: On 7 May 1807, Zebulon Pike reported passing by two springs, the first being the first water since leaving the Río Florido four miles above Guajuquilla and heading southeast. He showed two springs called San Bernarde and San Blas in that order as he was going south. In 1895 Coues reversed the order in his notes and identified a nearby stream as the Cerro Gordo near the town of the same name (Coues 1895:II.672).

On 5 May 1847, some 31 miles south of Guajuquilla, Wislizenus reported stopping at a spring whose water was so muddy that "the animals refused to drink, or rather to eat it," in a ravine on the left side of the road; it was called San Antonio. After three more miles he reached another spring which was just as muddy, and sulphurous, on the right side of the road. This spring was named San Blas. Five miles south of San Blas was the first good water since just below Guajuquilla, at a deserted rancho called San Bernardo. A creek began in one spring, just below a steep mountain and surrounded by willows and cottonwoods. Other springs appeared in a grassy plain about a mile below the rancho. Upon leaving, Wislizenus and the army crossed the mountains above San Bernardo heading south toward Pelayo (Wislizenus 1848:66).

**Ojo San Blas**: On 7 May 1807, Zebulon Pike reported passing by two springs, the first being the first water since leaving the Río Florido four miles above Guajuquilla and heading southeast. He showed two springs called San Bernarde and San Blas in that order as he was going south. In 1895 Coues reversed them in his notes and identified a nearby stream as the Cerro Gordo near the town of the same name (Coues 1895:II.672).

Some 31 miles south of Guajuquilla, Wislizenus stopped at a spring found in a ravine on the left side of the road; it was called San Antonio. After three more miles he reached another spring which was very muddy, and sulphurous, on the right side of the road. This spring was named San Blas and was reached on 5 May 1847 (Wislizenus 1848:66). Pike came to San Blas from Guajuquilla. [See also **PRESIDIO DE NUESTRA SENORA DE LAS CALDAS DE GUAJOQUILLA**]

**San Antonio**: Some 31 miles south of Guajuquilla, Wislizenus reported stopping at a spring whose water was so muddy that "the animals refused to drink, or rather to eat it," in a ravine on the , left side of the road. He and the army which he accompanied reached this spring, called San Antonio, on 5 May 1847 (Wislizenus 1848:66). Wislizenus came to San Antonio from the Hacienda de Dolores.[See also **HACIENDA DE DO-LORES**]

**Paraje or Aguaje de la Parida**: On 16 November 1597 the Oñate expedition left Cerro Gordo and traveled four leagues to La Parida (Pacheco, Cárdenas, y Torres 1871:XVI.230). On 28 December 1725, after leaving the Presidio San Miguel de Cerro Gordo, Rivera traveled northwest north and passed the *parajes* of La Partida and of El Alamo, and found the Río Florido (Alessio Robles 1946:40-41). In flat, dry country, five leagues northwest of El Gallo, this water hole was visited by Lafora on 19 May 1766 (Alessio Robles 1939:63).

**Paraje del Alamo**: On 28 December 1725, after leaving the Presidio San Miguel de Cerro Gordo, Rivera traveled northwest north and passed the *paraje* of El Alamo, and came to the Río Florido (Alessio Robles 1946:40-41). Lafora passed by the "Arroyo del Alamo" on 19 May 1766 after traveling in flat, dry country for ten leagues northwest of El Gallo (Alessio Robles 1939:63).

**Aguaje de Bauz**: On 16 November 1597 the Oñate expedition traveled a distance of three leagues from La Parida to the Aguaje de Bauz (Pacheco, Cárdenas, y Torres 1871:XVI.230). From here the Oñate expedition went to Río de Enmedio. [See also **RIO DE ENMEDIO**]

**Estancia o Rancho de Nuestra Señora de la Asunción**: This was found by Lafora, along with other haciendas, on the banks of the Río Florida fourteen leagues northwest of El Gallo on 19 May 1766 (Alessio Robles 1939:63).

**Arroyo de San Agustín**: This was a dry arroyo passed by Lafora a little south of Valle de San Bartolomé and north of Río Florida on 20 May 1766 (Alessio Robles 1939:63).

**Arroyo de los Mimbres**: This was an almost dry arroyo passed by Lafora a little south of Valle de San Bartolomé on 20 May 1766, between Arroyo de San Agustín and Arroyo de Balsequiilo (Alessio Robles 1939:63).

**Arroyo de Balsequillo**: On 20 May 1766, Lafora passed this almost dry arroyo a little south of Valle de San Bartolomé, just north of Arroyo de los Mimbres (Alessio Robles 1939:63).

**Hacienda de la Concepción**: On 29 December 1725, after stopping on the northern bank of the Río Florido, Rivera traveled northwest through flat and pleasant land, with very little mounts and with good pasture land, and came to the Hacienda de la Concepción (Alessio Robles 1946:41). Lafora passed by there, five leagues southeast of the Valle de San Bartolomé, on 20 May 1766. This hacienda is in the modern municipio de Jiménez, Durango (Alessio Robles 1939:63). In 1841 Josiah Gregg showed the road which he traveled going through Santa Rosalia and then almost directly south through Santa Cruz toward "Allende or Valle de S. Bartolomé" and southwest to Cerro Gordo. "Concepcion" was about one third of the way from Valle de San Bartolomé to Cerro Gordo (Gregg 1933).

**Rio Florido:** On 17 November 1597, the Oñate expediton left Bauz to the Río Florido a distance of two "good" leagues.

**Río de Enmedio**: On 17 November 1597 the Oñate expedition traveled one league from the Río Florido to Río de Enmedio (Pacheco, Cárdenas, y Torres 1871:XVI.230). On 29 December 1725, after passing the Hacienda de la Concepción, Rivera came to the Río de Enmedio and the valley of San Bartolomé (Alessio Robles 1946:41). Lafora used this name when he crossed it three leagues southeast of Valle de San Bartolomé on 20 May 1766. Later he said that it was the same as the Río de Santa Bárbara (Alessio Robles 1939:63-64).

**Río de los Buñuelos**: On 17 November 1597 the Oñate expedition left Bauz and traveled one league to Río de los Buñuelos. (Pacheco, Cárdenas, y Torres 1871:XVI.230).

**La Villa de Santa Bárbara** [26 48N  105 49W]: The 1581-1582 Sánchez Chamuscado expedition into New México was organized in Santa Bárbara and left there for the north on 5 June 1581, heading down the Río de San Gregorio toward its confluence with the Río Conchos (Hammond and Rey 1927:12-13;Mecham 1926:268).

According to Joseph Brondate, who was captain of the cavalry, the Oñate expedition began its trek to New Mexico at the mines of Santa Bárbara, the last settlement in Nueva Vizcaya, on 19 December 1597 (Hammond and Rey 1953:II.624). Bishop Mota y Escobar found ten or twelve Spaniards, stock-raisers and merchants, when he was there shortly after 1600. There were also two or three miners with mills and a Franciscan convent. This fertile region impressed Mota y Escobar with its produce, especially the grapes. The landscape was mountainous with large rivers from which the local Indians gathered fish. It was 25 sparsely populated leagues northwest of Indehe and seven west of El Valle de San Bartolomé (Ramirez Cabañas 1940:198-199). Santa Bárbara was settled in 1567 by Rodrígo del Río. It remained for a time the northernmost Spanish outpost (Mecham 1927:189). In 1759, Bishop Tamarón placed this *real de minas* six leagues west of Parral. There were 170 families totaling 1,020 people residing there (Alessio Robles 1937:124).

The following synthesised history of Santa Bárbara begins in 1567, when Rodrígo del Río de Losa officially opened the *Villa de Santa Bárbara*, whose mines had previously been discovered by Juan de La Parra. The *Villa de Santa Bárbara* was also the capital town of a province with the same name that encompassed the entire valley of the Río Florido (Cramaussel 1990:22-23).

During the rest of the 16th century, the mining activities never became very prosperous, and the Spanish settlement was often disturbed by Indian attacks and by the expeditions to New Mexico, in which many of the inhabitants of Santa Bárbara enlisted. As a result the mines were abandoned in favor of agricultural pursuits (Cramaussel 1990:38-42). Until the founding of the mines at Todos Santos around 1586, Santa Bárbara was the last settled area on the *Camino Real.*

There continued to be some commercial traffic through this small town but the expansion of Valle de San Bartolomé caused the road to be diverted towards the fertile streams of the Franciscan mission. In 1631, when the mines in Parral were discovered, new mining operations were established in Santa Bárbara, but by the end of the 17th century it was again almost abandoned because of the lack of new mines. Many of the inhabitants left to go to Cusihuiriachi (Documento de la cofradía del santísimo sacramento). During the 18th century the town was rejuvenated, and, by the end of the nineteenth century, under Porfirio Díaz, Santa Bárbara was connected by railroad to Parral. It was then transformed into a center of gold and silver production. In 1902 its population numbered at 2,406 (Rocha Chávez 1967:14), and in 1907 its production of precious metals was double the quantity that was produced in Parral (Ponce de León 1909:25).

**San José del Parral** [Hidalgo del Parral 26 56N  105 40W]: On 11 January 1726, after leaving the Valle de San Bartolomé, Rivera headed west through flat land that had some hills and ravines and came to the *real de minas* of San José del Parral. It is now identified as Hidalgo del Parral and is located on the northern side of a small river. Rivera described it as made up of Spaniards, mestizos and mulattoes. He wrote that in the past it was quite important and that the residence of the governor and captain general of Nueva Vizcaya was there (Alessio Robles 1946:41).

In 1759, Bishop Tamarón placed this "Real de San José del Parral" seven leagues northwest of the "Valle de San Bartholomé" and 20 leagues west of the Presidio de Conchos. There were mines of gold and silver there, as well as a convent of San Francisco, a Colegio de la Compañía de Jesús and some churches. There were 428 families totaling 2,693 people residing there (Alessio Robles 1937:124). The following information provides a summary of the history of San José del Parral. This place was known by the Spanish colonizers from the province of Santa Bárbara since the 16th century because it was located on the side of the *camino* heading to New Mexico. It was located about halfway between Santa Bárbara and Todos Santos. The name "Parral" means "vinyard, the place where grapevines grow." The mining activity began pretty early; in 1567, the *real* of San Juan was established just a few kilometers from Parral. But the mining operations never prospered and by the end of the 16th century most of the settlers had turned to agricultural activities (Cramaussel 1990:43-51).

By the end of the 1620s, the stabilized agricultural society and the pacification of the Indians led to a supply of grains sufficient enough to support large numbers of people (Alvarez 1989 and Cramaussel 1992a:31-38). In July of 1631, Juan Rangel de Biesma discovered a new rich vein which he named "La Negrita" (Cramaussel 1992a). Because of the vein's richness it attracted other people interested in mining, and the population of Parral increased. In 1632, there were 115 *vecinos* and miners registered in Parral; in 1635 there were 500 Spaniards and up to 4,000 Indians working in the mines (Alvarez 1989:130). By 1640, Parral had become the most populated place in Nueva Vizcaya, containing around 10,000 inhabitants (Cramaussel 1992b).

In January 1632, the governor of Nueva Vizcaya, Gonzalo Cervantes de Casaús, moved his residency to Parral, and his successors followed this same practice. From then on, Parral virtually became the capital of Nueva Vizcaya, even though Durango continued to be the official residence of the provincial governor. This situation changed when, in 1730, the governor moved to San Felipe el Real de Chihuahua (Bargellini 1992:218). In 1634, the office of assay and distribution of mercury opened in Parral, and it became an obligatory meeting place for the majority of the miners in the northern part of Nueva Vizcaya (Porras Muñoz 1988:59-60). This kind of traffic directed towards Parral became so important that by the middle of the 17th century a short *vía* from Zacatecas to Parral was opened, thus enabling those traveling to avoid having to pass through Durango, the official capital of the province (Porras Muñoz 1980b:55).

Two bridges were built over the *Camino Real* in Parral to connect the two banks of the Río San Gregorio that went through the *real*. Both bridges were built to facilitate the comings and goings of the carts and livestock on the road. One could be found at the exit of the mines in the direction of Durango; it was built of stone in 1681 (Bargellini 1992:218). The other bridge had to be crossed by those heading to Santa Bárbara. It was built of wood and had to be propped up several times during the colonial period.

Little by little, in the eighteenth century, the traffic on the *Camino Real*

## MAP 6: ROUTE FROM SANTA BARBARA TO NOMBRE DE DIOS

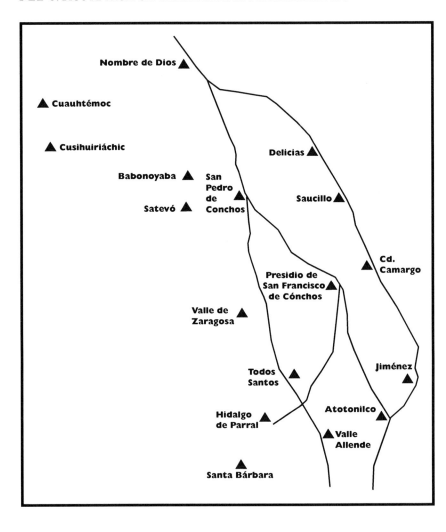

became diverted farther to the east: the merchants traveled from the Cerro Gordo to the Valle de San Bartolomé without going through Parral. This practice continued until the route going from Cerro Gordo to San Bartolomé and Nueva Vizcaya (Chihuahua) became the principal road of *tierra adentro*, and the Parral road became a secondary branch of the *camino* (Gerhard 1993:242). By 1760 the population of Parral had decreased to 3,000 inhabitants but by the beginning of the 19th century it had increased to near 10,000 (Gerhard 1993:218, and Alatriste 1983:76).

**Real de San Diego**: In 1634, this *real de minas* was founded a few kilometers from Parral (Parral Archives: Minas, solares y terrenos, 1634).

**Valle de San Bartolomé** [Valle de Allende 26 56N  105 24W]: Although Luxán's account of the Espejo expedition has them leaving from San Gregorio on 10 November 1582, Espejo and Obregón give their starting point as San Bartolomé (See also the Valle de San Gregorio entry). A year later, on 10 September 1583, they ended the expedition there. Obregón pointed out that San Bartolomé was in the jurisdiction of "Santa Bárbola" (or Santa Bárbara) at the time (Hammond and Rey 1929:45,128; Hammond and Rey 1928:317; Pacheco, Cárdenas, y Torres 1871:XV.103).

On 19 November 1597, the Oñate expedition left Río de los Buñuelos and traveled four leagues to the pueblo and Valle de San Bartolomé, in the province of Santa Bárbara. They stayed there until 17 December 1597, for an inspection. According to the 1598 itinerary of the Oñate expedition, the Río de San Bartolomé ran southeast to northwest (Pacheco, Cárdenas, y Torres 1871:XVI.231).

Soon after 1600, Bishop Mota y Escobar wrote that this valley lay seven leagues east of Santa Bárbara and four or five from the mountains. All manner of produce and animals were raised there with the aid of irrigation from a river. Mills ground flour to be sold to nearby mines. A nearby marsh supported ducks, geese, and cranes. It was subject to the rule of Santa Bárbara and visitations from the Franciscans there (Ramirez Cabañas 1940:199--200).

On 29 December 1725, after passing the Hacienda de la Concepción and the Río de Enmedio, Rivera came to the Valle de San Bartolomé. It was inhabited by Spaniards, mestizos and mulattoes. It contained the parish and convent of San Francisco, and its lands produced all types of seeds, fruit and vegetables (Alessio Robles 1946:41).

In 1759, Bishop Tamarón described this town as one of the larger and more splendid places of this bishopric. It was composed of merchants and farmers, and 202 families totaling 1,833 people resided here. There was a convent of San Francisco maintained only by the guardian, and there used to be a *presidio* that was removed in 1751. It was 15 leagues north from Las Bocas and 124 leagues from Durango (Alessio Robles 1937:121). In 1825 its name was changed to Valle de Allende (Alessio Robles 1937:125).

Lafora stayed there from 20 to 24 May 1766. It had a priest and an *Alcalde Mayor* whose jurisdiction covered a circumference of seventy leagues; he also described its boundaries and the rivers found in it. The population was 4,751 Spanish, mestizos, and mulattoes (Alessio Robles 1939:63-65).

Josiah Gregg, in 1841, went through Saucillo and Garzas before reaching Santa Rosalia. He then continued almost directly south through Santa Cruz toward "Allende or Valle de S. Bartolomé" and southwest to Cerro Gordo (Gregg 1933). From Valle de San Bartolomé Rivera and Lafora took different routes to Presidio de San Francisco de Conchos; from here Lafora went to Atotonilco. [See also **PRESIDIO DE SAN FRANCISCO DE CONCHOS** and **ATOTONILCO**]

**Valle de San Gregorio** [27 01N  105 30W]: Gallegos and Bustamante reported leaving the Valle de San Gregorio with the Sánchez Chamuscado expedition on 6 June 1581. They then continued down the river of the same name toward its confluence with the Río Conchos and Río Florido (Mecham 1926:268;Pacheco and Cárdenas 1871:XV.83,90; Hammond and Rey 1927:12-13).

According to the Luxán narrative, the Espejo expedition set out from San Gregorio on 10 November 1582. The accounts of Obregón and Espejo disagree on this point. It is probable that San Gregorio is located eight miles northwest of San Bartolomé on the Río Parral. The Río Parral of today and Río San Gregorio of the sixteenth century are the same (Hammond and Rey 1929:45; Hammond and Rey 1928:317; Pacheco, Cárdenas, y Torres 1871:XV.103).

**Río de San Gregorio**: Leaving Santa Bárbara on 5 June 1581, the Sánchez Chamuscado expedition followed this river to where it met the Río Conchos and Río Florido, a distance of some twelve leagues (Pacheco and Cárdenas 1871:XV.83,90;Hammond and Rey 1927:12-13). According to Luxán's account, the Río Parral of today and Río San Gregorio of the six-teenth century are the same. The Espejo expedition followed this river to its confluence with the Río Conchos, a distance of eighteen leagues. Along the way they named three places: Los Alamos, Los Charcos Hondos, and La Barranca (Hammond and Rey 1929:45-49,144; Hammond and Rey 1928:317; Pacheco, Cárdenas, y Torres 1871:XV.103-104).

**Estancia de Fuensalida**: On 17 December 1597, the Oñate expedition left the Valle de San Bartolomé and traveled three leagues to the Estancia de Fuensalida (Pacheco, Cárdenas, y Torres 1871:XVI.231).

**Arroyo de San Geronimo**: On 20 December 1597, the Oñate expedition left Fuensalida and traveled two and a half leagues to this arroyo. The sec-ond inspection was held here; they did not leave until 26 January 1598 (Pacheco, Cárdenas, y Torres 1871:XVI.232).

**Santa Cruz**: On 26 January 1598, the Oñate expedition left the Arroyo de San Geronimo and passed the "Torrente de la Cruz" (Pacheco, Cárdenas, y Torres 1871:XVI.232). In 1841 Josiah Gregg showed the road which he traveled going through Saucillo and Garzas before reaching Santa Rosalia. He then continued almost directly south toward "Allende or Valle de S. Bartolomé." Santa Cruz lay along this road, just south of the Río Parral (Gregg 1933).

**Todos Santos**: On 27 January 1598, the Oñate expedition spent the night at the mouth of the Todos Santos mines (Pacheco, Cárdenas, y Torres, 1871:XVI.232). Bishop Mota y Escobar defined this as the last settlement in the northwest part of Nueva Vizcaya (present Chihuahua) of the early seventeenth century. Beyond there commenced large uninhabited plains and the way to Nuevo México. It was five leagues to the north of El Valle de San Bartolomé. Eight or ten Spaniards processed ores in mills run by mules and raised crops and livestock. There was abundant water as well as wild game (Ramirez Cabañas 1940:199, 200-201). This area was known to contain ores during the 1570s but remained unsettled due to Indian hostilities (Mecham 1927:230).

This *real* was probably founded on 1 November (Day of the Dead, or All Saints) 1586. It became one of the most important mining centers in the province of Santa Bárbara. Nevertheless, this boom did not last more than a decade (Cramaussel 1990:Chapter 1). With the agricultural boom of Valle de San Bartolomé, those traveling to New Mexico stopped passing through Todos Santos, and the population of the *real* decreased drastically. It was almost abandoned by the beginning of the 18th century but it survived, largely due to its coal and agricultural industries.

**Ojo del Agua Hondo**: On 28 January 1598, the Oñate expedition traveled two leagues from the Todos Santos mines to this Ojo (Pacheco, Cárdenas, y Torres 1871:XVI.232).

**Arroyo Lamosso**: On 29 January 1598, the Oñate expedition left the Ojo del Agua Hondo and traveled one and a half leagues to this arroyo (Pacheco, Cárdenas, y Torres 1871:XVI.232). From Arroyo Lamosso Oñate went to Río de Conchos. [See also **RIO DE CONCHOS**]

**Hacienda de Dolores**: Wislizenus stopped and rested at this hacienda, three miles south of Guajuquilla, on 4 May 1847, before continuing south across a waterless stretch of 20 leagues. It was large and well-irrigated (Wislizenus 1848:65).

**San Pedro**: On 9 March 1726, after leaving San José del Parral, Rivera headed northwest through flat land that had some hills covered with hay; he did not see any woods. He arrived at a hacienda called San Pedro, located on the northern side of an arroyo of the same name (Alessio Robles 1946:42). From San Pedro Rivera went to Presidio de San Francisco de Conchos. [See also **PRESIDIO DE SAN FRANCISCO DE CONCHOS**]

**Atotonilco (in Chihuahua)** [Villa López 27 00N  105 02W]: In 1759 Bishop Tamarón placed this Indian town 10 leagues east of the Valle de San Bartolomé on the Río Florido. The mission there was administered by the Franciscans. There was a large water hole that provided plenty of water for the land. There were 83 families totaling 280 people residing there (Alessio Robles 1937:122).

This Franciscan mission and Tarahumara pueblo eight leagues northeast of Valle de San Bartolomé on the Río Florido was visited by Lafora on 24 May 1766. The road in the area was flat with brushy vegetation. One priest ministered to 300 Indians who produced some maize, wheat and wine. Later, the name changed to Villa López, in the municipalidad of the same name in the state of Chihuahua (Alessio Robles 1939: 65).

**Presidio de Nuestra Señora de las Caldas de Guajoquilla** [Ciudad Jiménez 27 08N  104 55W]: In 1759, Bishop Tamarón placed this Presidio de Nuestra Señora de las Caldas de Guajuquilla 5 leagues east of Atotonilco and 15 from San Bartolomé; it was next to the Río Florido. The *presidio* was founded in 1752 and was complete at the time of his visit. It was built of adobes and, although it was well-built, the Indians already knew how to break through the adobe; Tamarón noted that eventually the adobe began to decay. There were 65 *"plazas de"* soldiers, and 96 families totaling 1,400 people. The five *presidios* removed in 1751 from Mapimí, Gallo, Cerro Gordo, El Valle de Conchos were incorporated at this *presidio* (Alessio Robles 1937:122-123).

Lafora stayed there, fourteen leagues northeast of Valle de San Bartolomé, from 24 May to 7 June 1766. It was built in 1752 and contained forty troops and 195 people total. This became Ciudad Jiménez, Chihuahua (Alessio Robles 1939:65-66).

"Guajuquill" is the rendering given by Coues in 1895 of the town called "Guaxequillo" by Pike. Pike arrived there on 2 May 1807 (Coues 1895:II.670-671). "Guajuquilla" was the most impressive town which Wislizenus had seen since Chihuahua when he was there on 3 May 1847. The entire region was well-planted, especially in cotton, and he estimated that the city contained 6 or 7,000 people. Before entering it, the army crossed the Río Florido, and there, they left the river behind them as it turned to the west and they continued south (Wislizenus 1848:65).

**Río Florido**: Sánchez Chamuscado passed the mouth of this river, where both it and the San Gregorio flow into the Río Conchos, on 6 June 1581

(Pacheco and Cárdenas 1871:XV.83,90; Hammond and Rey 1927:12-13). Espejo and company passed the mouth of this river, where both it and the San Gregorio flow into the Río Conchos, shortly after beginning their journey. They returned to it by way of the Conchos on 6 September 1583, then continued for two days to the Valle de San Bartolomé, where the expedition ended (Hammond and Rey 1929:49).

On 17 November 1597, when the Oñate expedition left Bauz for the Río Florido, they traveled a distance of two "good" leagues northward (Pacheco, Cárdenas, y Torres 1871:XVI.230). On 28 December 1725, after passing the *parajes* of La Partida and El Alamo, Rivera came to the Río Florido and described its banks as covered with poplars (Alessio Robles 1946:41). It was crossed by Lafora, on 7 June 1766, one league north of the Presidio de Nuestra Señora de las Caldas de Guajoquillas. The land near it was flat with low brush and poplars, and it wound around the base of the Sierra de Chupaderos (Alessio Robles 1939:66).

Zebulon Pike and his Spanish captors followed the Río Conchos upriver to its confluence with the Río Florido on 1 May 1807. There they found a "poor miserable village" which Coues identified in 1895 as Santa Rosalia, Chihuahua. They then followed this river past "flourishing settlements" with good timber and continued up it until four miles beyond Guajuquilla (Coues 1895:II.669-670).

The U.S. Army and Wislizenus reached the Río Florido from the north by way of the Río Conchos on 30 April 1847. They crossed the Florido just above the confluence and there found the town of Santa Rosalia, between the two rivers just before they met. They continued to follow along the left bank of the Florido until they crossed it and left its shores to continue on south (Wislizenus 1848:64-65). From Río Florido Rivera went to Hacienda de la Concepción. See **HACIENDA DE LA CONCEPCION**]

**Hacienda de San Antonio de Ramada**: Lafora stayed there the night of 7 June 1766, near the Río Florida between the present Ciudad Jiménez and Camargo in Chihuahua. He described it as containing 210 people living in adobe houses formed into a square with two circular towers. They raised various crops and grazed horses and mules on abundant pastures. It is now a hacienda in the municipalidad of Camargo, Chihuahua (Alessio Robles

1939:66). Wislizenus, in the company of the United States Army, marched 24 miles south from Santa Rosalia before reaching La Ramada, "a small place on the Florido" on 2 May 1847 (Wislizenus 1848:65).

**Hacienda de Nuestra Señora de Aranzazú**: Lafora passed through there, four leagues west of the Hacienda de San Antonio de Ramada, on 8 June 1766. The country remained flat and covered with mesquite and huizache (Alessio Robles 1939:66-67).

**San Francisco**: This mission and pueblo, home to 200 Chizo and Tarahumara Indians administered by one Franciscan priest, was passed by Lafora seven leagues west of the Hacienda de San Antonio de Ramada on 8 June 1766 (Alessio Robles 1939:67).

**Presidio de San Francisco de Conchos** [27 35N 105 19W]: On 10 March 1726, Rivera arrived at the Presidio de San Francisco de Conchos, located on the bank of the river of the same name. The pueblo was located half a league to the east from the *presidio* and populated by the Tarahumaras, Chizos o Taguitatones, Conchos, and "Tovosos," all administered by the Franciscans (Alessio Robles 1946:42).

In 1759, Bishop Tamarón placed this Indian town of San Francisco de Conchos 20 leagues northeast of Valle de San Bartolomé. There were 89 Indian families, totaling 289 people; from the abolished *presidio*, which was removed in 1751, there were 139 families, totaling 1,330 people. The families from the *presidio* maintained a church and were located half a league from the Indian town, which also had a good church. Both had a view of the Río Conchos, the Indian town on the east and the *presidio* on the west side. Bishop Tamarón felt that this place needed a *presidio* to guard the *Camino Real* to Chihuahua because of the 20 uninhabited leagues, where there was a risk of attack by enemy Indians (Alessio Robles 1937:121).

This *presidio*, one league from the mission and pueblo of the same name in Nueva Vizcaya (Chihuahua), was already in ruins when Lafora passed by on 8 June 1766. The pueblo of San Francisco de Conchos sits on the site of the *presidio* (Alessio Robles 1939:67).

The following information provides a summary of the history of this *presidio*. The mission of San Francisco de Conchos, originally called San Francisco de Comayaos, was founded in 1604 (Griffen 1979:61). During the first half of the century this new mission became Nueva Vizcaya's most northern post on the *camino* of New Mexico. It was probably also the most populated mission in the province of Santa Bárbara during the first half of the 17th century, containing around 2,000 Indians in 1622 (Gerhard 1993:185).

After experiencing many hostilities with the Toboso Indians, the mission was rejuvenated in 1676, when Governor Lope de Sierra Osorio managed to capture a strong contingent of Tobosos (Hackett 1923-37:212). During the 1680s several *estancias, ranchos* and haciendas appeared in the area (Cuentas de la Real Caja de Durango, 1684-1688), and in 1683 there began to be talk about building a new *presidio* (Hackett 1923-37:218), which was accomplished in 1685 (Porras Muñoz 1980:345). During the 18th century the local Spanish population continued to grow, and new haciendas and ranchos began to appear, and the *presidio* became a real settlement. Later it would become like a military colony, under the name of Santa María de Guadalupe. Even after the *presidio* was abolished in 1751, San Francisco de Conchos continued existing as a pueblo for the rest of the century, and its population remained around 1,000 people (Gerhard 1993:184).

**Nuestra Señora de Guadalupe**: This small town was attached to the ruined Presidio de San Francisco de Conchos in Nueva Vizcaya (Chihuahua). It was on the bank of the Río Concho in a place where the riverbed was very wide and so deep that irrigation was impossible. Lafora described its inhabitants as 25 families of *gente de razón* who produced cotton cloth on two looms. He passed by on 8 June 1766. This town may have become part of San Francisco de Conchos; there is also a hacienda to the northeast with the same name (Alessio Robles 1939:67).

**Santa Rosalia** [Ciudad Camargo 27 40N  105 10W]: Zebulon Pike and his Spanish captors followed the Río Conchos upriver to its confluence with the Río Florido on 1 May 1807. There they found a "poor miserable village" which Coues identified in 1895 as Santa Rosalia, Chihuahua (Coues 1895:II.669-670). In 1841 Josiah Gregg showed the road which he traveled going through Saucillo and Garzas before reaching Santa Rosalia. He then continued almost directly south toward "Allende or Valle de S. Bartolomé" (Gregg 1933). The U.S. Army and Wislizenus reached the Río Florido from the north by way of the Río Conchos on 30 April 1847. They crossed the Florido just above the confluence and there found the town of Santa Rosalia, between the two rivers just before they met. It sat on a hill 100 feet above the rivers on a plateau which stretched south. Wislizenus estimated its population at 5,000 (Wislizenus 1848:64-65).

The Spanish first settled there for missionary reasons around 1740, but it was abandoned shortly afterwards because of Apache Indian attacks. In 1797 the place was resettled by 28 *vecinos* from San Francisco de Conchos under orders of the general governor Pedro de Nava (Almada 1968:83). By 1823 the population of Santa Rosalía numbered 1,581 (Ponce de León 1910:171). In 1897 the local government bestowed the title of city to Santa Rosalía, renaming it Ciudad Camargo in honor of Ignacio Camargo, who had been killed in Chihuahua during the independence movement (Almada 1968:83).

**Las Garzas** [27 49N  105 11W]: Pike arrived at the Río Conchos in the area of the later town of Saucillo, Chihuahua. He came down the Río San Pedro to its confluence with the Conchos on 30 April 1807 and found a small fort garrisoned by a detachment from "Fort Conchos" which, he wrote, was 15 leagues upriver. In 1895 Coues identified this small fort as Las Garzas (Coues 1895:II.668-669). Josiah Gregg, in 1841, showed the road which he traveled going through San Pablo and on to Saucillo and Garzas (Gregg 1933). As the U.S. Army and Wislizenus marched south from Saucillo on the Río Conchos on 30 April 1847, they entered a five mile wide gap between two mountains which led them into another valley over a hilly road. About half-way through they found the small town of La Cruz and beyond that the even smaller town of Las Garzas. There they crossed the Río Conchos from west to east and continued to follow it to the mouth of the Río Florido (Wislizenus 1848:64).

This small hacienda in the municipality of La Cruz was formerly known as "Ancón de las Garzas" (Almada 1968:221). In 1847 it had a population of only 100 to 200 inhabitants (Gregg 1944:109).

**La Cruz** [27 52N  105 12W]: As the U.S. Army and Wislizenus marched south from Saucillo on the Río Conchos on 30 April 1847, they entered a five mile wide gap between two mountains which led them into another valley over a hilly road. About half way through they found the small town of La Cruz (Wislizenus 1848:64). La Cruz was founded on 21 April 1797, and has been a municipality since 1868 (Almada 1968:305). In 1854 the population of the small town was 300 (Altamirano 1988).

**Saucillo** [28 01N  105 17W]: In 1841 Josiah Gregg showed the road which he traveled going through San Pablo and on to Saucillo and Garzas (Gregg 1933). When Wislizenus accompanied the U.S. Army south through Mexico in April 1847, he traveled on both branches of the road which forked about ten miles southeast of Bachimba. One crossed the Río San Pedro at Santa Cruz and the other at San Pablo. The two roads met again before Saucillo. That road approached Saucillo and the Río Conchos on the 29th on good road through the same valley as before but with more hills (Wislizenus 1848:63-64).

The following provides some details of the history of Saucillo. On 24 September 1717 Saucillo was titled over to the sergeant major Juan de Trasviña y Retes; later it would come into the possession of the *Compañía de Jesús* (Almada 1968:496;Benedict 1971:67). A mine was discovered in the vicinity around 1839, and it grew to be a village of two or three hundred "souls" (Gregg 1944:109). By 1851, however, Saucillo was abandoned and in ruins (Altamirano 1988). Then, in 1870, a group of *vecinos* headed by Don José María Armendáriz bought 100 lots of land for agricultural purposes, thus initiating the birth of a new pueblo (Almada 1968:497).

**Río Conchos**: After reaching this river by way of a tributary, the San Gregorio, on 6 June 1581, Sánchez Chamuscado followed it toward the place where it emptied into the Río Grande, crossing many dense ridges with great difficulty. They left it and turned north before reaching the confluence, encountering the Río Grande some five leagues north of the Conchos. Gallegos described the country along the Río Conchos as wretched, dry, and unproductive. Along this river, the expedition encountered different native groups which they called the Concha, Raya, and Cabri. The Cabri have been identified with the Pazaguantes from near Cuchillo Parado [29 26N  106 50W] (Mecham 1926:269,n.13,14). They cultivated beans and calabashes and also subsisted on roots, ground mesquite, prickly pears, and mushrooms (Pacheco and Cárdenas 1871:XV.83; Hammond and Rey

1927:14-18;Mecham 1926:269-270).

At the confluence of the San Gregorio, Florido and Conchos rivers, Luxán gave a description of the Conchos Indians who inhabited the region. According to him, they wore skins over their private parts (though he later described them as naked), lived in peace, and supported themselves on fish, mesquite, and mescal. Espejo added that they hunted rabbits, hares, and deer and grew some corn, melons, and gourds, and went into a little more detail about their diet and food preparation. He described them as going about naked but living in grass huts and having *caciques*, and noted that they used the bow and arrow. Beyond the Conchos were a people called the "Passaguates" or Pazaguantes, and others who all spoke similar languages and lived in a like manner. According to Luxán, along the Río Conchos, the party bestowed the names El Mesquital, El Bado, El Mohino, Los Sauces, El Xacal, El Paraje Seco, La Chorrera, El Calabazal, La Barreta, La Ciénaga Llana, El Puerto de la Raya de los Conchos, and La Paz (Hammond and Rey 1929:49-59; Pacheco, Cárdenas, y Torres 1871:XV.104-106).

On 30 January 1598 the Oñate expedition left the Arroyo Lamosso and traveled one and a half leagues to the Río de Conchos. In that area, the river flowed toward the east and southeast. They stayed there until 7 February (Pacheco, Cárdenas, y Torres 1871:XVI.232). Oñate was the first to redirect the route to New Mexico from along the Río Conchos to one aimed more directly northward (Reeve 1961:121-122).

On 4 April 1726 Rivera passed the "Río de Conchos" near Chancaples (Alessio Robles 1946:42). Pike seems to have arrived at the Río Conchos in the area of the later town of Saucillo, Chihuahua. He came down the Río San Pedro to its confluence with the Conchos on 30 April 1807 and found a small fort which Coues identified as Las Garzas (Coues 1895:II.668-669). Wislizenus and the United States Army, heading south, reached the Río Conchos at Saucillo on 29 April 1846. They followed it to the mouth of the Río Florida, near Santa Rosalia, crossing from west to east at Las Garzas. They then continued south along the Río Florida (Wislizenus 1848:64-65).

**Río San Pedro**: The Espejo party went four leagues downstream from a site which they called Los Sauces before passing the mouth of this tributary of the Río Conchos on 23 November 1582. Although it did not flow all year around, it contained many fish and the area was thickly settled by Concha Indians as a result (Hammond and Rey 1929:52).

On 10 February 1598 the Oñate expedition traveled three leagues to the San Pedro, noting that it flowed from west to east. They stayed by the river for one month. During this time Oñate sent Vicente Zaldivar to find a road for carts to the Río del Norte. The *Sargento Mayor* set out from the Río de San Pedro on 14 February with 17 men. After a road was discovered, half the party returned to camp on 7 March. Zaldivar and the rest of the party returned on the 10th (Pacheco, Cárdenas, y Torres 1871:XVI.233).

Pike left Chihuahua on 28 April 1807 and headed south to skirt the Bolsón de Mapimí. The first locale which he identified by name was a "Presidio de San Paubla" on a river of the same name, reached on the 29th. In 1895, Coues identified this as the later site of Ortiz on the Río San Pedro (Coues 1895:II.668). In 1841 Gregg showed that the road which he followed crossed the Río San Pedro at San Pablo (Gregg 1933). Wislizenus traveled along two different branches of the main road, which forked about ten miles southeast of Bachimba. One crossed the Río San Pedro at Santa Cruz and the other at San Pablo. He found both towns to be both picturesque and productive. The two roads met again before Saucillo on the Río Conchos (Wislizenus 1848:63-64).

**Portezuelo**: On 7 February 1598 the Oñate expedition left the Río de Conchos, turning to go directly north, and went through "Portecuelo" (Pacheco, Cárdenas, y Torres 1871:XVI.233). This was the first expedition to go directly north from the Río Conchos toward New Mexico (Reeve 1961:121-122).

**Agua de la Tentación**: On 7 February 1598 the Oñate expedition left the Río de Conchos, went through Portezuelo and continued toward the north. After three leagues they reached Agua de la *Tentación*, so named because they reached it on Temptation Sunday (Pacheco, Cárdenas, y Torres 1871:XVI.233)

**El Pizarral**: On 8 February 1598 the Oñate expedition left Agua de la *Tentación* and passed through El Pizarral (Pacheco, Cárdenas, y Torres 1871:XVI.233). This has been identified as the site of a slate quarry (Hammond and Rey 1953:I.311).

**Agua del Incendio**: On 8 February 1598 the Oñate expedition passed through El Pizarral and reached Agua del Incendio, two leagues farther north (Pacheco, Cárdenas, y Torres 1871:XVI.233).

**Barrancas del Río de San Pedro**: On 9 February 1598 the Oñate expedition left Agua del Incendio and traveled three leagues to these barrancas (Pacheco, Cárdenas, y Torres 1871: XVI.233). From here they went three more leagues to the Río San Pedro.[See **RIO SAN PEDRO**]

---

The route of the Espejo expedition into New Mexico is as follows: Espejo and his men set out from the jurisdiction of Santa Barbara on 10 November 1582. They followed the Río de San Gregorio (modern Río Parral) to its confluence with the Rio Conchos and continued along it to the Río del Norte, tracing it to the pueblo region of New Mexico. Below are place names bestowed by Espejo, many of which cannot be identified today (Hammond and Rey 1929:45; Hammond and Rey 1928:317;Pacheco y Cárdenas 1871:XV.103).

**Los Alamos:** This is the first of three place names bestowed by the Espejo expedition between the Valle de San Gregorio and the confluence of the river of the same name and the Río Conchos, according to the account of Diego Pérez de Luxán (Hammond and Rey 1929:49).

**Los Charcos Hondos:** This is the second of three place names bestowed by the Espejo expedition between the Valle de San Gregorio and the confluence of the river of the same name and the Río Conchos, according to the account of Diego Pérez de Luxán. It was after Los Alamos and before La Barranca (Hammond and Rey 1929:49).

**La Barranca:** This is the third of three place names bestowed by the Espejo expedition between the Valle de San Gregorio and the confluence of the river of the same name and the Río Con-

---

chos, according to the account of Diego Pérez de Luxán. It was after Los Alamos and Los Charcos Hondos (Hammond and Rey 1929:49).

**El Mesquital:** According to Luxán, the Espejo party named twelve places along the Río Conchos. The first, El Mesquital, was four leagues beyond the confluence of the Conchos, Florido, San Bartolomé, and San Gregorio Rivers. It was inhabited by people described as Conchos Indians and was named on 18 November 1582 (Hammond and Rey 1929:49-59).

**El Bado:** El Bado was the second of twelve sites along the Río Conchos named by the Espejo expedition. According to Luxán, it was four leagues downstream from El Mesquital and inhabited by people described as Conchos Indians; they found it on 19 November 1582 (Hammond and Rey 1929:49-59).

**El Mohino:** According to Luxán, El Mohino was three leagues downstream from El Bado and inhabited by people described as Conchos Indians. It was reached on 21 November 1582 (Hammond and Rey 1929:49-59).

**Los Sauces:** Luxán placed Los Sauces three leagues downstream from El Mohino. People described as Conchos Indians lived there. It was named on 22 November 1582, for the willow trees and poplar groves along the river. Just beyond it was the mouth of the Río San Pedro (Hammond and Rey 1929:49-59).

**Río San Pedro:** The Espejo party went four leagues downstream from Los Sauces before passing the mouth of this tributary of the Río Conchos on 23 November 1582. Although it did not flow all year around, it contained many fish and the area was thickly settled by Concha Indians as a result (Hammond and Rey 1929:52). [See SAN PEDRO]

**El Xacal:** El Xacal was two leagues downstream from the mouth of the Río San Pedro and was inhabited by people described as Conchos Indians. On 24 November 1582, Espejo encountered a hut built by slavers from Santa Bárbara, led by a Capitan Lope de Aristi, and named this site accordingly. Luxán reported that Capitan "Xamuscado" (Sánchez Chamuscado) was buried here. Espejo may have crossed the Conchos there (Bolton 1930:174), then the party left the Río Conchos for a few days although they continued to follow its course (Hammond and Rey 1929:49-59;Bolton 1930:174).

**El Paraje Seco:** The Espejo party marched five leagues from El Xacal and encountered this paraje on 25 November 1582. It was a difficult mountain crossing and the paraje was so-named because the waterhole was dry and there was no available firewood. (Hammond and Rey 1929:49-59).

**La Chorrera:** Beginning on 26 November 1582, the Espejo party rested at La Chorrera few days before continuing. It was in highlands with many pools and a waterfall, six leagues beyond El Paraje Seco (Hammond and Rey 1929:49-59).

**El Calabazal:** El Calabazal, named because of the fields of squash or gourds grown by the local Concho Indians was found on 2 December 1582. Evidently, the party returned to the Río Conchos here after leaving it at El Xacal, crossing some mountainous terrain, and spending the night of the first near a gorge with several waterholes. From La Chorrera to El Calabazal it was at least six leagues. Espejo reported finding promising mines along the way (Hammond and Rey 1929:49-59).

**La Barreta:** Espejo marched only two leagues from El Calabazal on 3 December 1582, and then stayed overnight at La Barreta because the party could not cross a watercourse during that day. The name was given after a small bar was stolen by Conchos Indians. Throughout this stretch of the journey Espejo regularly went away from and back to the Río Conchos (Hammond and Rey 1929:49-59).

**La Ciénaga Llana:** The Espejo party arrived at this marshy area after marching four leagues from La Barreta on 4 December 1582. They were guided by natives to usable water nearby. Leaving there they went from the land of the Conchos to that of the Passaguates (also known as Pazaguantes as Pasaguates) and the Patarabueyes (also Amotomancos, Otomoacos, Patazaguates, and Jamanas or Jumanos). These last were evidently called, at times, the Rayas as well (Hammond and Rey 1929:49-59; Hammond and Rey 1928:317; Hammond and Rey 1927:13-18; Mecham 1926:122-124).

**El Puerto de la Raya de los Conchos:** This was the first stop after leaving the land of the Conchos (see the La Ciénaga Llana note for names of the natives of this area). The expedition arrived here on 5 December 1582 after going four leagues and was warned that the natives ahead of them were preparing to fight them. Next, Espejo and company came to a Patarabueye ranchería where they were attacked at night through a dense stand of mesquite but succeeded in making peace with little trouble. In the process a boy was captured who continued with the expedition as an interpreter (Hammond and Rey 1929:49-59).

**La Paz:** This site, reached on 8 December 1582, after a journey of some 6 1/2 leagues, was so-named because the Espejo party was met here by two caciques from the place where the Conchos empties into the Río Grande who asked whether they came in peace or at war. Their people were called Abriaches, another branch of the Jumano family (see the La Ciénaga Llana note for names of the natives of this area). From this area, Espejo left the Río Conchos and went overland three leagues to the Río Grande (Hammond and Rey 1929:49-59).

After returning to the Río del Norte by way of the Pecos River the Espejo expedition retraced its steps to San Bartolomé. The following names were given during this return trip along the Río Conchos between the Río del Norte and the mouth of the Río Florido.

**El Toboso:** The Espejo expedition returned from New Mexico by way of the Río Pecos, cutting overland to reach the Río del Norte a little north of the mouth of the Río Conchos. From there they proceeded to Pueblo de Santo Tomás at the confluence of the Concho and Río del Norte. Along the Río Conchos between Santo Tomás and the mouth of the Río Florido Luxán mentioned six place names. The first, El "Tovoso" lay eight leagues from Santo Tomás, near a stream of running water and was reached on 26 August 1583. They name the stream El "Tovoso" after an elderly Toboso Indian found there after the rest of the populace had fled (Hammond and Rey 1929:126-128).

**Los Charcos de la Cañada:** The pools which the Espejo expedition named Los Charcos de la Cañada lay three leagues above El Toboso and were reached on 27 August 1583 (Hammond and Rey 1929:126-128).

**La Fuente de la Mala Paz:** The spring called by Luxán La Fuente de la Mala Paz was six leagues beyond Los Charcos de la Cañada; it was reached on 28 August 1583. The name stems from an incident in which some Toboso Indians came to the camp in peace, but later a horse and two mules were wounded by arrows (Hammond and Rey 1929:126-128).

**Los Charcos de los Llanos:** These pools were surrounded by a plain and were six leagues beyond La Fuente de la Mala Paz. The Espejo party came there on 29 August 1583 (Hammond and Rey 1929:126-128).

**La Elona:** The pools and Concho Indian ranchería labeled La Elona by Luxán were eight leagues beyond Los Charcos de los Llanos and were reached on 30 August 1583. Two leagues away was a large saline of good salt (Hammond and Rey 1929:126-128).

**El Espíritu Santo:** Espejo saw the pool which they called El Espíritu Santo, five leagues beyond La Elona, on 2 September 1583. Sixteen leagues beyond, past many more pools, the expedition reached the mouth of the Río Florido and then continued back to San Bartolomé (Hammond and Rey 1929:126-128).

Below are names given by Espejo as his party traveled northward along the Río del Norte from the mouth of the Río Conchos to the Piro Pueblos of New Mexico.

**San Bernardino:** Having left the Río Conchos on 9 December 1582, near the place they called La Paz, the Espejo expedition went directly north to the Río Grande. Upon reaching it they encountered a pueblo which they named San Bernardino. Before continuing north they traveled downriver and across it to visit the local inhabitants (Hammond and Rey 1929:60-61).

**Pueblo de Santo Tomás (Ojinaga or Junta de los Ríos)** [29 34N 104 25W]: The Espejo party reached the Río del Norte on 9 December 1582, a short distance upriver from the junction of the Río Conchos and Río del Norte. Before continuing north toward New Mexico they traveled down the Río del Norte to the Río Conchos to visit the local Indians. At the junction of the two rivers they found a pueblo of some 600 people, which they named

Santo Tomás. They passed here again during the return trip, on 22 August 1583. Across the Río del Norte from Santo Tomás was a pueblo which they called San Juan Evangelista (Hammond and Rey 1929:61-62,126). Modern Ojinaga, Chihuahua, Mexico and Presidio, Texas are near the confluence of the Río del Norte and Río Conchos.

**Pozo del Río Turbio:** Espejo evidently camped here on the night of 18 December 1582. It was the first place specified after the party left the area of the junction of the Río Conchos and Río del Norte, which they also called the Río Turbio (Hammond and Rey 1929:64).

**La Daga:** On 19 December 1582, the Espejo expedition camped near the Río del Norte at a place they called La Daga. Diego Pérez de Luxán, author of this journal, described the landscape as hilly and covered with mesquite (Hammond and Rey 1929:65).

**El Estrecho de Santo Tomás:** The Espejo expedition stayed here, near a narrows of the Río del Norte on the feast day of Saint Thomas, 21 December 1582. They had been traveling along the Río del Norte for only four days (Hammond and Rey 1929:65).

**Potreadero:** On 22 December 1582, the Espejo party left El Estrecho de Santo Tomás and followed the Río del Norte north three leagues to this place (Hammond and Rey 1929:65).

**La Hoya:** This Espejo campsite was located five leagues to the north of the place which they named Potreadero, along the Río del Norte. They camped here on 23 December 1582 (Hammond and Rey 1929:65-66).

**La Alamedilla:** La Alamedilla was located three leagues to the north of the place which they named La Hoya, along the Río del

Norte. It was the sixth place which Luxán named along this stretch of the Río del Norte north of the mouth of the Río Conchos; they arrived here on 24 December 1582, and stayed until the 27th. The land here was rough and sandy and covered with thistles (Hammond and Rey 1929:66).

**Las Bocas:** This site was located four leagues to the north of the place which they named La Alamedilla, along the Río del Norte. It was so-named because the river flowed out from between two rocky ridges and back between two others. Espejo was there 27 December 1582 (Hammond and Rey 1929:66).

**La Sabana Llana:** This Espejo campsite was located three leagues to the north of the place which they named Las Bocas, up the Río del Norte through a sierra. Some Otomoacos visited them during their stay on 28 December 1582 (Hammond and Rey 1929:66).

**El Real de Santa María:** The Espejo party traveled three leagues to the north from La Sabana Llana to camp here on 30 December 1582, staying next to the Río del Norte (Hammond and Rey 1929:66).

**La Deseada:** Espejo camped at this site on 31 December 1582. It was located five leagues to the north of El Real de Santa María, next to the Río del Norte. To reach it they went four leagues over a large mountain range on difficult road. It was the tenth place which Luxán named along this stretch of the Río del Norte north of the mouth of the Río Conchos and they were visited by many Otomoacos who brought gifts (Hammond and Rey 1929:66-67).

**El Año Nuevo:** Espejo and company arrived on 1 January 1583, after traveling four leagues from La Deseada and named the place accordingly. They were again visited by Otomoacos, this time with much mescal (Hammond and Rey 1929:67).

**La Guardia del Caballo:** Espejo and company arrived here on 2 January 1583, after traveling four leagues from the place which they called El Año Nuevo. Otomoacos and their cacique came with a horse which had been left by Sánchez Chamuscado. They were shown mines and erected crosses in the area (Hammond and Rey 1929:67-68).

**Las Vueltas del Río del Punzón:** The Espejo party named this campsite on 3 January 1583, after having gone four leagues up the Río del Norte from a site which they called La Guardia del Caballo (Hammond and Rey 1929:68).

**Los Reyes:** Members of the Caguate nation met the Espejo party peacefully on 4 January 1583, and they decided to stay for a few days at this campsite after having gone four leagues up the Río del Norte from a site which they called Las Vueltas del Río del Punzón. It was referred to as an inlet (Hammond and Rey 1929:68).

**Las Salinillas:** The Espejo party named this stop, three leagues up from Los Reyes, on 7 January 1583. The soil was so salty that they were able to boil it to obtain salt for consumption (Hammond and Rey 1929:68).

**La Ciénaga Grande:** Espejo came four leagues, on 8 January 1583, to this swamp formed by overflow from the river, here called Río Turbio. The surrounding country contained many salines and much waterfowl (Hammond and Rey 1929:68).

**Los Charcos del Canutillo:** The Espejo party first saw this campsite on 9 January 1583, after having gone three leagues up the Río del Norte from a site which they called La Ciénaga Grande. Its name came from the large number of pools and marshes near the river which were full of both reeds and fish. Tanpachoa Indians brought them food during the week which they stayed here

(Hammond and Rey 1929:68-69).

**Las Salinas:** On 15 January 1583, five leagues from Los Charcos del Canutillo, Espejo found this site. There were mountains across the river which Luxán was sure contained valuable minerals but they were unable to cross the river to reach them. They passed salines of white rock salt and camped near some pools which gave the site its name (Hammond and Rey 1929:70).

**El Charco de San Antonio:** Five leagues north of Las Salinas, the Espejo party named this pool on 16 January 1583. It was a pool formed by the river when it had run over its banks (Hammond and Rey 1929:70).

**Las Vueltas del Río:** The Espejo party named this campsite on 19 January 1583, after having traveled five leagues up the Río del Norte from a site which they called El Charco de San Antonio. According to Luxán, the river began to wind here, which suggested the name (Hammond and Rey 1929:70).

**La Barranca de las Vueltas:** This promontory overlooking the river was reached on 21 January 1583, five leagues up from Las Vueltas del Río (Hammond and Rey 1929:70).

**La Playa de las Salinas:** This site was seen on 22 January 1583, five leagues from La Barranca de las Vueltas. Despite evidence to the contrary, Luxán wrote that here they found the first salines that they had found along the river (Hammond and Rey 1929:70).

**La Ciénaga Helada:** There was a marsh here which was frozen so hard that the party had to break through the ice with bars and picks in order to water their horses on 23 January 1583. It was four leagues up the Río del Norte from the site which they called La Playa de las Salinas (Hammond and Rey 1929:70).

**El Frontón de las Minas:** The Espejo party named this campsite on 24 January 1583, after having traveled five leagues up the Río del Norte from a site which they called La Ciénaga Helada. They named it after some mineral veins which they had seen along the way to this place. Although they did not see any people around there, they saw abandoned dwellings and other signs of life (Hammond and Rey 1929:71).

**Los Humos:** The Espejo party named this campsite on 26 January 1583, after having traveled three leagues up the Río del Norte from a site which they called El Frontón de las Minas. With this day they and the course of the river began to travel directly toward the north. They named it after plumes of smoke which they observed in the mountains on both sides of the river. It has been suggested that the party was then in the neighborhood of Hatch, New Mexico. This was the twenty-fifth place named by Diego Pérez de Luxán, author of this journal, north of the confluence of the Río del Norte and Río Conchos. It has been claimed that the party crossed the river on this day though that is by no means clear from available sources (Hammond and Rey 1929:71; Bolton 1930:176).

**El Peñol de los Cedros:** This was reached on 28 January 1583, after a journey of five leagues up the Río del Norte from Los Humos. The day's journey took them over a mountain near the river which Luxán reported to be rich in silver. The region was full of black rock and covered with cedar groves (Hammond and Rey 1929:71-72).

**La Punta de Buena Esperanza:** This campsite was named 30 January 1583, seven leagues up the Río del Norte from El Peñol de los Cedros (Hammond and Rey 1929:72).

**El Malpaís:** The Espejo party named this "Mal País" on 31 January 1583, after having traveled four leagues up the Río del Norte from a site which they called La Punta de Buena Esperanza. It was a marsh surrounded by malpaís. This was the twenty-eighth place named by Luxán north of the confluence of the Río del Norte and Río Conchos (Hammond and Rey 1929:72). The next place mentioned was in the vicinity of the Piro pueblos of New Mexico. [See JUEVES DE LAS COMADRES]

**Chancaple** [Chancaplia 27 50N  105 41W]: On 4 April 1726, Rivera passed the Río de Conchos, traveled through flat land with some hills of mesquite brush, and stopped at Chancaple, which was uninhabited but contained a mine (Alessio Robles 1946:42-43).

In 1759, Bishop Tamarón placed this *ojo de agua* (spring) at a half-way point on the 20 uninhabited leagues on the *Camino Real* from Conchos to Chihuahua which he described to illustrate the need for a *presidio* in Conchos. He wrote that a *vecino* had built a good house there that had to be abandoned due to enemy Indian attacks. Because of these attacks and the lack of a *presidio*, the place was completely uninhabited (Alessio Robles 1937:121-122).

Lafora stayed here on 9 June 1766. During that day he had traveled on a flat round plain covered with mesquite and other brush and surrounded by hills with occasional signs of irrigation. He described it as two or three huts abandoned out of fear of hostile Indians and a small spring, fourteen leagues north-northwest of the Presidio de San Francisco de Conchos. It survived as a rancho in the *municipalidad* of Saucillo, Chihuahua (Alessio Robles 1939:67).

**Hacienda de San Lucas** [Rosales 28 12N  105 33W]: On 10 June 1766, Lafora was traveling west-northwest over mostly flat land with mesquite and a few small hills when he came to this hacienda, thirteen leagues out of Chancaple. It was located on the left bank of the Río San Pedro which, while carrying little water, was sufficient for irrigation by canal. By this means this land, described by Lafora as pleasant, was cultivated. In 1939, it was a hacienda in the *municipalidad* of Rosales, Chihuahua (Alessio Robles 1939:67-68).

**San Pedro**: On 5 April 1726 Rivera left Chancaple and traveled through flat land covered with mesquite brush and discerned some mountainous country. He stopped at a *hacienda de labor* located on the south bank of the Río de San Pedro. The luxuriant growth of the poplars made its shores pleasant (Alessio Robles 1946:43). Lafora passed by on 10 June 1766. He found a mission of Concho Indians administered by a Franciscan priest, located about one league upstream of the Hacienda de San Lucas on the Río de San Pedro. It is a modern pueblo in the *municipio* of Rosales, Chihuahua (Alessio Robles 1939:68).

**San Pablo** [Ortiz Rail Station 28 15N  105 31W]: Still a prisoner of Spain, Pike was taken south from Chihuahua on 28 April 1807, on the road skirting the Bolson de Mapimí. The first locale which he erronously identified by name was a "Presidio de San Paubla"--which he meant was obviously San Pablo-- on a river of the same name, reached on 29 April. This was 24 miles from the Río Conchos, according to Pike. In 1895, Coues identified this site as the later site of Ortiz on the Río San Pedro (Coues 1895:II.668). In 1841, Gregg showed the road which he traveled going through San Pablo and on to Saucillo (Gregg 1933).

The first time that Wislizenus left Chihuahua, he went to San Pablo. The second time he followed the fork which branched off about ten miles southeast of Bachimba, and went through Santa Cruz. The two branches met again before Saucillo. San Pablo was about eight miles downstream from Santa Cruz and contained some 4,000 people. Its location on the Río San Pedro allowed it to grow many crops, of which Wislizenus particularly noticed cotton and maize (Wislizenus 1848:63-64).

The following provides some details about the history of San Pablo. By the end of the 17th century, San Pablo was a *visita* of the Franciscan mission of San Pedro de Conchos; it had 30 Concho Indian families in 1693 (Griffen 1979:71). In 1709 it became the religious capital of that area (Almada 1968:331-332), although some believe that in the 18th century it was dependent on the mission at Julimes. In 1765, there were 36 people living there (Griffen 1979:72). In 1773, the capital of a flying company was established there, and in 1807 the presidio was still in existence (Almada 1968:331-332). And in 1817, one of the four flying companies of Nueva Vizcaya was still located there (Jones 1988:216-217). In 1866, Benito Juárez changed the name of this town to Meoqui, in honor of Pedro Meoqui (Almada 1968:331-332).

**Misión de Santa Cruz**: In 1759, Bishop Tamarón visited this Indian pueblo and Franciscan mission, which was also the head pueblo of this jurisdiction. He located it nine leagues south of Tulimes, 20 leagues west of Conchos and almost 20 leagues east of Chihuahua and described it as being on the banks of the Río San Pedro. He counted 23 Indian families, which totaled 79 people (Alessio Robles 1937:154-155). It has been identified as modern Santa Cruz Rosales or simply Rosales (Alessio Robles 1937:166).

Lafora noted that Santa Cruz was inhabited by Concho Indians. When he passed by on 10 June 1766, it was still administered by a Franciscan priest. He located it about one league upstream of the Hacienda de San Lucas on the Río de San Pedro. It was also called Santa Cruz de Tapacolmes and a *villa* of that name exists in the *municipio* of Rosales, Chihuahua (Alessio Robles 1939:68).

On 27 April 1847, Wislizenus arrived in Santa Cruz in the company of elements of the United States Army. He estimated its population at around 5,000, including nearby settlements. It was located on the Río San Pedro about eight miles above San Pablo. As he passed through this valley, heading southeast, Wislizenus reported that the Río Conchos followed a chain of mountains about 25 miles to the east and northeast. From Santa Cruz to Saucillo, on the Conchos, it was 23 miles. The main road forked about ten miles southeast of Bachimba, with one branch going through San Pablo and the other through Santa Cruz. The two branches met again before Saucillo (Wislizenus 1848:63-64).

**Pueblo de San Pedro**: In 1759, Bishop Tamarón located this pueblo seven leagues south of Santa Cruz de Tapacolmes, and counted nine Indian families, which totaled 74 people (Alessio Robles 1937:155).

**San Pedro (or San Greco)**: On 10 March 1598, the Oñate expedition left the Río San Pedro and went to the pools which they called either San Pedro or San Greco, a distance of three leagues (Pacheco, Cárdenas, y Torres 1871:XVI.234;Hammond and Rey 1953:I.312).

**Charcos de las Moxárras**: On 11 March 1598, the Oñate expedition found these ponds two leagues from San Pedro (or San Greco). They described them as deep and numerous (Pacheco, Cárdenas, y Torres 1871:XVI.234).

**Bachimba** [28 25N 105 41W]: After the conquest of Chihuahua by troops of the United States, Wislizenus joined the U.S. army as a surgeon and continued south with it. Twice he left Chihuahua and went through Mapula and Bachimba before continuing. Eventually he went south over the hills from Chihuahua into the valley which contained Mapula as one of its few settlements. It narrowed to a canyon which the road followed for five or six miles. In this pass were two ranchos, one destroyed and the other with a spring; about five miles beyond it was Bachimba. Wislizenus described it as consisting of around twelve houses in a plain, near a stream which was running even in that particularly dry season. About ten miles southeast of Bachimba the road forked, with one branch going through San Pablo and the other through Santa Cruz, Wislizenus taking the latter. The two branches met before Saucillo (Wislizenus 1848:62-63).

The following provides some details of the history of Bachimba. During the 1600s, there was a series of small ranches of Indians from this group living on the banks of the arroyo of Bachimba. Because this region was so close to the *Camino Real* of New Mexico, it was explored by the Spaniards from the beginning of the 17th century. In 1651, the first Spanish settlements appeared in this region, when a group of *encomenderos* from the Valle de San Bartolomé arrived in Tabalaopa and opened the first mines in what would later be known as Chihuahua. In 1653, another *encomendero* from San Bartolomé, Diego Rodríguez de Amaya, established the first mining operations in Bachimba (Alvarez 1995:174). In the 1650s and 1660s, the rebellions of the Conchas and Tarahumaras impeded Spanish settlement of this region, and it was not until after peace was achieved that the Spaniards returned. In 1673, Bachimba became a *visita* of the Franciscan mission of Babonoyaba (Alvarez 1995:178). In 1723, the Hacienda de San José de Bachimba was registered as one of the haciendas that provided grains to the Villa de San Felipe el Real (Cuaderno de providencias de Joseph López de Carvajal, 1723). During the second half of the 18th century, however, the hacienda as well as the Indian pueblo of Bachimba, suffered a severe depopulation. Nevertheless, the Hacienda de San José de Bachimba continued to exist until the independent period, and it continued to be a place of rest on the *Camino Real.*

**Mapula** [28 29N  105 58W]: Lafora found thirty people who cared for animals owned by citizens of Chihuahua, six leagues to the northwest, when he passed by on 11 June 1766. A small brook with little water flowed through, though Lafora pointed out that the land was very dry. He also commented on the pastureland along the *Camino Real.* Mapula remains as a hacienda in the *municipio* of Chihuahua (Alessio Robles 1939:68).

Wislizenus went through Mapula between Chihuahua and Bachimba on 26 April 1847. Mapula seemed to be a few miles west of the usual road, the detour being taken for the sake of finding additional water. Wislizenus described the road from Chihuahua as climbing the hills to the south of that city and then entering a valley some ten miles wide between mountain chains to the east and west. Mapula was one of the few settlements in this valley, which eventually narrowed to a canyon for five or six miles. Bachimba was beyond this pass (Wislizenus 1848:62-63).

**La Carretada**: On 6 April 1726, Rivera left a hacienda located on the south bank of the Río de San Pedro and traveled through flat land with dry arroyos and mesquite brush, then spent the night in la Carreta, which was uninhabited (Alessio Robles 1946:43).

**Chihuahua** [28 38N  106 05W]: On 7 April 1726, heading northwest, Rivera traveled through terrain that was uneven and bothersome because of the hills, arroyos, and rocks. He observed bare hills said to contain minerals and then came to the "villa of San Felipe del Real or Chiguagua" (Alessio Robles 1946:43). It was a settlement of Spaniards, mestizos and mulattoes. Having been established for only a few years, it was already populated by a considerable number of souls, and was located on the south side of a small river whose origin was in a mountain range between the pueblos of Chuvisca and San Andrés of the Tarahumara nation. Five leagues to the east was the *real y minas* of Santa Eulalia, also called el Realito. It was also considerably populated and abundant in silver (Alessio Robles 1946:43).

In 1759, Bishop Tamarón visited this settlement, which he described as one of the most populous in the bishopric. He stated that there were many silver mines but that firewood was far away. It was risky to travel to it because of the danger of enemy Indian attacks. Tamarón warned that if Chihuahua were ruined because of this danger, all of Vizcaya and New Mexico would be at risk because they depended on Chihuahua for their supplies as well as Sonora and part of Sinaloa. He wrote that Chihuahua's commerce was the best and that its inhabitants were Spanish, mestizos and mulattoes, He counted 692 families, which totaled 4,652 people. Bishop Tamarón located Chihuahua north of Durango by way of two roads, one for horses and the other for carts; the first was shorter. Although he gives a distance of 160 leagues, he does not say by which road (Alessio Robles 1937:152-153).

Lafora approached this *villa*, located on dry land next to a small stream, from the southeast, on 12 June 1766. He road over a generally good road through a wide valley, over a gentle pass, and then across a plain called El Bajío. Lafora found a population of 400 families of Spaniard, mestizos, and mulattoes and noted that it had decreased due to the decline of the mines in the area and the attacks of hostile Indians. The church of Nuestra Señora de Guadalupe was a little upstream of the city surrounded by thirty families of Yaqui Indians. Across from it was the mission and pueblo of El Nombre de Dios (now a pueblo in the municipio of Chihuahua), located in a pleasant canyon where various crops were cultivated. On its left side were some hills and on the right a range of high and steep hills where some gold mines were located which were left idle due to their lack of productivity. The stream that flowed through this canyon joined the Río de Chihuahua near the *villa*. The founding date of Chihuahua was 5 August 1705; it was elevated to a *villa* in 1718, and named a *ciudad* in 1823 (Alessio Robles 1939:68-70).

When Zebulon Pike was taken captive by the Spanish in modern southern Colorado he was escorted to Chihuahua for an interview with the commanding general of the *Provincias Internas*. He arrived on 2 April 1807 (Coues 1895:II.655). Dr. Wislizenus entered Chihuahua on 24 August 1846. He was impressed from afar by the encircling mountains, its aqueduct, groves of trees, houses, and churches. Unfortunately for him, the war with the United States had just begun and his experiences in Chihuahua belied his initial impressions of the city. He estimated the population as 12 to 15,000 and described a plaza with public buildings on three sides and a cathedral on the fourth. Another cathedral, dedicated to San Felipe, was begun by the Jesuits but left uncompleted after their expulsion in 1769. The south side of the city received water from the aqueduct while the north exploited the Río

Chihuahua and a stream called Nombre de Dios (Wislizenus 1848:48-60).

In 1803, the population of Chihuahua was at 5,000 (Florescano 1976, Document #2). When Chihuahua was named as capital of the state, the population had increased to 9,250 (Ponce de León 1910:171) and, ten years later, it reached 10,602 people (Altamirano 1988). Although the population had increased to 12,000 by 1851 (Altamirano 1988), Chihuahua was in a state of deterioration due to the decline of mining in Santa Eulalia (Frobel 1952:13). In 1847 the city was almost completely abandoned because of the Northamerican invasion. By 1895, however, Chihuahua had 19,520 inhabitants (Almada 1984:104), becoming one of the fastest growing cities in the Mexican republic. From Chihuahua Rivera went to Nombre de Dios (Chihuahua). [See **NOMBRE DE DIOS** (Chihuahua)]

MAP 7: ROUTE FROM CHIHUAHUA TO OJO LUCERO

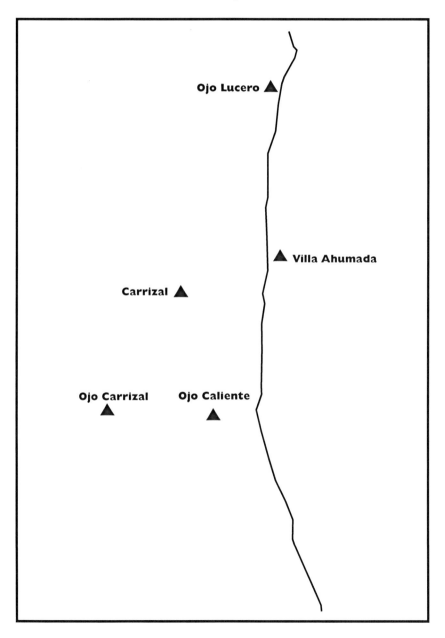

**Paraje de Tabalaopa** [28 40N  106 02W]: This was given by Lafora as the site of a famous Jesuit hacienda when he passed by it on 7 July 1766, one or two leagues north-northeast of the *villa* of Chihuahua on the left side of the road. It remains as a hacienda in the *municipio* of Chihuahua (Alessio Robles 1939:71).

The first mention of this place is in 1619 (Naylor and Polzer 1986:272-293). At that time it was a resting place for the people traveling on the *Camino Real* towards New Mexico; it was also visited frequently by the *encomenderos* from Valle de San Bartolomé (Alvarez 1995:174). In 1652, Pedro del Castillo opened the first mines in that area a few kilometers from Tabalaopa. There was also an important *ranchería* of Tarahumara Indians located there (Alvarez 1995:174). In 1681, Apresa Falcón acquired the lands as part of a land grant, and by the middle of that decade the Hacienda de Santo Domingo de Tabalaopa was well-established (Porras Muñoz 1993:109-110). In 1690 the Indian pueblo of Tabalaopa, along with Chuviscar and Nombre de Dios, became a *visita* of the important Franciscan mission of Santa Isabel (Griffen 1979:74). After the Jesuits acquired the hacienda in 1718, it grew to become one of the most important haciendas in the region and the most important Jesuit property in the northern part of Nueva Vizcaya. In 1767, the hacienda was valued at a little more than 22,000 pesos, and in 1770, its value went up to almost 26,000 pesos (Bradley 1971:130). Although the hacienda suffered losses during the second half of the 18th century, it continued to be an important place on the *Camino Real*, since it was the first point north of the. Villa de San Felipe and since one of its functions was to protect that *villa* from Indian attacks (Navarro García 1964:229).

**El Real de Santa Eulalia** [Cerro de Santa Eulalia 28 37N  105 51W]: Rivera noted that the *Real y minas* of Santa Eulalia, also called el Realito, lay five leagues east of Chihuahua. It was also considerably populated and abundant in silver (Alessio Robles 1946:43).

In 1759, Bishop Tamarón visited this real, located five leagues east of Chihuahua. He described some flat plains and some places, such as el Realito, that participated in commerce. This *real* had no *alcaldes*, just a *teniente de corregidor* from Chihuahua. He described the inhabitants as Spanish and mestizoes and counted 733 families, which totaled 4,755 people. Tamarón wrote that there were many silver mines that belonged to the citizens of both Chihuahua and this real. He also said that they lacked water and had to depend on wells that were dry the majority of the time. While he was there, Tamarón blessed the first stone for the new, larger parish (Alessio Robles 1937:153-154).

This was located on the right side of the road taken by Lafora on 7 July 1766, five leagues north-northeast of the *villa* of Chihuahua. It was in a rugged mountain range that Lafora said had given much silver but did not at the time of his passage. Silver was discovered there early in the eighteenth century. This is the *Cabecera* of the municipio of the same name (Alessio Robles 1939:71).

**Misión de Chiarras** [Aldama 28 51N  105 54W]: This was a Concho Indian mission administered, by a Jesuit priest, at the foot of the mountains of Santa Eulalia. Lafora went by on 7 July 1766. This could be the modern Villa Aldama, Chihuahua and could also include the missions of Santa Ana and San Gerónimo (Alessio Robles 1939:71-72).

**Misión de Santa Anna**: On 7 July 1766, north-northeast of Chihuahua, Lafora wrote that this mission was located a half league from the spot where he forded the Río Chihuahua, or Chuvíscar, in a wide valley. Alessio Robles guesses that it could also be part of the modern Villa Aldama (Alessio Robles 1939:71-72).

**El Río de Chihuahua**: Lafora forded this river six leagues north-northeast of the *villa* of Chihuahua on 7 July 1766, after crossing the plain called the Bajío.  It is now called Río Chuvíscar (Alessio Robles 1939:71).

**Misión de San Jerónimo or San Gerónimo**: Bishop Tamarón visited "San Jerónimo, located four leagues east of Nombre de Dios, in 1759. He described the church as nearly abandoned and the missionary's house as deteriorated.  He counted 23 families, which totaled 121 people, who lived in the "campos" (Alessio Robles 1937:154,165). Lafora placed the mission of "San Gerónimo" near the spot where he forded the Río Chihuahua or Chuvíscar north-northeast of Chihuahua in a wide valley on 7 July 1766. It contained Tarahumara Indians administered by a Franciscan priest. It may be part of the modern Villa Aldama (Alessio Robles 1939:71-72).

**Hacienda del Palo Blanco** [29 01N  105 56W]: Lafora described this as being abandoned for fear of Indians when he passed by on 8 July 1766. It was some eight leagues north of the present *municipio* of Aldama in a spacious valley formed on the left by the Sierra de San Gerónimo and on the right by the mountains which contained the "Realito de Santa Eulalia." Its small spring held the only water to be found in the area. It is probably a *ranchería* in the *municipio* of Aldama, Chihuahua (Alessio Robles 1939:72).

**El Puerto de Hormigas** [29 13N  105 48W]: This hacienda was abandoned when it was passed by Lafora on 9 July 1766. It was in a valley formed by the mountains of San Gerónimo and Santa Eulalia, running north and north east of Aldama, Chihuahua and eight to twelve leagues distant. Lafora found abundant water for humans and livestock, of which he saw much; this was the only water to found nearby. It remains as a *ranchería* in the *municipio* of Aldama.(Alessio Robles 1939:72). From this hacienda, Lafora to went to Encinillas. [See **ENCINILLAS**]

**Paraje de los Reyes** [29 33N  106 08W]: Lafora found this *paraje* in flat land on 11 July 1766, after traveling for two days in a northwesterly direction from the hacienda de Encinillas, Chihuahua. It was right next to the spring which he called San Bernardo. It is a rancho in the present municipio of Chihuahua (Alessio Robles 1939:73).

**Ojo de Agua de San Bernardo**: Located next to the Paraje de los Reyes in Chihuahua, Lafora found this spring on 11 July 1766. He described it as lying to the right of the *Camino Real* and three leagues to the south of Agua Nueva. The country was described as being of hills of varying size and steepness forming a narrow canyon (Alessio Robles 1939:73).

**Nombre de Dios (Chihuahua)** [28 41N  106 05W]: On 30 April 1726, Rivera left San Felipe el Real or Chihuahua heading west northwest through flat pasture land with no woods and with hills within sight, leaving on the east side the pueblo and mission of El Nombre de Dios (Alessio Robles 1946:45). In 1759, Bishop Tamarón visited this Indian pueblo, which was the head pueblo of its jurisdiction and which was also a Franciscan mission. It was located one league north of Chihuahua on very flat ground.

He counted 18 families, which totaled 100 people, who lived there (Alessio Robles 1937:154).

The first intents to colonize this area date from the years 1646-1652, when several miners and landowners from the province of Santa Bárbara undertook mining activities in the Río Sacramento, very close to the *Camino Real* (Almada 1984:10). In 1650, the Franciscans from San Francisco de Conchos made some attempts to convert Indians north of the Río Conchos. They renamed one of the principal Indian pueblos in the area "Nombre de Dios." It was classified as a pueblo of Conchos and Tarahumaras, and they designated it as a religious capital (Hackett 1923-37:166). The initial effort of the conversion of Nombre de Dios was abandoned a few years later, but, during the decade of 1670, Spanish settlement of this area increased. In 1673, there were several mining operations undertaken very close to the pueblo of Nombre de Dios (Almada 1984:19-20), and by 1677, Nombre de Dios was again a Franciscan mission, with the new name of San Cristobal de Nombre de Dios (Gerhard 1993:198). In the early 1700s, Nombre de Dios experienced a population growth, and in 1711, numerous mining operations were established in and around Nombre de Dios. Until the end of the colonial period, Nombre de Dios remained a Franciscan mission and an Indian town (Porras Muñoz 1982:514).

**Río Chuviscar or de Nombre de Dios**: On 12 March 1598, the Oñate expedition came to the Río del Nombre de Dios, five leagues from San Pedro (or San Greco). The river flows from west to east. The pools and marshes extend about a league and a half up river (Pacheco, Cárdenas, y Torres 1871:XVI.234-235). This river has been identified as the Río Chuviscar near Nombre de Dios, Chihuahua (Moorhead 1958:12).

**San Juan del Alamillo**: In 1759, Bishop Tamarón visited this pueblo located eight leagues north of San Jerónimo. He counted 28 Indians there (Alessio Robles 1937:154). It is possible that it may be modern San Juan de Urrutia (Alessio Robles 1937:166).

**Encinar de San Buenaventura**: On 14 March 1598, the Oñate expedition traveled five leagues from the Río de Nombre de Dios to this oak grove (Pacheco, Cárdenas, y Torres 1871:XVI.235).

**Valle de San Martín:** On 14 March 1598, the Oñate expedition crossed the Río de Nombre de Dios (or Río de Chuviscar), on their left, in order to enter the Valle de San Martín (Pacheco, Cárdenas, y Torres 1871:XVI.235).

**San José del Potrero:** On 30 April 1726, Rivera left Chihuahua heading west northwest over flat pasture land with no trees, within sight of hills. After going 12 leagues, he spent the night on an *estancia* called San José del Potrero (Alessio Robles 1946:45). Pike showed a "Delpotrero" just south of Agua Nueva but the text of his journal skips from that point to Chihuahua (Coues 1895:II.653-655).

**Río Sacramento:** On 19 March 1598, the Oñate expedition left "Sierrezuela de las Ogeras" and traveled one league to the Agua de "Sant Joseph" (Pacheco, Cárdenas, y Torres 1871:XVI.236). This was probably the Río Sacramento (Moorhead 1958:13). Wislizenus encountered this river from the then inappropriately named Arroyo Seco, Chihuahua, on 23 August 1846. In this area the broad plain, on which he had been traveling from the north, narrowed between mountain ranges. The valley of this river was soon to be famous for a battle fought against invading U.S. troops (Wislizenus 1848:47).

**Sacramento Mountains:** On 18 March 1598, the Oñate expedition traveled three leagues from the Valle de San Martín to the "Sierrezuela de las Ogeras." There was a large watering place to their left (Pacheco, Cárdenas, y Torres 1871:XVI.235). This has been associated with the range later called the Sacramentos (Moorhead 1958:13).

Wislizenus used the name Sacramento to identify the mountains just north of the city of Chihuahua in the vicinity of the river of the same name. He approached that city on a road below these mountains on 24 August 1846 (Wislizenus 1848:47-48).

**Rancho Sacramento** [28 50N  106 10W]: In 1759, while visiting Chihuahua, Bishop Tamarón described this rancho as being close to Ciudad Chihuahua; he counted six families, which totaled 56 people (Alessio Robles 1937:152). Wislizenus encountered this rancho, alongside a flooded Arroyo Seco, on 23 August 1846. In this area the broad plain on which he had been traveling from the north narrowed between mountain ranges. This was just above the Sacramento Valley of Chihuahua (Wislizenus 1848:47).

**Rancho de los Fresnos**: In 1759, while visiting Chihuahua, Bishop Tamarón described this rancho as being near Chihuahua City; he counted 32 families and a total of 115 people (Alessio Robles 1937:152).

**Arroyo Seco**: When Wislizenus crossed here on 23 August 1846, the arroyo was running so full as to make it almost impassable. The stream continued on to the east and emptied into the Río Sacramento. Across the arroyo was a rancho which was also called Sacramento (Wislizenus 1848:47-48).

**El Sauz** [29 02N  106 16W]: On 1 May 1726, Rivera left San José del Potrero and traveled northwest through flat land, which was fertile, pleasant, and good pasture. To the east and the west there were hills and mountainous country, which he thought may have contained minerals. He stopped at a rancho called El Sauz (Alessio Robles 1946:46).

In 1841, Gregg showed his road passing to the east of here and Laguna de Encinillas (Gregg 1933). Wislizenus passed to the east of this settlement on 23 August 1846, and noted that it lay nearer to the mountains than the road. It was shown southwest of El Peñol along the creek of that name (Wislizenus 1848:46).

The following is a brief history of El Sauz. The *paraje* called El Sauz, which would later become an hacienda, was settled towards the end of the 1670s (Alvarez 1995:183). In 1684, there is mention of a rancho called "Los Sauces" located three miles from the haciendas of Encinillas and Tabalaopa and north of the Laguna de Encinillas; this rancho belonged to Juan Domínguez de Mendoza (Porras Muñoz 1993:41). Domínguez de Mendoza was one of the early settlers of the Albuquerque area prior to the Pueblo Revolt of 1680 (Sánchez, Between Two Rivers, 2008:15-16). In 1721, El Sauz became the property of Francisco de Salcedo; at this time it was still a rather small place (Porras Muñoz 1993:41). Sometime soon after 1721, however, it passed into the hands of Andrés Facundo Carbonel, who was also the owner of the Hacienda de Encinillas. Thus, El Sauz became part of

Encinillas and a fixed point in the itinerary of those traveling the *Camino Real*. In 1734, Manuel de San Juan de Santa Cruz acquired Encinillas along with El Sauz, and when Encinillas was confiscated by the *Real Hacienda*, El Sauz was included as part of the package. By 1779, Juan Bautista de Anza found El Sauz to be a grand hacienda, with good crops and a luxurious house; it was an hacienda through which passed the many travelers of the *Camino Real* (Porras Muñoz 1993:42). In 1839, the hacienda passed into the possession of Prefect Angel Trías (Almada 1968:539). Then in 1854, it came into the possession of Pablo Martínez del Río, as did Encinillas, and finally it ended in the hands of Luis Terrazas (Porras Muñoz 1993:43).

**Descendimiento de la Cruz y Sancto Sepulcro**: On 21 March 1598, the Oñate expedition left the Agua de San Joseph and traveled three leagues to reach this place (Pacheco, Cárdenas, y Torres 1871:XVI.236).

**El Peñol** [29 08N   106 14W]: Wislizenus arrived at a large hacienda with this name, just south of Laguna de Encinillas and some 40 miles north of Chihuahua, on 22 August 1846 (Wislizenus 1848:46).

**El Peñol Creek**: On 22 August 1846, Wislizenus arrived at a large hacienda and creek named El Peñol. He described the creek as the main affluent of the nearby lake. It was, at the time, a torrent due to recent and ongoing rains (Wislizenus 1848:46).

**Encinar de la Resurreccion y Ojos Milagrosos**: On 22 March 1598, the Oñate expedition traveled three leagues to reach this oak grove. It was named this because a horse stepped in a bog near a large spring and a waterspout shot into the air and continued flowing about one span high (Pacheco, Cárdenas, y Torres 1871:XVI.236).

**Alameda de la Asumpcion de Nuestra Señora**: On 24 March 1598 the Oñate expedition traveled two leagues to reach this place. The waterholes are large and good (Pacheco, Cárdenas, y Torres 1871:XVI.236).

**Encinillas** [29 15N   106 21W]: On 2 May 1726, Rivera left El Sauz and traveled northwest through very fertile and fruitful land. He saw a small evergreen oak forest and several hot springs that contributed to the production of the seeds of the *hacienda de labor* called San Juan de las Encinillas (Alessio Robles 1946:46). In 1759, Bishop Tamarón described this hacienda as being located 18 leagues north of Chihuahua. He counted 48 families (Alessio Robles 1937:152).

On 9 July 1766, Lafora described the hacienda named Encinillas as being in a large valley which he found at the northeast end of the San Gerónimo mountains and to the left of the road. It remains as a hacienda in the *municipio* of Chihuahua in the state of the same name (Alessio Robles 1939:72).

In 1841, Gregg showed his road passing to the east of here and the lake of the same name (Gregg 1933). Wislizenus mentioned passing this hacienda or settlement at the southern end of the lake of the same name. He noted that it lay nearer to the mountains than the road. This site was shown as lying to the west of the road and near the mouth of the creek which he called El Peñol (Wislizenus 1848:46).

The following is a synthesized history of Encinillas. Following the 1650s, this region became colonized by settlers from Santa Bárbara, who established an agricultural base there (Alvarez 1995:174). In 1678, Benito Pérez de Rivera acquired land for livestock in the area which would later be called the Hacienda de Encenillas (Porras Muñoz 1989:4). With the support of the resources and people of Santa Bárbara this area was rapidly settled (Alvarez 1995:181). By the 1680s, Encinillas was fully operational, and some mining operations were undertaken in its outskirts. However, in 1684 and 1685 Encinillas and other settlements were temporarily abandoned because of the rebellion of the Conchos, Sumas and Janos (Navarro García 1964:27). After the hostilities ended, Encinillas was repopulated; Pérez de Rivera and his son Andrés Facundo Carbonel became the first owners of the *haciendas de minas* in the Real de Santa Eulalia (Limosnas por redención de cautivos por los vecinos de Santa Eulalia, 1708). In 1719, after the death of the original proprieter, the Hacienda de Encinillas, already one of the most important haciendas in the region, was designated as a chaplaincy (Testamentaría de Benito Pérez de Rivera, 1719). But, in 1734, it was sold for 20,000 pesos to Manuel Antonio de San Juan de Santa Cruz Jaques, nephew of Manuel de San Juan de Santa Cruz, ex-governor of Nueva Vizcaya (Porras Muñoz 1993:97). In 1752 the property of this family was confiscated and the hacienda was put in the charge of an administrator named by the *Real Haci-*

*enda* (Porras Muñoz 1993:98). Encinillas became one of the most important population centers north of the Villa de San Felipe el Real and an important point of defense on the *Camino Real* against enemy Indian attacks. In 1773, Hugo de O'Connor considered this hacienda to be one of the principal bastions in the protection of the *Camino Real* (Navarro García 1964:354). In the following years ownership of this hacienda changed hands several times. In 1862, Luis Terrrazas leased the hacienda and then became sole owner in 1868 (Porras Muñoz 1993:101). From Encinillas, Rivera went to San Martín. [See **SAN MARTIN**]

**Laguna de Encinillas** [29 28N  106 21W]: On 25 March 1598, the Oñate expedition traveled one league to reach "Laguna de San Benito y Ojuelas del Norte," which was two leagues around. The itinerary of the expedition noted that its waters and odor were like that of the lake of Mexico (Pacheco, Cárdenas, y Torres 1871:XVI.237). The writer was referring to Lake Texcoco (Hammond and Rey:1953:I.313). This was the lake later called Laguna de Encinillas (Moorhead 1958:14).

Gregg described this lake in 1839 as being ten or twelve miles by two or three in size, very salty, and with no outlets. The road beside it was flooded due to recent rains. Gregg commented on the large and rich haciendas in this valley but named no settlements of any kind. He showed the road passing east of the lake and the settlements of Encinillas and El Sauz (Gregg 1933:265-266).

When Wislizenus passed through this area on 21-22 August 1846, rains were plentiful and the lake was high. He estimated its area as 15 by 3 miles and explained that it had no outlet and rose and fell with the seasons and the fortunes of its feeder streams. The text of this entry in the Wislizenus journal is confusing, placing the road to both the east and west of the lake; his map shows the former case. Laguna de Encinillas was in a level plain at about 5,000 feet of elevation (Wislizenus 1848:46).

**Aguaje de la Cruz**: On 26 March 1598, the Oñate expedition traveled three leagues from the Laguna de San Benito y Ojuelas del Norte and reached this "Aguaxe" de la Cruz (Pacheco, Cárdenas, y Torres 1871:XVI.237).

**Agua Nueva** [29 40N  106 13W]: On 27 March 1598, the Oñate expedition traveled one league west from the Aguaje de la Cruz and reached the "Bocas del Peñol de Velez" and the end of the sierras of Levante and of Oñate. They enclose the "Sant Martín" valley. They remained here for two days (Pacheco, Cárdenas, y Torres 1871:XVI.237). The description and coordinates match Agua Nueva (Moorhead 1958:14-15).

Lafora came to Agua Nueva on 11 July 1766, from the southeast on the *Camino Real,* which he described as going through a narrow canyon formed by hills of varying size and steepness and then over a small pass. At the foot of this pass, the hacienda of Agua Nueva sat in a valley which, Lafora wrote, could be called pleasant due to its abundance of water, except that it was uncultivated because of the activities of hostile Indians. Next to the hacienda was a small *villa* surrounded by a wall with circular towers. Four leagues northwest of here, beyond Chivato and Gallego, Lafora wrote that they returned to the *Camino Real* that ran from Chihuahua through Encinillas and to "(el) paso del Río del Norte" (EL Paso). They had left it for a time, intending to go to the confluence of the Río Conchos and the Río del Norte. The name survives in a hacienda in the municipio of Chihuahua. (Alessio Robles 1939:73-75).

Pike did not name this spring when he was here on 31 March 1807, but noted that nearby a road to Sonora joined that which he was on. On his map the only road in that direction forks off near Carrizal, but the springs which he was at are labelled "Aqas Nueva" (Coues 1895:II.653). Wislizenus did not visit, but did mark on his map the spring at Agua Nueva. His road seems to have passed a short distance to the west (Wislizenus 1848).

**Ancón del Recelo**: On 30 March 1598, the Oñate expedition traveled three leagues from the Bocas del Peñol de Velez and reached Ancon del Recelo (Pacheco, Cárdenas, y Torres 1871:XVI.237).

**El Aguaje del Chivato**: On 31 March 1598 the Oñate expedition traveled two short leagues to the "Fuente de Sant Francisco de Paula," later known as Chivato (Pacheco, Cárdenas, y Torres 1871:XVI.237;Moorhead 1958:15). This spring, located at the foot of a hill called los Arados, north northwest of the hacienda of Agua Nueva, Chihuahua, was described by Lafora on 12 July 1766. The road near there was generally flat, surrounded by pastureland and a few hills (Alessio Robles 1939:74). On 20 August

1846, a few miles north of El Gallego, Wislizenus heard of a spring, whose name he recorded as "Chaveta," which was located in some mountains to the west of the road (Wislizenus 1848:45).

**San Martín**: On 3 May 1726 Rivera left the hacienda of San Juan de las Encinillas and traveled north northwest through fertile land, without any type of forests, seeing hills and mountainous country everywhere, some about four leagues apart, that form a delightful meadow in the distance. He came to a lake called San Martín whose length ran two from leagues northwest to southeast (Alessio Robles 1946:46).

**El Gallego** [Estacion Gallego 29 49N 106 22W]: On 4 May 1726, Rivera left San Martín and traveled north northwest to the uninhabited El Gallego, where he found a water hole (Alessio Robles 1946:46).

This spring was found on the right side of the road by Lafora as he traveled north northwest through hilly country on 12 July 1766. It has been identified with a train station in the *municipio* of Ahumada, Chihuahua. At this point, Lafora discusses the routes of the Apache from these hills to the various places where they raid (Alessio Robles 1939:75).

Pike did not name this spring when he was there on 30 March 1807, but only noted that it was 52 dry miles south of Ojo Caliente. He described a beautiful scene of a "spring on the side of (a) mountain, to the east of the road" and nearby ash trees, the first which he had seen in the region (Coues 1895:II.652-653).

Wislizenus described an "Oj de Callejo" about 50 miles south of Ojo Caliente which seems to fit the description and location of El Gallego. He saw a spring which formed a creek beginning to the east of the road and spreading across it, but noted that in the dry season one had to follow the course of the stream back up into the hills to find the spring itself. According to Wislizenus, the landscape became greener in this area than it had been further to the north, but he also noted almost daily thunderstorms (Wislizenus 1848:45-46).

**Las Boquillas**: On 5 May 1726, Rivera traveled north northwest through land with a few hills and glades, with mountainous country in sight. He came to the uninhabited place with no water called las Boquillas, which he considered the boundary of la Nueva México (Alessio Robles 1946:46).

**El Aguaje de Jesús María**: Lafora camped at this spring on 13 July 1766, some twelve leagues north-northwest of Agua Nueva. He described its setting as in a small ravine in a spacious valley at the foot of a steep hill near a pass formed by a hill. It was east of the valley of Santa Clara, abandoned due to Indian trouble (Alessio Robles 1939:75).

**Socorro del Cielo**: On 1 April 1598, the Oñate expedition traveled for nine leagues, during which they found no water. After traveling for three leagues a heavy downpour formed large pools of water, with which they were able to water more than seven thousand head of livestock of all kind. Because of this help from God, they named the place Socorro del Cielo (Pacheco, Cárdenas, y Torres 1871:XVI.237-238). This *paraje* was probably in the area of Jesús María (Moorhead 1958:15).

**Hacienda del Carmen**: In 1852, an optional road to Carrizal was described; it was located between Encinillas and this hacienda and traveled during times of drought (Frobel 1852:34). During times of rain the plains traversed by this road were flooded and made even more difficult to cross because some areas were very mountainous (Ruxton 1847:161-162). This detour was also one taken during the colonial period but in doing so the travelers were then not on the true *Camino Real* (Rivera 1726). The Río del Carmen flows from this hacienda towards Carrizal.

**Río del Carmen**: On 3 April 1598, the Oñate expedition left the *paraje* called "Socorro del Cielo" and traveled for two days. They reached the "Río de la Mentira,"--river of the lie--named this because even though it had a large bed and many trees it did not hold a drop of water (Pacheco, Cárdenas, y Torres 1871:XVI.238). This dry riverbed has been identified as the Río Carmen (Moorhead 1958:15-16).

On 14 July 1766, Lafora crossed this dry river bed just west of a hot spring where lay the abandoned hacienda of Ojo Caliente (Alessio Robles 1939:76). Wislizenus passed Laguna de Patos on 18 August 1846. He described it briefly as a small lake east of the road which was the "outlet of the Río Carmen." The next day he again passed the Río Carmen, this time below where the outlet of Ojo Caliente flowed into it. He characterized it as a river of fair size at that time which disappeared in the dry season. Wislizenus wrote that it began above Ojo Caliente and flowed southwest before turning to the north toward Laguna de Patos, but his map shows it beginning to the southwest of Ojo Caliente (Wislizenus 1848:44-45).

**Los Baños de San Isidro**: While at the Río de la Mentira, on 3 April 1598, the priest who wrote this itinerary described the "Cienega de Los Baños de San Isidro" as being "dos tiros de arcabuz" east of the Río de la Mentira. It is formed by some springs of nearly hot water and is located six short leagues from Socorro del Cielo. The remained there until the 6th of April (Pacheco, Cárdenas, y Torres 1871:XVI.238). This marsh was probably a seasonal overflow of the Río Carmen (Moorhead 1958:15-16).

**El Ojo Caliente** [Ojo Caliente de Santa Rosa 30 25N  106 36W]: On 6 May 1726, Rivera left Las Boquillas and traveled northwest through flat land with some rosemary thickets. He passed a dry arroyo and came to the small settlement of Ojo Caliente, the first in la Nueva México. It was made up of Spaniards and mestizos, and consisted of only four *ranchos de labor*, where they planted wheat and corn (Alessio Robles 1946:46).

Lafora found this hacienda abandoned when he passed by on 14 July 1766. It lay five leagues south of El Carrizal in Chihuahua at the foot of a small hill. Lafora noted this as the boundary of the jurisdiction of New Mexico at the time. Its modern name is Ojo Caliente de Santa Rosa, in the *municipio* of Carrizal, Chihuahua (Alessio Robles 1939:76).

Zebulon Pike only noted that the march from Carrizal to Ojo Caliente just took from late afternoon until sundown and that a fosse or acequia was crossed en route when he was here on 28 March 1807 (Coues 1895:II.652-653). Dr. Wislizenus described Ojo Caliente on 19 August 1846, after reaching it from Carrizal, some 10 miles to the north by his reckoning. He saw a basin of igneous rock, connected to a nearby ridge, with a sandy bottom, from which many warm springs of good water issued. A creek from it emptied into the Río Carmen not far away (Wislizenus 1848:45).

This place is located on the edges of the famous Médanos de Samalayuca, which were a principal obstacle to those traveling on the *Camino Real*. The first Spanish occupant was probably Cristóbal de Chávez, a *vecino* from

the town of Paso del Norte. Around 1700, he was given a land grant by Antonio de Valverde y Cosío, captain for life of the presidio of Paso del Norte
and *alcalde mayor* of the jurisdiction. This grant included Ojo Caliende, and
although some descriptions stated that the lands there were bad and that it
suffered from Indian invasions, the settlement of Ojo Caliente prospered.
Around the 1730s Manuel de San Juan de Santa Cruz acquired the lands
of Ojo Caliente (Testimonios de autos: Títulos de la hacienda de Ojo Caliente) and founded an important hacienda. From that point on, Ojo Caliente
became an important stopping place on this section of the *Camino Real*. But
by the end of the colonial period, the hacienda practically disappeared, and it
became a simple watering hole on the *Camino Real*.

**El Carrizal** [30 34N  106 39W]: On 6 May 1726, while at Ojo Caliente,
Rivera met seven Indians of the Suma nation who lived in the *paraje* called
el Carrizal. Since some of them spoke and understood Spanish, Rivera ad-
monished them to observe the peace, and, having received bread, meat and
tobacco, they went away content (Alessio Robles 1946:46-47).

In 1759, Bishop Tamarón wrote that this pueblo was new, founded in
the year 1758 by Captain Don Manuel de San Juan, who paid the expenses
of fifty settlers equipped as soldiers out of his own private means. A secular priest was appointed, and 20 soldiers from the *presidio* of El Paso were
stationed there. Bishop Tamarón's opinion was that, although it was an important outpost, it would not survive. It was 36 leagues south of El Paso on
the way to Chihuahua. There were 41 families, with 171 persons. Bishop
Tamarón stated that it belonged to New Mexico (Adams 1953:197).

Lafora described this as a small town of mestizos and mulattoes when he
camped here on 14 July 1766. A squad of ten soldiers from El Paso were stationed here due to Indian trouble but Lafora noted that there was sufficient
water to support many more settlers if peace were maintained. It is now the
pueblo cabecera of the *municipio* of the same name in the state of Chihuahua
(Alessio Robles 1939:76).

Pike arrived at the "Presidio of Carracal" from El Paso on 27 March
1807, after crossing the sand dunes between the two. His map showed a
road forking off to the west toward Sonora near this point, but it was not
mentioned in the text (Coues 1895:II.650-652).

Wislizenus made Carrizal on 18 August 1846 and described it as a "small country town" and as the only notable habitation between El Paso and Chihuahua. It still had a wall around it and a few soldiers although he said that it was no longer a *presidio* (Wislizenus 1848:45).

The following is a brief history of El Carrizal. When Fray Miguel Menchero visited the haciendas of El Carrizal, Ojo Caliente and Ranchería in 1744, he found a total of 40 families of mixed blood living there (Timmons 1990:34-35). In 1740, Mateo de la Peña had founded an *estancia* called El Carrizal that was situated on the *Camino Real* (Almada 1968:91), but by 1753, it was abandonded, after eight people were killed by Apache Indians (Griffen 1988:22). In 1750, Captain Tellez Girón also had a rancho called El Carrizal (Testimonio de las diligencias de Alonso Rubín de Celis). In 1758, about 20 soldiers from the presidio of El Paso were transferred to El Carrizal in order to provide protection for the travelers of the *Camino Real* and to open a new route from El Carrizal to Janos and Sonora. Soon about 45 familias and six individuals settled there; about 70% were from El Paso and the rest had been recruited from San Buenaventura, Valle de San Bartolomé (Jones 1979:152-155). By 1771, there were 161 inhabitants in the presidio of San Fernando del Carrizal (Moorhead 1958). Indians, who were prisoners of war, were also part of the population of El Carrizal; in 1821, they numbered 347 and 280 in 1825 (Griffen 1989:22). Although El Carrizal experienced a period of prosperity in the early 1800s, by 1852, it was in ruins because of constant Apache attacks. By then it was almost completely abandoned, with more than half of the inhabitants gone and without any sort of defense left (Altamirano 1988).

**Los Patos** [Laguna de los Patos 30 45N 106 29W]: On 7 April 1598, the Oñate expedition traveled two leagues to the sierra and cienega of "Alchicubite de Sant Vicente," already considered well-known. It had very good water (Pacheco, Cárdenas, y Torres 1871:XVI.239). This water was probably Los Patos (Moorhead 1958:16).

On 7 May 1726, Rivera traveled north northeast from El Ojo Caliente and Carrizal and came to an uninhabited place called Los Patos, where there was a hot spring and a fresh water lagoon (Alessio Robles 1946:47). Lafora also called this los "Platos" and described it as an abundant source of water in an otherwise flat and dry area, though one given to marshiness in wetter seasons. He passed it, four leagues north northeast of El Carrizal, Chihuahua, on 16 July 1766. The Río del Carmen empties into this lake (Alessio Robles 1939:86).

In his 1839 trip through this area, Josiah Gregg was surprised to find the road flooded by "Lake Patos" due to recent rainfall being carried in seasonal streams. He was pleased at finding such amounts of water in this arid region but struggled for hours in crossing it. He showed the road passing to the west of the lake (Gregg 1933:264-265). Dr. Wislizenus passed "Laguna de Patos" on 18 August 1846. He described it briefly as a small lake east of the road which was the "outlet of the Río Carmen." Near here, the two south-bound roads from El Paso joined and continued into Carrizal (Wislizenus 1848:44-45). From Los Patos, Rivera proceeded to Sierra de la Ranchería. [See **SIERRA DE LA RANCHERIA**]

## MAP 8: ROUTE FROM OJO LUCERO TO EL PASO

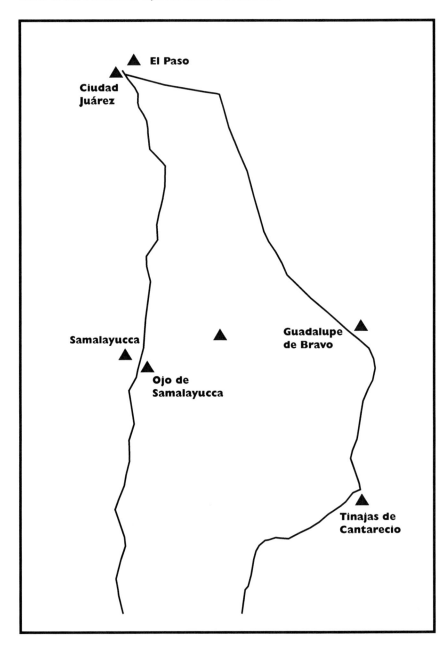

**Ojo del Lucero** [30 50N  106 30W]: On 8 April 1598, the Oñate expedition traveled three leagues to the "Cienega de la Concepcion," probably formed by the overflow from Ojo del Lucero (Pacheco, Cárdenas, y Torres 1871:XVI.239; Moorhead 1958:16-17).

Lafora passed this spring, eight leagues north northeast of El Carrizal, on 16 July 1766. He described its water as salty and hard. The same name is found on both new and old maps (Alessio Robles 1939:86). Wislizenus described Ojo del Lucero on 18 August 1846. It was a sizable spring of good water which poured out of a small depression in the plain within 100 yards to the east of the road. The water formed a creek which crossed the road and emptied into a pond (Wislizenus 1848:44).

**El Puerto del Bordo**: Lafora camped by a small pool of rainwater in this spot on 17 July 1766. It was some sixteen leagues to the south of El Paso. He had just come from the southwest through a large plain covered with mesquite, *huizache*, and pasture land between las Sierra de la Ranchería on the east and the Sierra de la Candelaria on the west. Lafora later refers to this as a *puertecito*. It was probably located , near the rail station of Candelaria (Alessio Robles 1939:86).

**Sierra de la Ranchería** [31 04N  106 20W]: On 8 May 1726, Rivera left Los Patos and traveled north northeast through flat land with dense mounts of mesquite, *huizaches* and *uñas de gato*, leaving the *sierra* called de Ranchería to the east (Alessio Robles 1946:47).

**Ranchería de Candelaria** [31 07N  106 29W]: On 8 May 1726, Rivera traveled north northeast through flat land with thickets of mesquite, huizaches and uñas de gato. On the east was the *sierra* called la Ranchería and on the west the *sierra* called Candelaria. He passed a canyon formed by these two *sierras* and spent the night at the uninhabited place and lagoon of Candelaria. Northwest of this lagoon he could see a smaller one (Alessio Robles 1946:47).

**Los Médanos** [Rail Station 31 12N  106 31W]: On 12 April 1598, the Oñate expedition left the spring of San "Ermengildo" and traveled three leagues to the openings of the sand dunes called Bocas de los Médanos.

They buried an Indian boy there and remained until the 19th because the preceding watering places did not have enough water for the livestock They had to take the animals down to the Río del Norte. On the 19th they actually entered the sand dunes and traveled three leagues (Pacheco, Cárdenas, y Torres 1871:XVI.239-240).

On 9 May 1726, Rivera traveled northeast through sand dunes which were difficult to cross, especially the last two leagues. Here the dunes were higher than some of the ones Rivera has seen on the beaches. He noted that this chain of dunes ran northeast and southeast and deduced that they began in the north, in the land of the Apaches de "Xila" and ended near the junction of the rivers del Norte and Conchos.

In 1839, Gregg traversed this area and wrote that the road wound for six miles through the lowest gaps between the hills, some of pure sand totally lacking in vegetation. Gregg wrote that since "teams are never able to haul the loaded wagons over this region of loose sand, we engaged an *atajo* of mules at El Paso...," implying that this was a usual practice (Gregg 1933:263-264).

In August 1846, Wislizenus described "the much-dreaded sand hills" south of El Paso as "an immense field of steep sand ridges, without shrub or vegetation of any kind, looking like a piece of Arabian desert transplanted into this plain, or like the bottom of the sea uplifted from the deep." He heard of some springs scattered through the area but only named one, which he called "ojo de malayuque," located at the foot of the hills (Wislizenus 1848:43-44).

**Fuente de San Leon:** On 10 April 1598, the Oñate expedition traveled a league and a half from the Cienega de la Concepcion into Los Médanos and reached the Fuente de Sant Leon, a small water hole a short distance *"del camino"* (Pachecho, Cárdenas y Torres 1871:XVI.239). This or the spring mentioned below may have been the Charcos de Grado of later years (Moorhead 1958:17).

**Spring of San Ermenegildo**: On 11 April 1598, the Oñate expedition traveled three leagues from the Fuente de San Leon and reached the manantial de Sant Emenegildo, named for a Spanish prince and martyr (Pachecho, Cárdenas y Torres 1871:XVI.239). This or the Fuente de San Leon may have been the Charcos de Grado of later years (Moorhead 1958:17).

**Bocas de Los Médanos** [Rail Station 31 12N 106 31W]: On 12 April 1598, the Oñate expedition left the spring of San "Ermengildo" and traveled three leagues to the openings of the sand dunes called Bocas de los Médanos. They buried an Indian boy there and remained until the 19th because the preceding watering places did not have enough water for the livestock. They had to take the animals down to the Río del Norte. On the 19th they traveled three leagues to the gap known as Bocas de los Médanos. By this route, the *carretas* avoided the worst of the sand dunes and reached the Río del Norte about eight and a half leagues below El Paso (Pacheco, Cárdenas, y Torres 1871:XVI.239-240; Moorhead 1958:17-18).

**El Ojo de Agua de Samalayuca** [31 21N 106 28W]: Lafora visited this spring and pool, surrounded by trees, twelve leagues south of El Paso on 18 July 1766. He had just come through the sand dunes and then crossed a brushy plain. He went on through seven dry and unpopulated leagues before he camped. A train station and *ranchería* carried this name into modern times; a spring with this name lies south of it and three others are to the northwest. (Alessio Robles 1939:87).

On 26 March 1807, a short distance out of El Paso heading south, Pike noted camping at "Ogo mall a Ukap," the only water source for 60 miles, which he labeled "Ojo Malalka" on his map. From these names and the location, Coues deduced in 1895, that Pike was at the springs of Samalayuca. Coues delineated two roads from El Paso to Carrizal, one direct and the other down the Río del Norte far enough to avoid the sand dunes which lay between the two points (Coues 1895:II.648-649). Wislizenus called this spring "ojo de malayuque" when he came by in August 1846, but his map is marked "Ojo de S. Malayuque. Although he described it as lying at the foot of the nearby sand dunes and a usual camping place, his party evidently did not stop here (Wislizenus 1848:43). From Samalayuca Lafora traveled to El Paso. [See **PRESIDIO DE NUESTRA SENORA DEL PILAR Y SAN JOSE DEL PASO DEL RÍO DEL NORTE** (Ciudad Juárez)]

**El Ojito**: On 9 May 1726 Rivera traveled northeast through sand dunes to an uninhabited watering place called el Ojito (Alessio Robles 1946:47). He mentioned this spring again on 7 October 1726, during his return from New Mexico (Alessio Robles 1946:56).

**La Cañada**: On 10 May 1726, Rivera left El Ojito and traveled north through flat land made difficult by sand, stopping at an uninhabited place called La Cañada (Alessio Robles 1946:47).

**Camp Comanche**: This is the name given on the 1846 Wislizenus map for the point where the long road from El Paso to Carrizal leaves the Río del Norte and went southwest to meet the direct road near Los Patos (Wislizenus 1848).

**Presidio San Elizario**: Zebulon Pike reported stopping at a "Fort Elisiaira" just a few hours south of El Paso on 23 March 1807. There was a fort and settlement as well as a number of friendly Apache Indians. Coues interpreted this to be a *presidio* called San Elizario which, he said, sat at the boundary between Nueva Vizcaya and North (or New) Mexico. In 1895, Coues delineated two roads from El Paso to Carrizal, one heading directly south and the other down the Río del Norte far enough to avoid the sand dunes which lay between the two points. Pike's map showed San Elizario just south of El Paso and away from the river (Coues 1895:II.648-650). Gregg did not mention passing here in 1839, but his map shows it midway between the road and the Río del Norte (Gregg 1933).

When Wislizenus went from El Paso to Carrizal in August 1846, he discussed the two roads between the them and went on to describe his journey through the direct route over Los Medanos. He did not mention the *presidio* at San Elizario but his map, which showed both roads, had a "San Eleazario" on the Río del Norte a short distance south of El Paso and on the longer route along the Río del Norte (Wislizenus 1848).

**Sierra el Paso**: On 10 May 1726, after leaving El Ojito and stopping at La Cañada, Rivera could see a *sierra* to the west called El Paso (Alessio Robles 1946:47).

**Río del Norte (Río Grande)**: The Sánchez Chamuscado expedition encountered this river some five leagues north of its confluence with the Río Conchos on 6 July 1581. They gave it, and its valley, several names depending upon the writer and locale.

Gallegos and Bustamente coined several names for different segments of the Río del Norte. Baltasar Obregón used the same titles and added a few others. Gallegos and Obregón provided the most detail and are summarized at greater length below (Pacheco and Cárdenas 1871:XV.83,90; Hammond and Rey 1927:18-21; Hammond and Rey 1928:276-285; Mecham 1926:270).

The route followed by Francisco Sánchez Chamuscado and his men is noted by Gallegos. Valle de Nuestra Señora de la Concepción: Gallegos gave this name to the Río Grande valley in the area just north of the mouth of the Río Conchos. The Sánchez Chamuscado expedition entered the Río Grande valley some five miles north of the Río Conchos on 6 July 1581. He gave a flattering description of the inhabitants and their permanent settlements and called the river the largest in the Indies and the first seen since the Vera Cruz. According to Gallegos, the people here described Cabeza de Vaca and his companions and gave them information about other villages further north. Obregón's history agreed with Gallegos on the main points (Hammond and Rey 1927:18-21;Hammond and Rey 1928:278-283).

**Valle de los Carneros:** Leaving the Valle de Nuestra Señora de la Concepción, still following the Río Grande north, Sánchez Chamuscado went twelve leagues to the Valle de los Carneros, so named because of a quantity of ram's horns found in an abandoned ranchería. According to Gallegos, it took the expedition nine days to traverse this valley and to go on to the Valle de la Madalena (Hammond and Rey 1927:21). Obregón has the group in this valley for six days before entering the Valle de la Laguna (Hammond and Rey 1928:283).

**Valle de la Madalena:** Despite the time discrepancy noted above, the Valle de la Madalena of Gallegos seems to be Obregón's Valle de la Laguna (Hammond and Rey 1928:283). This valley marked the terminus of the territory of the Jumano Indians. It has been identified as a site some ten miles south of Fort Quitman on the south side of the Río Grande (Mecham 1926:271). Beyond it was a swampy region, which they christened Valle de los Valientes (Hammond and Rey 1927:21-23;Hammond and Rey 1928:283-285).

**Valle de los Valientes:** Leaving the land of the Jumanos, the Sánchez Chamuscado expedition entered the area of the Caguates or Caguases and then an uninhabited swampy region which they named Valle de los Valientes (Mecham 1926:271-272;Hammond and Rey 1927:23;Hammond and Rey 1928:284-285).

**Río Guadalquivir:** The Sánchez Chamuscado expedition gave this name to the Río Grande in the Piro area of New Mexico due to its large size and volume of water. Obregón described its beauty and surrounding farms, with corn, beans, calabashes, and cotton (Hammond and Rey 1927:25;Hammond and Rey 1928:291).

Espejo reached the Río Grande on 9 December 1582, upriver from the mouth of the Río Conchos. Apparently they were the first to refer to it as the Río del Norte, although Luxán wrote that Sánchez Chamuscado's men had coined the name. They also referred to it as El Río Turbio. Diego Pérez de Luxán, author of a journal of the expedition, described the river at this point as being very large but quiet as it flowed through a plain covered with poplars and willows. He added that they always followed the river, straying as much as a league but returning to camp nearby. They called the natives which they found in the area near where the two rivers met Abriaches (or Abriadres) and Caguates. These may have been the people later called the Suma and Manso (Hammond and Rey 1929:59; Pacheco, Cárdenas y Torres 1871: XV.106; Mecham 1926:123-124; Bolton 1930:174).

The Oñate expedition of 1598 was the first to travel directly north to New Mexico from the Río Conchos. Sánchez Chamuscado and Espejo had followed the Conchos eastward to its confluence with the Río del Norte and continued along the Río del Norte into New Mexico. On 20 April, after crossing the difficult sand dunes to the south, Oñate came to the Río del Norte in the area of modern El Paso. The itinerary of the expedition described the river as being larger than the Conchos river and as carrying more water than the Río de las Nasas. The water was sluggish and muddy, and there was plenty of vegetation and trees, as well as fish. There were also willows, mesquite and some salines with salt like that of the salines of Guadalquivir.

The itinerary noted that it was called the Río del Norte because it flowed from that direction. It added that after the river turned to the east it was called the Río Bravo where the Conchas and other rivers joined it. The Oñate expedition remained here until the 26th while Captain Aguilar went ahead to explore the road, traveling some 16 leagues.

Over the next three days they traveled two and a half leagues and found other salines, and on 30 April 1598, Oñate took possession of all the kingdoms and provinces of New Mexico in the name of King Philip. On 4 May they continued on to the pass of the river and the ford, where they met 40 Indians who were described as having Turkish bows, long hair that resembled little Milan caps, and headgear colored with blood or paint. Their first words were "manxo," "manxo," "micos," "mico," which meant "peaceful ones" and "friends." They also made the sign of the cross and helped the Oñate expedition cross the river (Pacheco, Cárdenas y Torres 1871:XVI.240-244).

According to Joseph Brondate, who was captain of the cavalry, after going upriver about fifty leagues from the ford, the Oñate expedition reached the first pueblos. Brondate described the land as being good, except for about eight leagues where there was no water (Hammond and Rey 1953:II.624-625). He also stated that the Río del Norte was the main river in the province and that it rose in the month of May. Many kinds of fish could be found in it (Hammond and Rey 1953:II.626).

In 1726, Rivera noted that the origin of the Río del Norte was 50 leagues northwest of the capital, Santa Fe. Poplars grew on its banks, and fish such as dog-fish, trout, ahuja, sea-bream, and remora were abundant (Alessio Robles 1946:54). Bishop Tamarón wrote that all the way to New Mexico from El Paso one did not lose sight of this river, but also mentioned difficulties with regard to the dearth of water in the Jornada del Muerto (Adams 1953:198).

Domínguez noted the reason for the name Río del Norte, agreeing with Oñate's chronicler that it stemmed from its northern origin. He added that it began many leagues beyond Taos, sometimes entering mesas, where it formed canyons, sometimes flowing through plains, broadening out more in some places than in others, winding in still others, but always tending toward the south. He thought that even the settlers and the Indians had been unable to find the source of the river. Domínguez went on that many large and small rivers joined the Río del Norte from the east and west, from above Taos to below El Paso. It was in flood from mid-April to the end of June (Adams and Chávez 1956:7).

Wislizenus approached the Río del Norte from the east in the area of Albuquerque on 12 July 1846. He found it shallow, flat, and not very imposing. His caravan was delayed north of Albuquerque when rain damaged part of the road which followed the river. Eventually they made it to a higher road to the east which, itself, became impassable just south of Albuquerque. Wislizenus wrote that some caravans crossed to the west bank of the river at Albuquerque and recrossed at Socorro, but that his did not (Wislizenus 1848:33-34).

**Presidio de Nuestra Señora del Pilar y San José del Paso del Río del Norte** [Ciudad Juárez 31 44N 106 29W]: After his 1591 arrest by Capitan Juan Morlete, Castaño de Sosa was taken by wagon down the Río del Norte. Seven years later Oñate saw the tracks from these wagons in the vicinity of modern El Paso and Juárez. This would have been the first wagon traffic on the later route of the *Camino Real* (Schroeder and Matson 1965:175-176).

On 11 May 1726, Pedro de Rivera traveled northwest and came to the Presidio de Nuestra Señora del Pilar y San José del Paso del Río del Norte, now known as Ciudad Juárez, Chihuahua. It was located on the south bank of the river and next to it was a settlement of Spaniards, mestizos and mulattoes. There was a separate pueblo in two districts that were inhabited by the two nations of Manos and Piros. Four leagues to the east of the settlement were the pueblos of Socorro, La Isleta, Senecú and San Lorenzo, inhabited by Indians of the Tiwas, Sumas and Piros nations. All of these Indians were administered by the Franciscans.

Nearby was a large *vega de labores* where wheat, corn, beans, and all types of vegetables were grown as well as vines that produced grapes better than those at Parras. A large acequia system supplied by the Río del Norte added to the natural abundance of the land, guaranteeing good harvests no matter what the weather (Alessio Robles 1946:48).

On 23 April, 1760, Bishop Tamarón began his visitation of New Mexico at "Presidio del Paso." He reported a population of 354 families of Spanish and "Europeanized" citizens, totaling 2,479 persons, and 72 Indian families totaling 249 persons. There was a royal *presidio* with a captain and fifty soldiers in the pay of the king. Two Franciscan friars of the Province of the Holy Gospel of Mexico served there: the Custos, who was prelate of all the New Mexico missionaries, and the parish priest of the town, who had the title of guardian. Two secular priests were also in residence; one holding the office of vicar and ecclesiastical judge.

Bishop Tamarón wrote that the inhabitants irrigated many vineyards with a large ditch from the Río del Norte that divided into arroyos which ran through broad plains. They grew wheat, maize, and other grains as well as fruit trees, apples, pears, peaches and figs (Adams 1953:192-194).

Tamarón made the statement that, although he arrived at the "Presidio del Paso" in April, he actually entered New Mexico in May (Adams 1953:195). He called the *presidio* the gateway to the interior of New Mexico and wrote that it was considered as such because it was on the most direct and well used route to the north (Adams 1953:198).

In 1766, Lafora referred to this *presidio* as both "Presidio del Paso del Río del Norte" and "Presidio de Nuestra Señora del Pilar del Paso del Río del Norte." He stayed from 18 July to 5 August 1766. He had just come from the south through brushy hills over a broken road along which he had seen little pasture land. His route through the region called "Tierra Blanca y Mesa" followed the later route of the National Railroad of Mexico. At the time, the *presidio* housed a company of cavalry composed of forty-six men. There were five Franciscan priests, who ministered to the five missions in the area, and an alcalde mayor. Between the *presidio*, nearby town, missions, and a hacienda, the populated area covered seven leagues and contained 5000 people. The nearby land was well-cultivated, and Lafora especially commented on the abundance of wine produced there (Alessio Robles 1939:88-89).

In 1776, Fray Domínguez wrote that the province of the Holy Gospel of Franciscan Observants of New Spain had in its charge the kingdom of New Mexico, the Custody of the Conversion of St. Paul. This custody had two branches, the smaller one at "Presidio del Paso del Río" and the larger one in the interior of the kingdom of New Mexico. The "Presidio del Paso" branch consisted of a Spanish *villa* and four Indian pueblos; all were established on the west bank and were supplied with water from the Río del Norte. The distance from the *villa* to the last pueblo downstream was 10-12 leagues (Adams and Chávez 1956:6).

When Anza traveled along the *Camino Real* from Fray Cristóbal to the "Presidio del Paso" on 23 November 1780, he described the journey as difficult because of the continuous snow (Thomas 1932:199). Pike arrived at "Passo" or "the passo" (modern Juárez) on 21 March 1807. He opined that the "second cities of the province (of New Mexico) were Albuquerque and Passo del Norte." Pike discussed two roads heading south from El Paso. One went directly south while the other followed the river far enough to the southeast to avoid the great sand dunes before turning back to the west to join the first (Coues 1895:II.641-647,739). In 1839, Josiah Gregg's caravan rented an extra team of mules in El Paso for the crossing of Los Medanos to the south (Gregg 1933:263).

Wislizenus stayed in El Paso for about a week in August 1846, during his trip from Santa Fe and points east to Chihuahua. He described it as stretching along the right bank of the Río del Norte (where modern Juárez is located), with only a few houses on the other side of the river. Here the river emptied from a canyon into a fertile plain which seemed like an oasis after the crossing of the Jornada del Muerto. The houses were spread among many gardens, orchards, and fields, making this the most abundant area which Wislizenus had seen. He mentioned seeing large quantities of maize, wheat, and many fruits, especially grapes, and estimated the total population of all the communities spread along this valley at 10-12,000. Wislizenus also knew of the two roads from El Paso to Carrizal, and noted that the two reunited at Los Patos (Wislizenus 1848:39-43).

The census of 1823 stated that there were 8,544 inhabitants in the jurisdiction of El Paso, of which 5,247 lived in the actual settlement (Ponce de León 1910:171). In 1826, El Paso was given the title of *villa* (Almada 1968:293). Despite the fact that the population did not increase much during the following years, El Paso became an important center of commerce after 1824, with the establishment of an annual fair which took place from December 8 to December 16 (Timmons 1990:81). In 1860 there were 428 inhabitants in the American territory on the northern bank of the river and 6,000 on the Mexican side, where the pueblo of Zaragoza was founded just east of Senecú by settlers from New Mexico, who had rejected the North American rule (Timmons 1990:156). Between 1865 and 1866 the city of El Paso del Norte was transformed into the Mexican republican see when President Benito Juárez took refuge there (Almada 1968:293). And, in 1888, El Paso became Ciudad Juárez in honor of said Mexican hero. In 1890, 8,000 people lived on the American side, and ten years later the population had doubled (Timmons 1990:185). El Paso-Ciudad Juárez continued to be an important commercial center, thanks to the railway lines that connected Mexico City with Kansas and that traversed the southern part of the United States (Martínez 1982:39-51).

**Guadalupe (Conversión de los Mansos):** Fray Benavides described the Manso in his Memorial of 1634, writing that they subsisted on fish and meat, all eaten raw. He also noted that they lived near a ford of the Río del Norte which the Spanish used often, Christianizing them in passing. The Mansos later lived in the area of Las Cruces and were moved south to the region where "Presidio del Paso" was constructed in 1659, when the mission of Nuestra Señora de Guadalupe de los Mansos was built (Hodge, Hammond, and Rey 1945:52-54,243-244).

In the 1663 trials of Don Bernardo López de Mendizábal, the former governor of New Mexico, the opening and maintenance of the "Conversión de los Mansos" was characterized as a major bone of contention between the governor and the New Mexican Franciscans (Primera Audiencia de don Bernardo López de Mendizábal, 1663). In 1692, Vetancurt described the 1659 founding of the Convento de Guadalupe de los Mansos, dedicated to the conversion of the Mansos, also called the "Lanos". It sat the foot of a rocky hill beside the Río del Norte "en el passo" (Vetancurt 1971:98).

On 24 August 1726, Rivera met with the Indians of the Suma nation, who agreed to settle in several places, among them the *real* de San Lorenzo, the *paraje* of Guadalupe and in Carrizal (Alessio Robles 1946:53). In 1749, Father Varo reported that the mission of Our Lady of Guadalupe near the "Presidio del Paso" had a population of "more than 200 Indians and more than 1,000 Spaniards and other Europeanized individuals" (Adams 1953:198). Lafora reported on "El Pueblo de Nuestra Señora de Guadalupe" of Spaniards, mestizos, mulattoes, and Tiwa, Piro, and *genízaro* Indians during his stay at "Presidio del Paso" from 18 July to 5 August 1766. It was contiguous with the *presidio* and a part of the pueblo was shown on the official plan of the *presidio* (Alessio Robles 1939:88-89).The Convento de Guadalupe has been described as "in the vicinity of the ford of the Río Grande, crossed by Oñate in 1598," and was founded by Fray Garcia de Zuñiga in 1659 (Twitchell 1911:I.367).

**El Pueblo de San Lorenzo de Real**: On 11 May 1726, Rivera described San Lorenzo, east of the "Presidio de Nuestra Señora del Pilar y San José del Río del Norte." He reported that it was inhabited by Indians of the Tiwas, Sumas and Piros nations, and was administered by the Franciscans (Alessio Robles 1946:48).

In 1760, Bishop Tamarón stated that this pueblo was called the Realito although he remarked that he had not been told there were mines there. It consisted of 32 families of "Europeanized" citizens totaling 192 persons. There were also 21 Indian families totaling 58 persons. A Franciscan parish priest ministered to all of them in a church which was 23 *varas* long and five and a half wide. Tamarón located San Lorenzo one league over a plain to the east of "Presidio del Paso", downstream. Its location at that time has also been given as three leagues from "Presidio del Paso" and three from Senecu. According to Father Varo, there were about 150 Suma Indians and 150 Spaniards in the vicinity in 1749 (Adams 1953:196).

Lafora also thought that San Lorenzo was peopled by Suma Indians along with some *gente de razón*, all administered by the Franciscans. This was the first of the pueblos to the east of "Presidio del Paso" along the south bank of the Río del Norte which he discussed in his report on 18 July 1766 (Alessio Robles 1939:88-89).

**El Pueblo de San Antonio de Senecú** [31 43N  106 23W]: On 11 May 1726, Rivera noted that this was one of four pueblos located four leagues to the east of the "Presidio de Nuestra Señora del Pilar y San José del Paso del Río del Norte" (Alessio Robles 1946:48). In 1760, Bishop Tamarón wrote that this pueblo was two leagues from San Lorenzo and three from "Presidio del Paso", downstream over the plain to the east. Its Franciscan mission had 111 families of Piro Indians, totaling 425 persons and 18 families of Suma Indians, totaling 52 persons, as well as some "infidel" Sumas who were being taught the catechism. There were also 29 families of citizens and "Europeanized" mixtures, totaling 141 persons. The church was thirty-six and three-fourths *varas* long, five and a half wide, and the priest's house measured nine *varas* (Adams 1953:196).

This was the second of the pueblos to the east of "Presidio del Paso" along the south bank of the Río del Norte discussed by Lafora in his report on that *presidio* (18 July 1766). It was peopled by Piro Indians and some *gente de razón* and administered by the Franciscans (Alessio Robles 1939:88-89).

The missions of Isleta, Socorro, and Senecú were founded in the region of "Presidio del Paso" after the Pueblo Revolt of 1680 and the first attempt at reconquest in 1681 (Twitchell 1911:I.377).

**El Pueblo de San Antonio de la Isleta**: The Tiwa pueblo of Isleta, just south of modern Albuquerque, did not participate in the 1680 revolt. When Governor Otermín passed by there in late 1681, at least 385 Isletans were moved to the region of "Presidio del Paso", where Isleta del Sur was established (Hodge, Hammond, and Rey 1945:64-65,253-258;Lummis 1894:4;Twitchell 1911:I.377). Vetancurt put the number of Isletans taken south by Otermín at 519 (Vetancurt 1971:99).

On 11 May 1726, Rivera mentioned El Pueblo de San Antonio de la Isleta in connection with the nearby *presidio* (Alessio Robles 1946:48). In 1760, Bishop Tamarón thought that there were Piro Indians in the charge of the Franciscan missionary. He counted 80 families of Indians totaling 429 persons, and 18 families of "citizens" totaling 131 persons. It was two leagues east of Senecú and five from "Presidio del Paso", downstream. The church was thirty-six *varas* long by five and one half wide, and the priest's house measured nine *varas* (Adams 1953:196-197). On 18 July 1766, Lafora noted that Isleta was peopled by Tiwa Indians and some *gente de razón* (Alessio Robles 1939:88-89).

**El Pueblo de la Purísima Concepción del Socorro**: On 11 May 1726, Rivera noted Socorro as one of the pueblos east of the *presidio* at "Presidio del Paso" (Alessio Robles 1946:48).

In 1760, Bishop Tamarón called this pueblo "Our Lady of Socorro;" it had a Franciscan missionary and 46 families of Suma Indians totaling 182 persons. It was one league east of Isleta and six from "Presidio del Paso", downstream. There were 82 families of "citizens," including those of Tiburcio, totaling 424 persons. The church was thirty-six *varas* long and seven wide, and the transept measured fourteen and three-fourths *varas*. The land was as "fertile and luxuriant" as "Presidio del Paso", with irrigation ditches filled from the river (Adams 1953:197).

Lafora mentioned Socorro in his report of 18 July 1766. Franciscans ministered to Piro Indians and some *gente de razón* (Alessio Robles 1939:88-89). Anza also went by Socorro when he left "Presidio del Paso" in 1779, marching northward along the *Camino Real* (Adams and Chávez 1956:154). It was founded after the Pueblo Revolt of 1680 and the first attempt at reconquest in 1681 (Twitchell 1911:I.377).

**La Hacienda de los Tiburcios**: Located to the east of the *presidio* and pueblos in the "Presidio del Paso" area, this hacienda of *gente de razón* was mentioned by Lafora in his report on that *presidio* of 18 July 1766 (Alessio Robles 1939:88-89).

**Los Puertos, crossing of Río del Norte**: On 4 May 1598, the Oñate expedition forded the Río del Norte, with the help of Indians, at a crossing they named Los Puertos because it was used by the Indians to go inland. The itinerary stated that there was no road for carts for many leagues. On that day they passed the ruts made by the ten carts that Castaño de Sosa and Morlete took out from New Mexico (Pacheco, Cárdenas y Torres 1871:XVI.244-245).

**Toma del Río del Norte**: Spanish colonial travelers usually commented that New Mexico began at the Toma del Río. This was the name used in the 1663 trials of Don Bernardo López de Mendizábal, the former governor of New Mexico, when supposedly referring to the ford of the Río del Norte, which was at or near it. The place name Toma del Río was in general use at the time. It likely was, in the vicinity of the later site of El Paso (Primera Audiencia de don Bernardo López de Mendizábal, 1663). Before the 1680 Pueblo Revolt, a Capitan Andrés López de Gracia lived at the Toma del Río del Norte (Concurso á los bienes de don Diego de Peñalosa y don Bernardo de Mendizábal, 1660-1668).

**El Vado de Balisan** [Vado 32 06N 106 39W]: This was the point at which

Lafora's party crossed the Río del Norte by raft on 5 August 1766. He described the country as being of rough, brushy hills but gave no specific location for the crossing point (Alessio Robles 1939:90).

## MAP 9: ROUTE FROM EL PASO TO LAS CRUCES

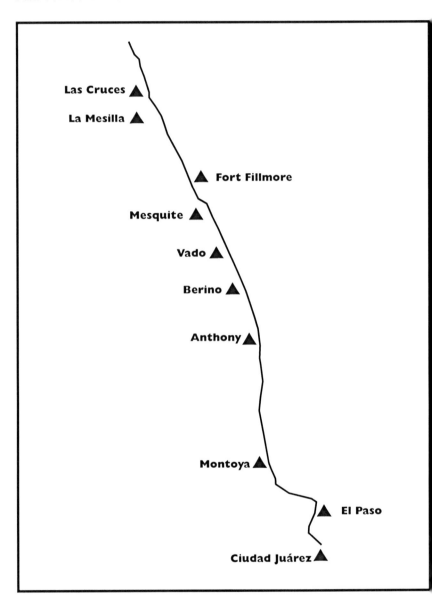

**The "upper crossing of the Río del Norte"**: In 1839, Josiah Gregg described what he knew as the "usual ford of the Río del Norte" six miles above El Paso (Gregg 1933:260). Wislizenus crossed the river from east to west about six miles to the north of El Paso on 7 August 1846. Above this crossing he described a good road which went through a narrow pass between mountains for several miles. The water was low and the crossing easy, however the road soon became impassable because of deep sand. Therefore, he retraced his steps and took another road which stayed east of the river until it crossed right at El Paso. This road traversed rocky hills through a canyon but allowed for easier travel than the first (Wislizenus 1848 39-40).

**Ancón de la Cruz de Juan Téllez**: Lafora followed the Río del Norte from his crossing near "Presidio del Paso" to this point on 5 August 1766. He described a range of mountains to the east as the "Sierra de la otra Banda" or "de los Mansos". The next day he referred to this range as being called "los Organos", or the Organ Mountains as they are known today. He described the landscape along the river as rough and hilly with much low brush (Alessio Robles 1939:90).

**El Paraje de los Cacaxtitos**: This Lafora campsite was about twelve leagues north-northwest along the Río del Norte from the spot where he crossed it. He stayed there, near the river, on the night of 6 August 1766 (Alessio Robles 1939:90).

**El Puerto de los Alamitos**: Lafora mentioned this as a place in the Organ Mountains one league north-northeast of El Paraje de los Cacaxtitos on 6 August 1766 (Alessio Robles 1939:90).

**La Salinera**: On 20 May 1726, Rivera left the Presidio del Paso and traveled northwest through stony hills and thickets of *quiotes* (maguey) and wild lettuce, and followed the bank of the Río del Norte, leaving the "sierra grande los Mansos" a short distance from the road. He stayed at a *paraje* called La Salinera (Alessio Robles 1946:48).

**El Paraje de los Bracitos** [Brazito 32 10N 106 41W]: This campsite, between the east bank of the Río del Norte and the Organ Mountains, was used by Lafora on 7 August 1766. He located it some twenty leagues north of the place where he crossed the river (Alessio Robles 1939:90-91). Rancho del Bracito was later the exchange point for mail runs between Santa Fe and Chihuahua (Moorhead 1957:112). From this *paraje*, Lafora went to Robledillo. [See **ROBLEDILLO**]

**Organ Mountains (Sierra de los Mansos and Sierra del Olvido)** [32 19N 106 33W]: From 5 May to 13 May 1598, the Oñate expedition traveled about 11 leagues up river over a road that was difficult in time of rain but very good when dry. On the 11th, they stopped at the same place where Captain Morlete hanged four Indians for having stolen some horses. On the 13th, they left the Río del Norte to the left and the Sierra del Olvido (Mountain of Forgetfullness, or more poetically, the Mountain of Oblivion) to the right. It was named this because none of Oñate's guides who had been with Morlete six years prior, and who had passed it before, remembered it (Pacheco, Cárdenas y Torres 1871:XVI.245-246). Teasing them, Oñate and his settlers had a good laugh about it. The Sierra del Olvido was undoubtedly the Organ mountains, which were an imposing sight (Hammond and Rey 1953:I.316). Near Sombrerete is a similar geologic formation aptly called Sierra de Organos.

On 20 May 1726, Rivera left the Presidio del Paso, traveled northwest, and followed the east bank of the Río del Norte, seeing the "sierra grande los Mansos" a short distance from the road (Alessio Robles 1946:48). In 1760, Bishop Tamarón wrote that on the eastern route from "Presidio del Paso" to New Mexico, he did not see a single stream from the west flank of the Sierra de los Mansos (Adams 1953:198).

Lafora followed the Río del Norte north from his crossing near "Presidio del Paso". On 5 August 1766, he described a range of mountains to the east as the Sierra de la otra Banda or de los Mansos. The next day he referred to this range as being called los Organos, or the Organ Mountains, as they are known today (Alessio Robles 1939:90).

During his 1839 passage, Gregg used the name "Los Organos" and described this range as an Apache Indian stronghold (Gregg 1933:262-263). On 5 August 1846, Wislizenus described the "broken, pointed, basaltic appearance" which led to the naming of the mountains, which he said were called "Organon." In his map, however, he labeled them properly as the Organ Mountains (Wislizenus 1848:39).

**Punta del Estero Largo**: On 21 May 1726, Rivera left La Salinera and traveled northwest, following the bank of the Río del Norte through flat land covered with poplar groves, and stayed at a *paraje* called La Punta del Estero Largo (Alessio Robles 1946:49).

**La Ranchería**: On 22 May 1726, Rivera followed the bank of the Río del Norte and stayed at a *paraje* next to the river called Ranchería, which used to be inhabited frequently by the Mansos Indians before they were contained to a pueblo (Alessio Robles 1946:49).

**Doña Ana** [32 23N   106 48W]: On 11 May 1760 Bishop Tamarón described Doña Ana as the *sierra* on the east side of the river. He camped between Doña Ana and the river (Adams 1953:199). Lafora described a place between mountain ranges which he labeled Doña Ana, to the east, and Roblerito, across the river to the west. The name Doña Ana is given elsewhere as the name of a *ranchería* (Alessio Robles 1939:91).

In August 1846, Wislizenus mentioned that "Doñana" was the first town reached south of the Jornada del Muerto. He said that it was 12 miles south of Robledo but did not describe it as he passed through (Wislizenus 1848 39).

## MAP 10: ROUTE FROM LAS CRUCES TO LAGUNA DEL MUERTO

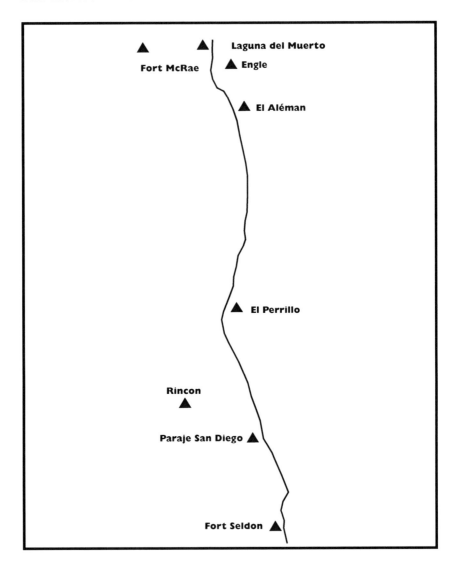

**Jornada del Muerto—Deadman's Journey**: [about 80 miles long] On 25 May 1726, Rivera came to the Jornada del Muerto (Alessio Robles 1946:49). On 12 May, 1760, Bishop Tamarón arrived at the Jornada del Muerto. To prepare for it, Tamarón made a detour to find the river at a place called San Diego and filled barrels with water. He wrote that since the river turned away from the Jornada del Muerto water supply was a problem (Adams 1953:198-200). Lafora crossed this dry stretch away from and to the east of the Río del Norte from 9 to 11 August 1766 (Alessio Robles 1939:92-93).

In the summer of 1846, Wislizenus traveled across the Jornada and noted that the crossing was made necessary by the westward bend of the Río del Norte and the rough mountains which followed the river in this region. He noted that there was plenty of water in the rainy season but that otherwise it was totally dry. He described it as a high, dry plain with much grass and more mesquite and palmilla, and as a "ridge-like elevation" in which little water could accumulate. It ran south between two steep mountain ranges; the one to the east he called the Sierra Blanca (Wislizenus 1848:37-39).

Two place names have survived along the dry wastelands north of El Paso to remind New Mexicans of Bernardo Gruber's final test, the Jornada del Muerto and Alemán (Sánchez 1987:120-128). Gruber was a German trader from Sonora who became a target of the Holy Office of the Inquisition in New Mexico sometime between 1668 and 1670. He became the focus of Fray Joseph de Paredes's investigation when a mulatto named Juan Nieto reported that Gruber was handing out *papelitos* with "+ABNA+ADNA+" written on them and telling people that if they swallowed them no harm could come to them from "that hour of this first day to that same hour of the second day." On April 19, 1668, Captain Joseph Nieto, the *alcalde mayor* of the Jurisdiction of Salinas, Fray Gabriel Toríja, the Franciscan minister of San Gregorio de Abó and notary for the Inquisition, and Juan and Joseph Martín Serrano, left Abó for Quarai to arrest Gruber on charges of practicing magic.

After being held for nearly a month in a cell at Abó Gruber was transferred to an *estancia* called San Nicolas, owned by Captain Francisco de Ortega, in the Jurisdiction of Sandía Pueblo. Gruber remained a prisoner there for nearly two years, during which there was no action from the Inquisition authorities in New Mexico. On June 22, 1670, Gruber made his escape with the aid of two accomplices: his guard, Juan Martín Serrano; and one of his Apache servants, Atanasio.

Although Ortega was able to pick up Gruber's trail on the *Camino Real*, he was unable to catch up with him or his servant Atanasio. However, it was Atanasio who later provided information regarding what happened to Gruber. According to Atanasio, he and Gruber spent June 24 on the trail somewhere near Senecú. That night they camped at a place called Fray Cristóbal, and the next day they made it through the "hot wasteland" to Las Peñuelas. After Atanasio returned from two days of searching for water, he discovered that Gruber was gone; apparently he had taken one horse and gone south on the *Camino Real*. Atanasio tried unsuccessfully to locate Gruber and then decided to report the incident to Fray Francisco Nicolás Hurtado, *ministro de doctrina* of the Convento de Senecú, not far from Socorro. Later it was said that Atanasio murdered Gruber. Although searches were conducted for Gruber, the only evidence found were what was believed to be his remains at a point which would later be called Alemán; New Mexico lore would then commemorate the trail as *La Jornada del Muerto*—Deadman's Journey (Sánchez 1987:120-128).

In his brief history of New Mexico, Dan Murphy wrote that the Jornada del Muerto was named for the death of a man named Robledo, for whom the *paraje* was named, during Oñate's 1598 entrada (Murphy 1985:39). James L. Haley thought that the name Jornado del Muerto came from Mescalero attacks on caravans in the area (Haley 1981:30). Tenorio Oclides explained that it was given because of the deaths of many people and animals from thirst and fatigue (Oclides 1975:2).

**The Jornada del Muerto begins approximately at "Robledillo" and ends at "Fray Cristóbal;" it is a stretch of about 80 miles:**

**Robledillo** [Robledo Mountain 32 26N  106 54W]: Between 14 May and 21 May 1598, the Oñate expedition traveled about four leagues after passing the Sierra del Olvido [Organ mountains]. The road was very bad, and the train had to be divided. On the 21st, they buried Pedro Robledo but did not refer to the burial site as Robledillo (Pacheco, Cárdenas y Torres 1871:XVI.246-247).

On 23 May 1726, Rivera left La Ranchería and traveled northwest through land with some small hills, glades and mesquite thickets, then stayed at a *paraje* called Robledillo (Alessio Robles 1946:49). On 11 May 17, 1760, Bishop Tamarón reached the "dread site" of Robledo. The river flowed between two *sierras*; the one on the west he called Robledo, and the one on the east Doña Ana. He camped between Doña Ana and the river and described the place as frightening because of attacks by "infidel" Indians, although he didn't personally experience any attacks (Adams 1953:199).

On 8 August 1766, Lafora named "Ancón de Roblerito" as a campsite on the bank of the Río del Norte. It was also called "Robles" and "*Paraje* de Robledillo." Lafora placed this point at 29 leagues upriver of his crossing near "Presidio del Paso," in a hilly area with brush that was thicker than it had previously been and between mountain ranges which he labeled Doña Ana, to the east, and Roblerito, across the river to the west (Alessio Robles 1939:91).

The caravan carrying Wislizenus "at last" arrived at the river after their crossing of the Jornada del Muerto on 5 August 1846. Wislizenus wrote that the country was mountainous and described the Organ Mountains to the east, though he called them the "Organon." He also noted that "Doñana," which was the first town south of the Jornada, was 12 miles to the south (Wislizenus 1848 39).

**San Diego** [San Diego Mountain 32 36N 106N 59W]: On 24 May 1726, Rivera left Robledillo and traveled northwest, then west, through land with hills, flat mesas, and thickets of gorse, mesquite and rosemary. He stayed at a pleasant *paraje* located between the bank of the river and a high hill called San Diego, said to contain minerals (Alessio Robles 1946:49).

On 12 May, 1760, Bishop Tamarón, to prepare for the Jornada del Muerto, made a detour to find the river at a place called San Diego and filled barrels with water (Adams 1953:200). On 9 August 1766, Lafora gave this name to a mountain range at the southern end of the Jornada del Muerto. He described the landscape as flat and barren with wild palms that gave dates comparable to those found in Spain. At San Diego, travelers prepared themselves and their livestock for the crossing of the arid Jornada (Alessio Robles 1939:92).

**Paraje del Perrillo**: Between 21 May and 23 May 1598 the Oñate expedition traveled about six leagues, doing very badly because of the lack of water. They were traveling five or six leagues to the right, or east, of the Río del Norte. On the 23rd a dog appeared with muddy paws, and they searched for some water holes. Captain Villagrá and Cristóbal Sánchez both found one, toward the river (Pacheco, Cárdenas y Torres 1871:XVI.247-248).

On 25 May 1726 Rivera left San Diego and traveled north-northwest through flat land, leaving the Cerros de Perrillo to the east (Alessio Robles 1946:49). On 9 August 1766, Lafora referred to a campsite and to a nearby mountain range as simply "Perrillo." He camped near pools of rainwater and identified the mountains to the east as the Organ range and to the west as the Sierras del Perrillo and del Muerto. He described the Río del Norte as running through a canyon beyond the mountains to the west (Alessio Robles 1939:92).

Wislizenus called this spring "Barilla" when his party stopped here on 3 August 1846. They had been at a spring to the north which they found dry and then had pushed on until they found sufficient amounts of stagnant water to provide for their stock here. Wislizenus observed that spurs from the mountains to the east approached the area and that the soil was more solid than it had been to the north (Wislizenus 1848 39).

**Las Peñuelas**: On 25 May 1726, Rivera left San Diego and traveled north northwest through flat land, leaving the hills called "el Perilloto" the east, and stopped at an uninhabited *paraje*, with no water or fire-wood, called Las Peñuelas (Alessio Robles 1946:49).

**Paraje del Alemán (Arroyo de Muertos or Parras)** [Alemán Ranch Headquarters 32 59N  106 59W]: Between 24 May and 25 May 1598, the Oñate expedition traveled six leagues north of the Paraje del Perrillo without any water. They finally came to some small pools where they drank and rested. The river was more than six leagues off to their left, where it was extremely hilly and very rough. On the 25th, they descended to the Arroyo de Muertos or Parras, which had running water. Because the water was not very good they continued another league to the Río del Norte (Pacheco, Cárdenas y Torres 1871:XVI.248-249). After reaching Socorro, Villagrá reflected on the hardship of the passage from Las Peñuelas to the Río Grande:

| Vino a faltar el agua de manera | Water became so scarce |
| Que, secas las gargantas miserables, | That, with their throats miserably dry, |
| Los tiernos niños, hombres y mugeres | The tender children, women and the men, |
| Traspassados, perdidos y abrassados, | Afflicted, ruined, quite burnt up, |
| Socorro al soberano Dios pedían, | Did beg for aid from sovereign God, |
| Por ser aqueste el ultimo remedio. | For this was their last hope. |

(Miguel Encinias, et al. 1992:128, Canto XIV, lines 203-208. Translated by Joseph P. Sánchez ).

Lafora passed by this spot, six leagues north of El Perrillo and eight south of Laguna del Muerto, in the Jornada del Muerto of New Mexico, on 10 August 1766. He found the pools which often gathered rainwater dry (Alessio Robles 1939:92-93).

"Alamos" was the name used by Wislizenus to describe what was, on 3 August 1846, a dry pool, some 16 miles north of Paraje del Perrillo (Wislizenus 1848 39).

**Horse Mountain** [Caballo Cone 33 06N   107 13W]: On 16 March 1807, Pike reported passing to the east side of Horse Mountain and Mountain of the Dead. Both were peaks of the Sierra de los Caballos, the former later known as Caballo Cone. Throughout this area, Pike noted seeing abundant signs of Indians and pursuing Spanish troops (Coues 1895:II.637-638).

**Sierra del Muerto or Mountain of the Dead**: Pike reported passing to the east of Horse Mountain and Mountain of the Dead on 16 March 1807. These were peaks in the Sierra de los Caballos. Pike saw evidence of Indians and Spanish troops near these mountains. According to his map, Pike crossed the Río del Norte from west to east just south of this mountain and headed back to rejoin the main road on 19 March. On the same day that the river was crossed, he noted the first signs of vegetation for some time (Coues 1895:II.637-638).

**Laguna del Muerto**: On 26 May 1726, Rivera left Las Peñuelas and traveled more than 10 leagues off the road to water the horses at the Laguna del Muerto (Alessio Robles 1946:50). Lafora camped at the Laguna del Muerto on 10 August 1766 although it was dry. He reported that it was 10 leagues to the southeast of the Paraje de Fray Cristóbal at the north end of the Jornada del Muerto of New Mexico (Alessio Robles 1939:93). On 2 August 1846, Wislizenus found this lake bed dry, so his party went to water their animals at the nearby Ojo del Muerto (Wislizenus 1848 38).

**Ojo del Muerto**: On 2 August 1846, Wislizenus reached the bed of the Laguna del Muerto but it was dry, so his party went to water their animals at the nearby Ojo del Muerto. He wrote that it was five miles to the west over a sandy plain and through a canyon, at the foot of a mountain. It provided good, but warm, water and was surrounded by cottonwood trees (Wislizenus 1848 38).

**Sierra Blanca** [33 31N 105 43W]: In 1839, Gregg mentioned this name in connection with one of the ridges to the east of the Río del Norte (Gregg 1933:262). This was the name given by Wislizenus to the mountain chain visible to the east of the Jornada del Muerto for its entire course when he came through in 1846 (Wislizenus 1848 38).

Go to Oñate's Itinerario for Frá Cristóbal's place name

## MAP 11: ROUTE FROM FRA CRISTÓBAL TO PUEBLITO

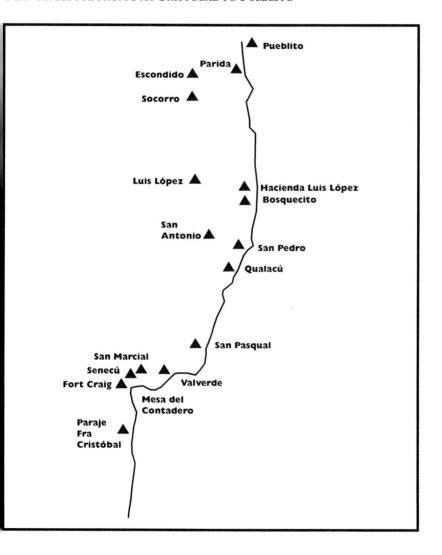

**Fray Cristóbal (mountain):** When Oñate and his 60 horesemen camped near the mountain in May 1598, one of them noticed an effigy made by shadows on the mountain and commented that it looked like Fray Cristóbal de Salazar, the Commissary of the Expedition. Laughingly they said "es feísimo" literally, he is so ugly, meaning, in this case, pitiful looking. Thus the mountain and the paraje took the place name Fray Cristóbal or Frá Cristóbal. On 27 May 1726, Rivera traveled north northwest past the Sierra de San Cristóbal on his way to the *paraje* called Fray Cristóbal (Alessio Robles 1946:50). On 13 May 1760, after coming to the Jornada del Muerto, Bishop Tamarón stopped opposite the Sierra of Fray Cristóbal (Adams 1953:200). Lafora placed this range five leagues into the Jornada (Alessio Robles 1939:93). On 14 March 1807 Zebulon Pike reported seeing a mountain which he called "Friar Christopher," where, he said, the road turned away from the river for two days and went due south. Pike and his captors continued along the Río del Norte and crossed to the west bank eight miles to the south. They rejoined the main road on 19 March two days north of El Paso (Coues 1895:II.634-635,639-641).

**Fray Cristóbal (paraje)** [33 28N   107 05W]: El Paraje del Fray Cristóbal marked the northern terminus of the Jornada del Muerto of New Mexico. On 27 May 1726 Rivera traveled north northwest, passing the Sierra de San Cristóbal, and stayed at a *paraje* called Fray Cristóbal, located on the bank of the Río del Norte (Alessio Robles 1946:50). On 11 August 1766, Lafora recounted camping there on the bank of the Río del Norte five leagues north of the northern end of the Sierra de San Cristóbal (Alessio Robles 1939:93). On 22 November 1780 Anza left Valverde and traveled five leagues south to "Fray Cristóval" (Thomas 1932:199).

In 1895, Coues characterized this as an area more than a specific point (Coues 1895:II.635-636). In August of 1846, Wislizenus understood this title to refer to the last camping place before entering the Jornada del Muerto heading south rather than a particular site. His caravan camped two miles from the Río del Norte but he noted that others stayed nearer or further and that there were no buildings with which to identify the name (Wislizenus 1848:38).

Fray Cristóbal marks the northern end of the Jornada del Muerto just before the Camino Real passes toward the Río Grande and the area of present Socorro at Ciénega de Mesilla de Guinea [see below].

**Piro pueblos**: In 1634, Fray Benavides reported that the Piro pueblos enjoyed three convents, at Senecú, Socorro, and Sevilleta, and the inhabitants lived Christian lives. As many as 42 Piro villages had once stood along the Río Grande, but that number was reduced to fourteen or less by 1630. Benavides reported that Sevilleta had already been burned (probably by the Apache) and rebuilt during his stay. By the time of the 1680 revolt, only Senecú, Socorro, Alamillo, and Sevilleta remained, due mainly to attacks by hostile Indians and the concentration policy of the Spanish missionaries (Hodge, Hammond, and Rey 1945:63-64,246-252).

**Jueves de las Comadres**: On 1 February 1583, the Espejo expedition reached the southern limit of the Piro pueblos of New Mexico. They visited many pueblos, both occupied and deserted. They neither named them, except for a group of pueblos which they called El Gallo, nor provided descriptions sufficient for identification. On 7 February, they camped at a place on the river which they named for the date that they arrived, then they continued to the two Piro pueblos called El Hosso and La Pedrosa by Gallegos (Hammond and Rey 1929:72-75).

**San Felipe (or San Phelipe)** [Ruins of Fort Craig 33 38N  107 00W]: Not to be confused with the Keres pueblo north of Bernalillo, New Mexico, this name was also given by the Sánchez Chamuscado expedition to the first Piro pueblo that they encountered in New Mexico and the Piro region in general. They reached it on 21 August 1581, after going several days without seeing any sign of human habitation. Sánchez Chamuscado first found a pueblo which was abandoned and in ruins and then a nearby inhabited pueblo, both on the west side of the river (Hammond and Rey 1927:24-25,45;Hammond and Rey 1928:288-290).

This pueblo has been linked to a site some two leagues south of Trenaquel (or San Miguel), near Fort Craig (Mecham 1926:272-273) and with a ruin at the foot of Milligan Gulch, just south of Fort Craig, which carries the label of site LA 597 (Marshall and Walt 1984:140,229,248-249).

**El Contadero**: This was a narrow pass which Lafora encountered on 12 August 1766, one league north of Fray Cristóbal and which extended north as far as the mesa of Senecú (Alessio Robles 1939:94).

**Ciénega de Mesilla de Guinea** [San Marcial 33 42N 106 59W]: Between 25 May and 27 May, the Oñate expedition traveled nine leagues from the "Arroyo de Muertos" or "Parras" without their carts because it was impossible to proceed with them. On the 27th they arrived at "Ciénaga de Mesilla de Guinea," named this because the mesa was made of black rock (Pacheco, Cárdenas y Torres 1871:XVI.249). This marsh was on the east bank of the Río Grande, near San Marcial (Hammond and Rey 1953:I.317).

**Senecú**: In 1634, Fray Benavides reported that there were three convents located in Piro pueblos and that their inhabitants lived Christian lives. One of these convents was San Antonio Senecú (Hodge, Hammond, and Rey 1945:63). In 1692, Vetancurt described the organ and rich adornments of the Convent of San Antonio de Padua at Senecu as well as its grape and wine production. When he wrote it had been deserted as a result of the 1680 Pueblo Revolt and was in ruins (Vetancurt 1971:98).

Lafora commented on a mesa and a nearby abandoned pueblo with this name on 12 August 1766, four leagues northeast of Fray Cristóbal. He wrote that the pueblo had been depopulated in the second entrada of the Spanish in 1692 (Alessio Robles 1939:94). In one provisional map placement and description, Senecú seems as if it could conform to Sánchez Chamuscado's San Miguel. It is located the proper distance above San Felipe and is across the river from and within view of another pueblo, as well as in the area of Contadero Mesa, as mentioned by Lafora (Marshall and Walt 1984:140,252-254).

**San Miguel**: This was the name given to the second Piro pueblo encountered by the Sánchez Chamuscado expedition to New Mexico in 1581. It was located on the west side of the Río Grande and has been identified with Trenaquel or Tzenaquel, possibly another name for Senecú (Mecham 1926:274;Hammond and Rey 1927:24-25,45;Marshall and Walt 1984:140,252-254).

**San Pasqual** [Little San Pascual Mountain 33 43N   106 51W]: When Otermín led his party and many Indian refugees south from Isleta toward "Presidio del Paso" on the east side of the Río Grande early in 1682, he recorded his route past the "Serillo de Tome," "Vega de las Nutrias," Sevilleta, "El Alto en frente del Nogal," a *vega* opposite Socorro, the hacienda of Luis Lopez, and the ruins of Qualacu and San Pasqual (Hackett 1915:391).

On 28 May 1726, Rivera left Fray Cristóbal and traveled north northwest through flat sandy land, with thickets of aromatic rosemary. He followed the bank of the Río del Norte and stopped at a *paraje* called San Pascual, which was uninhabited. Its name was taken from that of a pueblo located on the east bank of the river. From this *paraje* one could see traces of another called Senecú, located on the west side of the river (Alessio Robles 1946:50).

On 15 May 1760, Bishop Tamarón came to San Pascual. He reported that there had been a pueblo there before the "revolt of the kingdom," of which traces of the church and houses were still visible (Adams 1953:200). Lafora passed by the "Paraje de San Pasqual", six leagues northeast of Fray Cristóbal, on 12 August 1766. He described it as setting on the east bank of the Río del Norte (Alessio Robles 1939:94).

**Santiago**: In 1581, Sánchez Chamuscado gave this name to a Piro pueblo which was found across the Río Grande (on the east bank) from San Miguel in central New Mexico. Sánchez Chamuscado's Santiago was probably the pueblo later called San Pasqual or San Pascal. It has been noted that Senecú and San Pasqual were within view of one another across the river (Marshall and Walt 1984:140:251-252). It has, however, been identified with Qualacú (Mecham 1926:274; Hammond and Rey 1927:45).

**San Juan**: This name was given by Sánchez Chamuscado in 1581, to a Piro pueblo which they found on the west side of the Río Grande upriver from the pueblo of San Miguel. Sánchez Chamuscado may have crossed from the west to the east bank of the Río Grande at this pueblo. It has been provisionally identified as Senecú, at San Antonio, New Mexico (Mecham 1926:272-274; Hammond and Rey 1927:45; Marshall and Walt 1984;140,251-254).

**Qualacú** [San Marcial 33 42N 106 59W]: According to Marcelo de Espinosa, captain of cavalry on the Oñate expedition of 1598, "Cuelaqu" was the first pueblo in the provinces of New Mexico. From this pueblo to the last pueblo, which was Taos, there was a distance of 70 leagues, all in the upper valley of the Río del Norte (Hammond and Rey 1953:II.633). Between 27 May and 28 May 1598, the Oñate expedition traveled about four leagues from the Mesilla de Guinea. On the 28th they camped across from the second pueblo called Qualacú, toward the bank of the Río del Norte. The Indians had abandoned the pueblo, but the Spaniards reassured them with gifts and went to stay on the bank of the river in order not to frighten them. They remained there for a month, living in tents (Pacheco, Cárdenas y Torres 1871:XVI.249-248).

Qualacú has been called the most southerly of the Piro settlements on the east bank of the river, at the foot of the Black Mesa, near San Marcial (Hammond and Rey 1953:I.318). In 1682, however, Otermín noted passing the ruins of Qualacú between the hacienda of Luis López to the north and the ruins of San Pasqual further south (Hackett 1915:391).

**Piastla**: One map of the Sánchez Chamuscado expedition of 1581 shows the party crossing the Río Grande from the Piro pueblo of San Juan to that which they named Piastla. It has been identified as San Pascual, but this is by no means certain (Mecham 1926:274-275;Hammond and Rey 1927:45)

**Bosque del Apache** [33 50N 106 50W]: Lafora camped here, twelve leagues to the northeast of Fray Cristóbal, on 12 August 1766. The road in the area was hilly with plenty of pasture. Across the river was a mountain which was called los Ladrones which, he wrote, connected with the Mimbres range to the south and other mountains which extended all the way to Sonora (Alessio Robles 1939:94). On 20 November 1780, Anza left Pueblito and traveled four leagues south to the spring of the Apaches, or Apache Wood (Thomas 1932:198). Although Pike's description goes little beyond the sighting of many deer, Coues, in 1895, decided that he probably stayed within the boundaries of the Bosque del Apache on 13 March 1807 based on distances mentioned in his journal (Coues 1895:II.633-634).

**Valverde**: On 20 November 1780, Anza left the spring of the Apaches, or the Apache Wood, and traveled to Valverde (Thomas 1932:198). In 1839, Gregg observed the ruins of Valverde and wrote that it had been founded only twenty years earlier, in some of the richest land in New Mexico, and was deserted due to Indian attacks (Gregg 1933:258). On 30 July 1846, Wislizenus wrote of passing the "ruins of Valverde," which he described as "the mud walls of a deserted Mexican village," in an area of sand hills and cottonwood trees within twelve miles to the south of Luis López (Wislizenus 1848:37). In 1846, Abert identified a river crossing at Valverde and recommended that southbound wagons be taken to the west side of the Río del Norte at Albuquerque and back at this ford (Abert 1962:120).

**Magdalena Mountains** [34 02N  107 11W]: On his second day south out of Sevilleta, Pike, under arrest for trespassing on Spanish territory, noted the "mountains of Magdalen" to his west (Coues 1895:II.632). Of the mountain, Herbert E. Ungnade writes "There is an almost bare volcanic mountain on the west side of the range which has on its eastern slope the profile of a woman's face (Magdalena Peak, 8,152'). This mountain was sacred and a sanctuary to the Indians. It was named for Mary Magdalena by the Spaniards and the name was then given to the whole range" (Ungnade 1965:141).During the administration of Governor Fernando de Villanueva (1665-1668), the Piros rebelled under El Tanbulita. They joined a band of Apaches in the "Sierra de Madalena" where they ambushed and killed six Spanish settlers. (Sánchez 1989:41)

**Sierra Oscura** [33 38N  106 22W]: Two days from Sevilleta, heading south, Pike noted the "Black mountains" to the east. In 1895, Elliot Coues identified the latter as the Sierra Oscura (Coues 1895:II.632).

**Acomilla (or Hacienda de Luis López)** [Luis López, across the river from the original site, 33 59N  106 53W]: Otermín passed the hacienda of Luis Lopez on the east side of the Río Grande early in 1682 (Hackett 1915:391). On 29 May 1726, Rivera left San Pasqual and traveled north, then northwest through flat land and pleasant meadows. The bank of the Río del Norte were full of poplars. He saw some rosemary thickets and encountered some small sand dunes called Acomilla (Alessio Robles 1946:50).

On 16 May 1760, after leaving San Pascual, Bishop Tamarón came to this site, named for Luis López, who had a hacienda there before the revolt (Adams 1953:200). There were ruins on both sides of the Río del Norte when Lafora passed by on 13 August 1766, four leagues north of Bosque del Apache. He had been traveling over swampy ground covered with high grass and reeds. Lafora also described some fairly high, steep, rocky hills which the road passed through for three leagues that he called las vueltas de Acumilla or de Luis López. Across the river from these lay the ruins of the pueblo of Socorro (Alessio Robles 1939:94-95).

On 29 July 1846, Dr. Wislizenus mentioned a small town named Lopez; on his map he marked it L. Lopez. He commented that the mountains came closer to the river there and that this area contained the last settlements before the Jornada del Muerto (Wislizenus 1848:37).

**Socorro** [34 03N 106 53W]: On 14 June 1598, the Oñate expedition traveled three leagues from Qualacú and stopped opposite Teipana, the pueblo they called Socorro because it provided them with corn. Indeed, the word Socorro means succor or help. The chieftain, Lectoc, gave them an accurate and truthful account of the pueblos of the country (Pacheco, Cárdenas y Torres 1871:XVI.251). Teypana was a pueblo of the Piro, on the west bank of the Río Grande, near the modern town of Socorro (Hammond and Rey 1953:I.318).

In 1634, Fray Benavides mentioned a convent called Nuestra Señora del Socorro and claimed that the inhabitants of the pueblo of Socorro, which he also referred as Pilabo, lived Christian lives (Hodge, Hammond, and Rey 1945:63). In Vetancurt's 1692 description, he wrote that the Convent of Nuestra Señora del Socorro was so-named because the residents brought relief and bread to arriving carts. It was deserted in 1681 (Vetancurt 1971:98).

Otermín reported going past a *vega* opposite Socorro while retreating south along the east bank of the Río del Norte in 1682 (Hackett 1915:391). On 29 May 1726, from Acomilla, Rivera could see some structures of the uninhabited place called Socorro, located on the west side of the river (Alessio Robles 1946:50). Later, on 17 May 1760, Bishop Tamarón saw the remains of the pueblo of Socorro across the Río del Norte. The walls of the church were still standing, and he could see peach trees. He wrote that the pueblo was also "lost with the kingdom" (Adams 1953:201).

Lafora described the ruins of this pueblo on the west side of the Río del Norte when he passed by on the other side on 13 August 1766. He said that they lay at the foot of a mountain of the same name which was south of Sierra de los Ladrones and across from las vueltas de "Acumilla" or de Luis López (Alessio Robles 1939:95). Dr. Wislizenus's caravan also passed by Socorro on the other (or east) side of the Río del Norte, on 28 July 1846. He crossed the river for a visit and also observed some abandoned mines nearby (Wislizenus 1848:36-37)

**Piña and Elota**: These Piro pueblos were mentioned by Gallegos in his relation of the Sánchez Chamuscado entrada of 1581 as being above Piastla and evidently on the east side of the Río Grande. they seem to have been in the area of Socorro, New Mexico (Mecham 1926:275; Hammond and Rey 1927:45).

**Alamillo** [Modern town of Alamillo, across the river from the original site 34 15N  106 54W]: In 1692, Vetancurt wrote of the church dedicated to Santa Ana and mentioned that the people lived on fish gathered from the Río del Norte. The pueblo was burned in 1680 (Vetancurt 1971:98). On 29 May 1726, from Acomilla, Rivera could see several ruins on the east side of the river, where there had been *haciendas de labor* before the revolt. He found the pueblo of El Alamillo, located on the east side of the river, and stayed in an uninhabited place near it (Alessio Robles 1946:50).

On 17 May 1760, after seeing the remains of Socorro, Bishop Tamarón stopped at the site of "Alamito" (Adams 1953:201). Lafora saw ruins when he camped nearby on 13 August 1766. He located it four leagues to the south of the ruins of the pueblo of Sevilleta. The road leading to it was flat but quite rough (Alessio Robles 1939:95). On 17 November 1780, Anza left the Vueltas de Romero and traveled five leagues south to the region of Alamillo (Thomas 1932:198).

**El Hosso (or El Oso) and La Pedrosa**: These Piro pueblos were mentioned together in the Gallegos account of the Sánchez Chamuscado entrada of 1581. Both were located on the east bank of the Río Grande. It was evidently in the area of Alamillo, New Mexico (Mecham 1926:275;Hammond and Rey 1927:45).

On 1 February 1583, the Espejo expedition reached the southern limit of the Piro pueblos of New Mexico. They visited many pueblos, both occupied and deserted, but neither named them nor provided descriptions sufficient for identification. These were likely the El Hosso and La Pedrosa mentioned by Gallegos during the Sánchez Chamuscado expedition. Luxán, author of this Espejo expedition journal, calls these El Termino de Puala, meaning the border of the lands of Puala, by which he means Puaray or the Tiwa. There, Espejo received word that two priests of the Sánchez Chamuscado party who had remained at Puaray had been killed, news which had already reached Mexico. From this area, some of the party went to the Salinas pueblos east of the Manzano Mountains and then returned, whereupon the expedition began north into the country of the Tiwa (Hammond and Rey 1929:72-75).

**Parida**: Dr. Wislizenus wrote that the caravan which he was traveling with stopped near "Parida," some 15 miles south of La Joya [or Sevilleta], on 26 July 1846. Modern maps show an arroyo with this name just north of Socorro, New Mexico on the east side of the Río del Norte (Wislizenus 1848:36). Abert also mentioned Parida in 1846 and noted sandy bluffs nearby. He located across the river from, and one mile above, Socorro (Abert 1962:119,132).

**Sabino**: Anza noted a deserted rancho named "Savina" in this area in 1780 (Thomas 1932:102). Wislizenus, heading south, reported passing "through the town Sabino," on the east side of the river, on the morning of 26 July 1846 after camping at La Joya. He noted that large yucca as well as mesquite became more common here than they had been further north (Wislizenus 1848:36). Abert noted that the citizens of Sabino had been fighting with the Navajo in 1846 (Abert 1962:119).

**Sevilleta (Nueva Sevilla or La Joya)** [La Joya 34 21N  106 51W]: On 15 June 1598, the Oñate expedition traveled seven leagues from Socorro to the little pueblo which they named Nueva Sevilla. This was the first pueblo in which they camped since they thought it was safer to take refuge in the houses in case the Indians of the area decided to attack. They stayed there until 21 June. Between 15 June and 22 June 1598, the *Maese de Campo*, Juan de Zaldivar, and *Sargento Mayor*, Vicente de Zaldivar, encountered what they called "the pueblos of Abo" (Pacheco, Cárdenas y Torres 1871:XVI.251-252). This came to be known as Sevilleta, so named probably because of its resemblance to the landscape around Sevilla, Spain. This Piro pueblo was located on the east bank of the Río Grande, about 20 miles north of Socorro (1953:I.318).

In 1634, Fray Benavides reported that the Piro pueblo of Sevilleta boasted a convent and Indians who lived Christian lives. He wrote that when he arrived in New Mexico at the beginning of 1626, Sevilleta was burned and in ruins due to warfare with other Indians, likely the Apache. During the tenure of Benavides as Custodian of New Mexico, the pueblo was rebuilt and resettled and the convent erected and dedicated to San Luis Obispo. Benavides also used the name "Seelocú," evidently the Piro name for Sevilleta (Hodge, Hammond, and Rey 1945:63-64,252-253). Apparently, the inhabitants of Sevilleta were removed to nearby Alamillo during the 1650s, by Governor Juan Manso de Contreras and then returned in 1659 by the next governor, Bernardo López de Mendizábal, despite protests by the Franciscans in the area (Primera Audiencia de don Bernardo López de Mendizábal, 1663;Scholes 1942:29).

Otermín passed Sevilleta in 1682, as he retreated to the south (Hackett 1915:391). In 1692, Vetancurt said that this pueblo received its name due to its large Piro population. It was razed before he wrote (Vetancurt 1971:98).

On 30 May Rivera left El Alamillo and traveled north, northeast through flat land with hills, ravines and mounts and came to the ruins of a pueblo called Sevilleta, located on the east side of the river (Alessio Robles 1946:50-51). On 18 May 1760, after stopping at Alamito, Bishop Tamarón came to the site where the pueblo of Sevilleta stood, and a little beyond it the ruined *estancia* of Felipe Romero. Tamarón wrote that both were "lost with the kingdom" (Adams 1953:201). Lafora viewed the ruins of Sevilleta when he passed through on 14 August 1766. He placed it across from the mouth of the Río Puerco in an area of steep hills (Alessio Robles 1939:95).

On 10 March 1807, Pike described "Sibilleta" as "the neatest most regular village I have yet seen." It was a square, with a mud wall facing the outside and the windows and doors pointing inward toward the plaza. He thought the population to be 1000. This was the last village Pike stayed in before entering "the wilderness" on his trip to Mexico as a Spanish prisoner and he noted that caravans gathered there before heading south (Coues 1895:II.628-632). Wislizenus simply called it "Joya, another small town" when he went through on 25 July 1846. His map shows the road continuing straight south as the river curved to the west (Wislizenus 1848:36).

Between the visits Lafora and Pike, La Joya had been repopulated. In the 1790s, landless families from Taos, Las Vegas, and Mora who had experience fighting Indians had been moved to the area. They were to provide protection for caravans to and from Mexico. An 1819, a land grant to 67 individuals confirmed their defensive responsibilities (Calkins 1937:20).

**Ponsitlan and Pueblo Nuevo**: In his account of the Sánchez Chamuscado entrada, Gallegos named the two northernmost Piro pueblos in New Mexico Ponsitlan and Pueblo Nuevo, the latter was still being built at that time. They were both on the east side of the Río Grande and one may have been Sevilleta, later the northern border of the Piro nation (Mecham 1926:275;Hammond and Rey 1927:46).

**La Joyita**: Wislizenus camped near this small town on 24 July 1846, and noticed that, coming from the north, this was the first time that substantial bluffs approached the Río del Norte (Wislizenus 1848:35-36). In 1846, Abert commented on the abundant fields where the valley widened at La Joyita (Abert 1962:119).

San Juan Bautista (Piro or Tiwa pueblo): Between 15 June and 24 June 1598, while at Nueva Sevilla [Sevilleta], the Oñate expedition traveled four leagues to the pueblo of "Sant Joan Baptista," a deserted pueblo where there was a great deal of corn and many paintings which the Oñate party took for pagan idols (*ídolos pintados*). Many Indians came to see them in order to spy; among them was the one they called Don Lope, sent by Thomas and Xupal (Cristóbal), Indians that had remained since the time of Castaño de Sosa (Pacheco, Cárdenas y Torres 1871:XVI.252-253).

**El Corvillo**: After passing through the Piro region some of the Espejo party conducted a reconnaissance of the area east of the Manzano Mountains. On 13 February 1583, they returned to the Río Grande and set up camp at this spot. According to one map they crossed Abo Pass going in both directions and El Corvillo is on the east bank of the river near the mouth of the Río Puerco (Hammond and Rey 1929:78).

**Vueltas de Romero**: On 16 November 1780 Anza left Las Nutrias and was able to travel only three leagues because of the rain and snow; he was forced to stop at Vueltas de Romero (Thomas 1932:198).

**Las Nutrias** [34 28N  106 46W]: When Otermín led his party and many Indian refugees south from Isleta toward El Paso on the east side of the Río Grande early in 1682, he recorded his route past "Vega de las Nutrias" among other places (Hackett 1915:391).

On 30 May 1726, Rivera traveled north then northeast from Sevilleta through flat land dotted with hills, glades and thickets. He passed some arroyos without water after the ruins of Sevilleta he stayed at a *paraje* on the bank of the Río del Norte called Las Nutrias (Alessio Robles 1946:51). When Lafora was here on 14 August 1766, he described it as a recently formed town of thirty families. The ruins of las casas de Felipe Romero lay in the same area (Alessio Robles 1939:95-96). On 15 November 1780, Anza left the area near Belen and traveled five leagues south to Las Nutrias (Thomas 1932:198).

**Casa Colorado** [34 34N  106 45W]: On 19 May 1760, after coming to Sevilleta, Bishop Tamarón passed the house they called Colorada, also in ruins, and from that point on they began to see pens of ewes, corrals, and small houses (Adams 1953:201). Wislizenus only referred to the nearby sand hills and the location of "Casas Coloradas," six miles south of Tomé, when he camped here on 22 July 1846 (Wislizenus 1848:35). Later in the same year Abert commented on some large ponds north of town which were filled with water birds. His party had reached the Río del Norte near here after descending from Abó Pass (Abert 1962:117-118).

**Las Barrancas**: This was an *estancia* located between Sevilleta and Isleta on the east side of the Río Grande where Otermín camped the night of 5 December 1681 before attacking Isleta on the sixth (Hackett 1915:383).

**Jarales** [34 36N  106 445W]: Zebulon Pike reported passing "Xaxales" on 10 March 1807, on the east side of the Río del Norte between Tomé and Sevilleta, south of Sabinez or Sabinal. He recorded a population of 300. In 1895, Coues guessed that the name was probably a poor rendering of Jarales, a town in that area, but not in the same location (Coues 1895:II.628-629). Los Jarales was considered as one of the main *genízaro* settlements of New Mexico in the late eighteenth century (Chávez 1979:199).

**Sabinal** [34 29N  106 48W]: In his reminiscences, recorded in 1766, Juan Candelaria described the founding of many towns after the Spanish reconquest of New Mexico in the 1690s. He thought that Sabinal was founded in 1741 (Candelaria 1929:280). Zebulon Pike reported passing "Sabinez" on 10 March 1807, on the west side of the Río del Norte between Tomé and Sevilleta (Coues 1895:II.628-629).

**Belén (Bethlem)** [34 39N  106 46W]: In his 1766, reminiscences, Candelaria described the founding of "Nuestra Señora de Belen" in 1741 (Candelaria 1929:280). On 19 May 1760, the houses of the settlement of Belén on the other side of the Río del Norte came into Bishop Tamarón's view, and from there on the countryside was covered by great poplar groves. Tamarón was received by the alcalde of Tomé with the citizens of his town, of Belén and of Isleta (Adams 1953:201). On 14 August 1766, Lafora commented that this settlement of 38 *genízaro* and Spanish families lay across the Río del Norte from Tomé in a well-cultivated and pastured area (Alessio Robles 1939:96).

   When Anza left El Paso in 1779, he marched northward along the *Camino Real* past Belen (Adams and Chávez 1956:154). On 14 November 1780, on his trip back south, Anza left the pueblo near Valencia and traveled six leagues south, stopping for the night opposite the pueblo of Belen (Thomas 1932:198).

Map 12: Route from Tomé to Pajarito

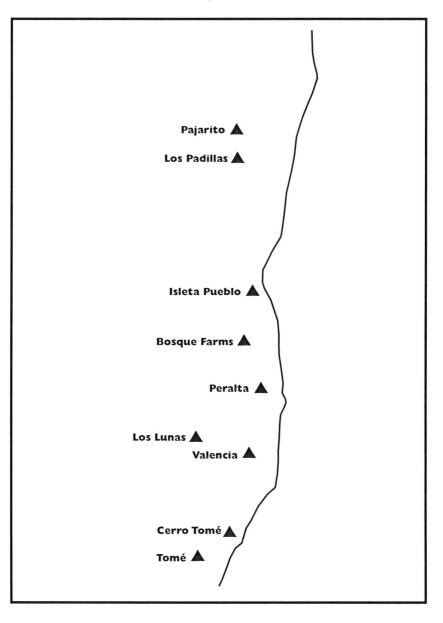

**Tomé** [34 42N   106 43W]: When Otermín led his party and many Indian refugees south from Isleta toward El Paso on the east side of the Río Grande early in 1682, he noted passing "Cerillo de Tomé"--Tomé Hill. (Hackett 1915:391).

On 19 May 1760, Bishop Tamarón was received by the alcalde of Tomé with the citizens of this town, of Belén and of Isleta. Tomé was a new settlement of Spanish citizens which, according to Tamarón, had the potential of becoming the best in the kingdom because of its extensive lands and the ease of running an irrigation ditch from the river. He wrote that they were already building a church, which was 33 *varas* long by 8 wide with a transept and three altars, that was dedicated to the Immaculate Conception. Bishop Tamarón confirmed 402 persons that afternoon. He did not record the population of this settlement until later because it was included in the census of the town of Albuquerque, to which it was subordinate (Adams 1953:201).

Lafora passed by Tomé on 14 August 1766, and wrote that it was also called "pueblo de la Limpia Concepción" and "Fuenclara." He located it six leagues north of Las Nutrias on good, flat road and across the Río del Norte from Belén. It contained a population of seventy Spanish *vecinos* and their families. The entire region was well-cultivated and small livestock grazed on ample pasture (Alessio Robles 1939:96).

When Juan Bautista de Anza left "Presidio del Paso" in 1779, he marched northward along the *Camino Real* past Tomé. Twenty-one residents of Tomé had been killed by Comanche warriors in the summer of 1777, and another 30 in the summer of 1778 (Adams and Chávez 1956:154).

Pike stayed near what he called St. Thomas on 9 March 1807. He reported that the population was 500 and that the camp was constructed to be able to withstand an attack (Coues 1895:II.628). Wislizenus noted the fine irrigated fields of Tomé, which, he wrote, was stretched along the road. He passed by on 21 July 1846, and camped nearby (Wislizenus 1848:35). Earlier, Tomé was one of the main *genízaro* settlements of New Mexico in the middle of the eighteenth century (Chávez 1979:199).

**Caxtole and Piquinaguatengo (or Piguina-Quatengo):** These were the first Tiwa pueblos found by the Sánchez Chamuscado party in 1581, as they traveled north along the Río Grande through New Mexico. They faced each other across the river, with Caxtole being on the east side and much smaller. Piquinaguatengo has been identified with the Tiwa pueblo of San Clemente, on the modern site of Los Lunas, New Mexico (Mecham 1926:276; Hammond and Rey 1927:46).

**Valencia** [34 47N   106 41W]: On 31 May 1726, Rivera left Las Nutrias and traveled through flat land, seeing meadows and poplars on both sides of the Río del Norte. He found many ruins of *haciendas de labor* and livestock *estancias*. He stayed at one called Valencia (Alessio Robles 1946:51). On 13 November 1780, Anza left the Ranch of Juan Sanches and traveled five leagues south to the pueblo of Valencia (Thomas 1932:198).

Wislizenus noted the rich soil when passing through this area of New Mexico between Peralta and Tomé on 21 July 1846 (Wislizenus 1848:35). Historians have noted that Valencia was one of the main *genízaro* settlements of New Mexico in the middle of the eighteenth century (Chávez 1979:199).

**Peralta** [34 50N   106 41W]: Wislizenus also referred to this settlement as Ontero's hacienda. He passed it on 21 July 1846, and commented on the richness of its walled and irrigated fields and stock (Wislizenus 1848:35).

**Hacienda of Mariano Chávez's Widow**: Wislizenus mentioned this hacienda, some seven miles south of Isleta, New Mexico and one mile north of Peralta, on 21 July 1846. He called it the largest which he had seen in that region. Its large fields and pastures were walled and irrigated and its quarters reminded him of plantations in the southern United States (Wislizenus 1848:35).

**Bosque, or Alamos, de Pinos**: The caravan containing Wislizenus camped here, five miles south of Isleta pueblo, New Mexico, and a mile east of the Río del Norte after crossing some difficult sand hills (Wislizenus 1848:35).

**Tiwa (or Tigua)**: After the Espejo party came up the Río del Norte in 1583, through the lands of the Tiwa and Keres, they followed the Jemez River to the north and then turned west, going as far as Arizona. They returned to the Río Grande valley in the northern Tiwa area, at which point Luxán recorded the names of all of the Tiwa pueblos. These do not include some of the names given earlier by Luxán or by preceding expeditions. This list includes Poguana, Comise, Achine, Guagua, Gagose, Simassa, Suyte, Nocoche, Hacala, Tiara, Tayçios, Casa, and Puala (Hammond and Rey 1929:115).

In his Memorial of 1634, former Custodian of New Mexico, Fray Benavides reported that the "Tioas" nation consisted of fifteen or sixteen pueblos and two convents. One was San Antonio de la Isleta and the other San Francisco de Sandia, where the body of Fray López of the Sánchez Chamuscado expedition was interred. According to Benavides, the Tiwa had been superstitious, belligerent, and great sorcerers but had been converted to good docile Christians (Hodge, Hammond, and Rey 1945:64-65,253-258).

In 1591, Castaño de Sosa reported seeing fourteen pueblos within sight of each other in "the province where the Franciscans were slain." Most were deserted by their inhabitants at the approach of the Spaniards. The last which they visited was Isleta, where they were told of the presence of the party which had come to arrest Castaño de Sosa for his illegal entrada (Hull 1916:329-330; Schroeder and Matson 1965:167-173; Pacheco, Cárdenas y Torres 1871:IV.352). Charles Fletcher Lummis gave the Tiwa name of Isleta as Teé-wahn (Lummis 1894:3). Lummis also said that Isleta's native name was reported to be Shi-e-hwib'-bak (Lummis 1894:4).

**Los Despoblados**: On 14 February 1583, Espejo left El Corvillo and continued north along the Río Grande for four leagues before coming upon two pueblos whose residents had fled to the mountains at the approach of the Spaniards. One of the pueblos had 250 houses, the other was not described. They stayed for a day but no one returned, so they continued on. Luxán, author of this Espejo journal, commented on the variety of produce which were grown and preserved here. They have been placed in the land of the Tiwa at this time, probably in the southern part of that region, near Los Lunas or Isleta (Hammond and Rey 1929:79).

**Mexicalcingo and Tomatlan**: These Tiwa pueblos on the east side of the Río Grande were identified by Gallegos in his account of the Sánchez Chamuscado entrada of 1581. They were located next to each other and across the river from Taxumulco, possibly near Isleta, New Mexico (Mecham 1926:276; Hammond and Rey 1927:46).

**El Pueblo de Isleta** [34 54N  106 41W]: It was at Isleta that Castaño de Sosa was told of the arrival of the Morlete party which came to arrest him for his illegal entrada (Hull 1916:330; Schroeder and Matson 1965:167-173; Pacheco, Cárdenas y Torres 1871:IV.352).

In his Memorial of 1634, former Custodian of New Mexico Fray Benavides reported that a convent was located at "San Antonio de la Isleta" of the "Tioas" nation. This first convent was erected around 1613, and was considered to be unusually fine (Hodge, Hammond, and Rey 1945:64-65,253-258). The large church and convent were dedicated to San Antonio de Padua (Vetancurt 1971:99).

Isleta did not participate in the 1680 revolt, but after its capture in 1681, at least 385 Isletans were taken south to the region of El Paso, where Isleta del Sur was established (Hodge, Hammond, and Rey 1945:64-65,253-258). During his attempt at reconquest, Otermín captured Isleta on 6 December. It was on the west bank of the Río del Norte and the first pueblo found to be inhabited as Otermín entered New Mexico from the south (Hackett 1915:383-384). Vetancurt, writing at a different time and place, put the number of Isletans taken south by Otermín at 519. He also noted that the road to Acoma, Zuñi and Moqui (Hopi) left the river at Isleta (Vetancurt 1971:99). Scattered Tiwas were settled on the sight of the old pueblo after the reconquest and the church was rebuilt in 1709 (Hodge, Hammond, and Rey 1945:64-65,253-258).

On 1 June 1726, Rivera left Valencia and traveled north-northeast following the river; to the west side of the river he recognized the pueblo of Isleta, inhabited by a small number of Tiwa families (Alessio Robles 1946:51). On 19 May 1760, Bishop Tamarón was received by the alcalde of Tomé with the citizens of this town, of Belén and of Isleta (Adams 1953:201). Lafora passed through the neighborhood of this Tiwa pueblo, following north along the Río del Norte, on 16 August 1766. It was ministered by a Franciscan priest. He reported that it lay along the road on the other (west side) of the river in a large *alameda* (poplar grove) which covered both banks of the river (Alessio Robles 1939:52).

Wislizenus camped below some sand hills across the Río del Norte from the pueblo of Isleta on 19 July 1846. He commented on the church, orchards, fields, and cottonwood trees. His party ate apples from the pueblo that night. To the south, the sand hills became more difficult to cross (Wislizenus 1848:35).

**Taxumulco (or Taxomulco):** This Tiwa pueblo, possibly Isleta, was seen by Sánchez Chamuscado in 1581 and was located directly across the Río Grande from a pueblo called Tomatlan (Mecham 1926:276; Hammond and Rey 1927:46).

**Los Padillas** [34 58N   106 41W]: Wislizenus mentioned this hacienda south of Albuquerque on 19 July 1846. He was on the east side of the Río del Norte, and noted that the more verdant west bank contained many ranchos and haciendas, among them one called Padillas (Wislizenus 1848:35).

**Pajarito:** In 1643, a land grant was given to a small family of settlers. Later, a serious dispute over land between the Pueblo of Isleta and the nearby *estancia* of "Paxarito" was discussed during the 1663 trial of Governor López Mendizábal of New Mexico before the Inquisition in Mexico City (Primera Audiencia de don Bernardo López de Mendizábal, 1663). Although this area has also been known by other names, in the 1894 hearings on the Atrisco Land Grant before the United States Court of Private Land Claims, Pajarito was given as the southern boundary of the Atrisco grant (Town of Atrisco Grant, 1894. See also, Sánchez 2008:14).

**St. Fernandez:** Upon leaving Albuquerque heading south, Pike crossed the Río del Norte, apparently at the ford to Atrisco. On 8 March 1807, he reported going south for three miles, still on the west side of the river, to a town which he called Tousac. Leaving "Tousac," Pike crossed the river to the east side and came to a town which he reported to be St. Fernandez. His map showed it to be the first village to the south of Albuquerque on the east bank of the Río del Norte with a population of 500. This name is a mystery, but the village was evidently some 11 miles north of Tomé, probably in the neighborhood of the pueblo of Isleta (Coues 1895:II.625;III.1946).

**Sandoval's Hacienda:** Wislizenus mentioned this hacienda, two miles south of Albuquerque on the east side of the Río del Norte, on 17 July 1846. He was traveling on a road above and east of the river until it became impassable a little south of this hacienda. The caravan then backtracked and returned to the road along the east bank, despite it being muddy enough to mire the wagons (Wislizenus 1848:34).

Antonio Sandoval was a very successful individual with tremendous vision. In 1843, he served as acting-governor of New Mexico while Governor Manuel Armijo arrested an invading army from Texas and had them marched down the Camino Real to Mexico City for trial. While at his hacienda at Lagunitas near present Barelas in Albuquerque, Sandoval planned the Barelas Acequia which ran from the Griegos-Candelaria Acequia through what would become Martineztown and downtown Albuquerque to Barelas. The Barelas Acequia was a landmark in Albuquerque into the 1960s when urban renewal took its toll and it was covered up (Sánchez and Miller 2009:55-58).

The Lagunitas Land Grant also ran its historical course. Between 1807 and 1815, Sandoval developed his grant and purchased land near it to enlarge his holdings. Eventually he lost his land. Three or four years after the occupation of New Mexico by the United States, a group of musicians from the American military band stationed in Albuquerque broke into Sandoval's house while he was away, assaulted his mayordomo, looted the premises, and upon leaving, set the place afire. Many of his valuable papers including the title to Las Lagunitas Grant were destroyed as a result of this foul deed. Sandoval died in 1862. When his heirs filed a claim to the land, the U.S. Surveyor General refused to acknowledge their ownership to the grant. Sandoval's heirs knew the land was lost unfairly because there was so much evidence that Sandoval had developed and lived on the land since before the end of the Spanish Colonial period that ended in 1821. Indeed, Wislizenus noted Sandoval's hacienda and its appurtanences when he passed by it in 1846. Still, Antonio Sandoval left a lasting mark on Albuquerque, for the Barela Acequia can still be seen on older maps of the city (Sánchez and Miller 2009:50-51).

**Tousac**: Upon leaving Albuquerque under Spanish escort heading south, Pike crossed the Río del Norte, apparently at the ford to Atrisco. On 8 March 1807, he reported going south for three miles, still on the west side of the river, to a town which he called Tousac (population 500). This name is unknown; in 1895, Coues deduced that the description conformed to Pajarito, the next town below Atrisco to the west of the Río del Norte, though the distance to Pajarito would have been more than three miles (Coues 1895:II.625;III.946).

MAP 13: ROUTE FROM ATRISCO TO SANTA FE

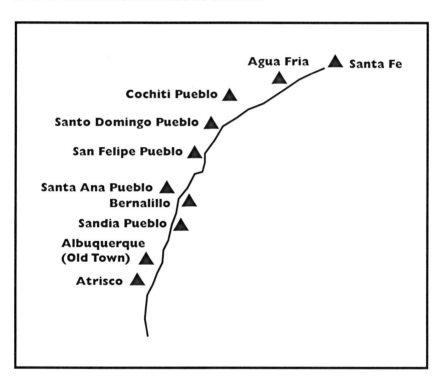

**Atrisco** [35 04N  106 41W]: Historians point to a 1662 attempt by Governor Peñalosa "to found a *villa* in the midst of the settled region, in a valley called Atrisco" as the earliest evidence for the existence of this settlement (Greenleaf 1967:5; Metzgar 1977:269). This document went on to call Atrisco "the best site in all New Mexico." (Hackett 1937:III.265). Before the 1680 Pueblo revolt, this area was well populated, according to documents cited by Charles Wilson Hackett (Hackett 1911:129). *Maestro de Campo* Juan Domínguez de Mendoza testified to going by his old hacienda "in the jurisdiction that they call Atrisco", on 8 December, during the 1681 attempt to reconquer New Mexico (Hackett and Shelby 1942:II.258; Hackett 1915:383-384; Sánchez 2008:15).

In 1692, Governor Diego de Vargas granted the land of Atrisco to Fernando Durán y Chávez whose family had been among the early settlers of the land in Albuquerque's south valley. The Atrisco Land Grant survived intact until 2006, when much of the land holdings were sold by the heirs. (Sánchez 2008:163-174).

Fray Domínguez gave a brief description of "Atlixco" in 1776. He placed it directly across the river from Alburquerque on a beautiful sandy plain and cited a population of 52 families, 288 persons. He also referred to it as Atlixco and *Atrisco de Alburquerque* (Sánchez 2008:11-12; Adams and Chávez 1956:154,207,243). When Zebulon Pike traveled down the Río del Norte as a Spanish prisoner in 1807, he crossed the Río del Norte from east to west "a little below Albuquerque" on 7 March. In 1895, Coues identified the ford as Atrisco, a common crossing before the advent of roads and the railroad (Coues 1895:II.621, 625; III.946).

In 1760, Atrisco was an ecclesiastical dependency of Alburquerque, a fact demonstrated by complaints of the priest in Alburquerque about having to cross the Río del Norte to minister to its citizens (Simmons 1973:10).

**La Villa de Alburquerque** [35 05N  106 39W]: Albuquerque was founded in 1706, by Governor Francisco Cuervo y Valdes. On his orders, Juan de Ulibarrí selected a site on the high ground on the east bank of the Río Grande. The importance of the Villa de Alburquerque was its preeminent position in the valley. Its strategic location on the Camino Real, its relationship to Tijeras Canyon, and the later settlement at Carnuel, as well as a string of at least fifteen land grant settlements along the river from

Bernalillo to Atrisco to Pajarito. Its military importance to the area conveyed prestige to the twelve founding families, whose political influence increased in the early decades of the eighteenth century. The Camino Real passed through present "Old Town" northward to settlements at Alameda, Ranchos de Albuquerque, and Los Poblanos. Beyond there were the pueblos and Santa Fe.

On 1 June 1726, after passing the pueblo of Isleta, Rivera came to the *villa* of Alburquerque, a settlement of Spaniards, mestizos and mulattoes who lived in various ranchos. The name was changed (dropping the middle "r") to Albuquerque after the United States conquered New Mexico (Alessio Robles 1946:51). On 20 May 1760, Bishop Tamarón described Alburquerque as a *villa* composed of Spanish citizens and Europeanized mixtures. He wrote that their priest and missionary was a Franciscan friar, and that it was located 10 leagues north of Tomé. He counted 270 families totaling 1814 persons (Adams 1953:202).

In 1776, Fray Domínguez wrote that the "mission of the Villa of San Felipe Neri de Alburquerque" was four leagues down the road to the south on the same plain as the mission of "Our Father Santo Domingo." The church and convent were about "two musket shots" from the Río del Norte. Until 1706, the general area of Albuquerque was variously called "Valle de Atrisco," *"Bosque Grande," "Bosque Grande de Doña Luisa," "Estancia de Doña Luisa de Trujillo,"* and *"Bosque Grande de San Francisco Xavier"* (Sánchez, 2008:11-16; Adams and Chávez 1956:144).

Lafora camped at this *villa* of seventy Spanish families on 16 August 1766 and commented on its militia of eighty well-armed and mounted men, its civil officials, and the Franciscan priest (Alessio Robles 1939:96). In 1779, Anza marched northward along the *Camino Real* past the Albuquerque area (Adams and Chávez 1956:154).

When Zebulon Pike traveled down the Río del Norte as a Spanish prisoner in 1807, he described the Albuquerque area as the best cultivated and inhabited that he had yet seen. He later referred to Albuquerque and El Paso as the second cities of the province of New Mexico. As he passed through on 7 March, he observed the residents opening irrigation canals from the river for the purpose of cultivating the plains and fields on both sides of the river (Coues 1895:II.619-621,739).

Wislizenus came into Albuquerque from the east on 12 July 1846, after going away from the Río del Norte to explore some mines to the south of Santa Fe. He commented on the abundance of stock grazing on the plain to the east of town and wrote that the surrounding countryside was well-irrigated and cultivated. He also noted that Albuquerque was spread along the river for several miles and was comparable in size to Santa Fe. His caravan was delayed north of Albuquerque when rain damaged part of the road which followed the river. Eventually they made it to a higher road to the east which, itself, became impassable just south of Albuquerque. Wislizenus wrote that some caravans crossed to the west bank of the river at Albuquerque and recrossed at Socorro, but that his did not (Wislizenus 1848:33-34). Later in the same year Abert advised travelers to cross to the west at Albuquerque and back in the area of Fray Cristóbal (Abert 1962:120).

Evidently, the decision to settle the "great riparian woods [bosque grande] of Doña Luisa" was made in 1698. A manuscript from February 1706 showed that Governor Cuervo y Valdéz authorized the actual settlement, which took place shortly thereafter. A church, dedicated to Saint Francis Xavier, was quickly built and soldiers were sent to guard against Indian raids (Greenleaf 1964:6-7). The pre-revolt *estancia* of Doña Luisa de Trujillo has been placed three leagues south of Sandia Pueblo. The area of Alburquerque contained 19 Spanish landholding Spanish families before the 1680 revolt (Twitchell 1911:I.364).

Among the reasons for Governor Cuervo's choice of site were that it was on the *Camino Real*, near a good ford of the river to the west, and directly west of a pass (Tijeras) to the plains (Simmons 1980:191). In addition, *estancias* were already scattered for a league up and down the river, from Alameda to the swamps of Mejía, before the 1680 revolt (Simmons 1980:197-202).

**Rosa de Castilla**: On 1 June 1726 Rivera traveled north northeast from Alburquerque, following the bank of the Río del Norte. He stayed at an uninhabited place called la Rosa de Castilla, on the bank of the river (Alessio Robles 1946:51).

**Los Guajolotes**: On 14 February 1583, Espejo's party left El Corvillo and continued north along the Río Grande for four leagues before coming upon two pueblos whose residents had fled to the mountains at the approach of the Spaniards. They called these Los Despoblados. On 16 February, they again headed north, and after five leagues encountered another deserted pueblo. This time they took provisions, including turkeys, after which they named the pueblo of Los Guajolotes (Hammond and Rey 1929:79).

**Alameda** [35 11N  106 37W]: The church at Alameda was dedicated to Santa Ana, according to Vetancurt, and it was burned in the 1680 revolt (Vetancurt 1971:99). In 1681, Alameda was located on the west bank of the Río Grande seven and a half to eight leagues above Isleta. Early travelers said it was reached from Isleta and Atrisco without a river crossing and then the river was forded to reach Sandia (Hackett 1915:381). In his reminiscences, recorded in 1766, Juan Candelaria gave a post-conquest history in which Alameda was repopulated in 1702 by Tiwa Indians; they were relocated to Isleta in 1708; and the town was settled by Spaniards in 1711 by a land grant given in 1710 (Candelaria 1929:276). In 1872, the river shifted, leaving the Alameda Grant on the east bank of the Río Grande.

**Santa Catalina**: In his account of the Sánchez Chamuscado entrada, Gallegos located this Tiwa-speaking pueblo on the west side of the Río Grande and upriver of those pueblos generally agreed to be in the vicinity of Isleta, New Mexico. This was probably the site of Alameda pueblo at the time (Mecham 1926:277; Hammond and Rey 1927:46).

**Tria**: On 29 July 1598, the Oñate expedition discovered Tria, near Puaray. Juan and Vicente de Zaldivar and Padre Salazar were sent to Tria, which was given as its patron saints San Pedro and San Pablo (Pacheco, Cárdenas y Torres 1871:XVI.254).

**Puaray**: Vetancurt thought that the name, which he spelled "Puray," meant worms, (probably millipedes) which abounded there. The pueblo was beside the Río del Norte, one league from Sandia, and the church was dedicated to "San Bartholome" (Vetancurt 1971:99). The Tiwa pueblo which Gallegos, of the 1581 Sánchez Chamuscado entrada, called Puaray may actually have been that which was later known as Sandia. It was located on the east side of the Río Grande and above the pueblo then called San Mattheo. Two of the priests with the expedition stayed here upon the return of the rest to Mexico and were later killed (Mecham 1926:277,285-289;Hammond and Rey 1927:46-47,50,53). In February of 1583, the Espejo expedition passed through the Tiwa province, counting thirteen pueblos, all deserted out of fear of the Spaniards. At that time they named Los Despoblados and Los Guajolotes. Two leagues north of this last, on 17 February, they encountered "Puala" (or Puaray), where two priests from the Sánchez Chamuscado expedition had been killed and added "los Mártires" to its name in their honor. Luxán described it as three stories high and containing 400 houses. The residents fled to the nearby mountains and refused to return. The Spanish helped themselves to provisions there as well as at other pueblos and continued on to visit the Keres. They returned to the Tiwa area and again approached Puala on 22 June 1583. This time they determined to teach this pueblo a lesson. According to Luxán, they executed sixteen Indians and burned others to death along with their pueblo (Hammond and Rey 1929:80-82,115-116).

On 25 June 1598, the Oñate expedition traveled six leagues from San Juan Baptista in search of Puaráy, observing many pueblos, *granjas* and *heredades* on both sides of the river. On the 26th they traveled five more leagues and on the 27th five more, finally reaching Puaráy, the pueblo where Fray Augustin and Fray Francisco, first discoverers and priests of New Mexico, were killed. At this time, Puaray was given San Antonio de Padua as its patron saint (Pacheco, Cárdenas y Torres 1871:XVI.253-254). When describing the Acoma events, the author of the Oñate itinerary wrote that one could reach the Peñol of Acoma by going west from Puaray (Pacheco, Cárdenas y Torres 1871:XVI.272-273).

Puaray has been placed on the east bank of the Río del Norte about one league above Alameda at the time of the revolt of 1680. It could be reached from Isleta and Atrisco without a river crossing, but the river had to be forded in order to reach Puaray and Sandia, within a league of each other on the east side of the river (Hackett 1915:381).

**San Mattheo (or San Mateo):** In his account of the Sánchez Chamuscado entrada of 1581, Gallegos located this Tiwa-speaking pueblo on the east side of the Río del Norte, across from Santa Catalina (probably Alameda) and upriver of those pueblos generally agreed to be in the vicinity of Isleta, New Mexico. This was probably the site of Puaray pueblo at the time, although Gallegos also identified another pueblo by that name (Mecham 1926:277; Hammond and Rey 1927:46-47).

**Sandia** [35 15N  106 34W]: In his Memorial of 1634 Benavides counted "San Francisco de Sandia" as one of the two convents of the "Tioas" nation. He noted that the body of Fray López of the Sánchez Chamuscado expedition was interred in that convent (Hodge, Hammond, and Rey 1945:64-65). In 1692, Vetancurt described a large church, dedicated to Saint Francis, and a good convent at "Zandia." It was razed in the revolt of 1680, by then the padres had escaped (Vetancurt 1971:99).

In 1681, Sandia was one league above Puaray on the east side of the Río Grande (Hackett 1915:381). Many of the inhabitants of Sandia fled to the Hopi region after the revolt of 1680 and the pueblo was destroyed by Otermín in 1681. It was then rebuilt by Fray Juan Miguel Menchero in 1748, and settled with Tiwas brought back from Hopi (Hodge, Hammond, and Rey 1945:64-65,253-258). In 1766, Juan Candelaria recalled that Sandia was resettled in 1746 by Father Menchero with Tiwas and some Moquis (Hopis) from Moqui (Candelaria 1929:280).

On 2 June 1726, Rivera found only the remnants of the pueblo of Sandia (Alessio Robles 1946:51). In 1759, Bishop Tamarón wrote that this pueblo of Moqui and Tiwa Indians was new and located four leagues north of Albuquerque. He found one Franciscan missionary parish priest who administered 35 families of settlers, totaling 222 persons. He described the Indians as living apart in their tenements, separated after the "manner customary in this kingdom." The Tiwa section housed 51 families totaling 196 persons while that of the converted Moqui Indians held 16 families, totaling 95 persons (Adams 1953:203).

In 1776, Fray Domínguez wrote that from Santo Domingo one traveled south some seven leagues downstream along the meadow of the Río del Norte, which was on the east bank. He described the pueblo and mission of "Nuestra Señora de los Dolores de Sandia" as being located 16 leagues from Santa Fe. In the Sandia registers the title was also given as "Our Lady of Sorrows and St. Anthony" (Adams and Chávez 1956:138-139).

Fray Domínguez described the convent as resembling nothing more than the old half-fallen houses that are usually found in Indian pueblos near Mexico City (Adams and Chávez 1956:141). He wrote that the pueblo lay to the east of the church and convent, below their facade. It was arranged and built in three small blocks, or buildings, to the north and two small plazas to the south. Everything was made of adobe and distributed and arranged like the other missions. The pueblo still housed Indians of two nations, the majority being Tiwas and the others Moquis. In his census the Indians number 92 families, totaling 275 persons (Adams and Chávez 1956:141-144).

On 17 August 1766, Lafora estimated that this pueblo was five leagues north-northeast of Albuquerque. Accordingly, the Tiwas and "Moquiños" there were administered by a Franciscan cleric (Alessio Robles 1939:97). Pike referred to this as "St. Dies" when he passed by it on 6 March 1807. He noted that it was administered by the priest from San Felipe and contained a population of 500 (Coues 1895:II.618-619).

**San Pedro:** In his account of the Sánchez Chamuscado expedition of 1581, Gallegos mentioned this Tewa pueblo as being upriver from Santa Catalina on the west side of the Río Grande (Mecham 1926:277; Hammond and Rey 1927:46-47).

**Analco, Culiacán, Villarrasa, La Palma**: According to the Gallegos account of the Sánchez Chamuscado 1581 journey into New Mexico, the Tiwa pueblos of Analco, Culiacán, Villarrasa, and La Palma (names given them by the members of the expedition) were encountered, in that order, going north along the west side of the Río Grande. They were probably located in the area of modern Bernalillo (Mecham 1926:277; Hammond and Rey 1927:46-47).

**Zenpoala (or Sempoala or Cempoalla), Nompe, Malpais, Caseres**: According to the Gallegos account of the Sánchez Chamuscado 1581 journey into New Mexico, the Tiwa pueblos of Zenpoala, Nompe, Malpais, and Caseres (names given them by the members of the expedition) were encountered, in that order, going north along the east side of the Río Grande. They were all north of Puaray and probably located in the area of modern Bernalillo. Malpais was named for a nearby area which it described. Caseres seems to have marked the northern end of the Tiwa pueblos (Mecham 1926:277-278; Hammond and Rey 1927:47-48).

**Upper Corrales** [35 14N   106 36W]: In 1776, Fray Domínguez wrote that the second group administered by the mission of Sandia is to the west called Upper Corrales. In 1762, the full name was Santa Rosalia de Corrales and ten families with 42 persons resided there. (Adams and Chávez 1956:144). Corrales was settled from the Alameda Land Grant in 1748

**Rancho de Juan Sanches**: On 12 November 1780, Anza left Bernalillo and traveled six leagues south to reach this rancho (Thomas 1932:198).

**Bernalillo** [35 18N   106 33W]: In 1776, Fray Domínguez wrote that the mission in Sandia was also has charge of the administration of some citizens divided into two small groups, one two leagues to the north was called Bernalillo. It had 27 families with 81 persons (Adams and Chávez 1956:144). Lafora gave this name to a collection of *ranchitos* scattered along both sides of the Río del Norte between the pueblos of Sandia and San Felipe in New Mexico on 18 August 1766 (Alessio Robles 1939:97). On 11 November 1780, Anza placed Bernalillo six leagues south of Santo Domingo (Thomas 1932:197-198).

The name "Bernalillo" may have come from a priest in New Mexico named "Bernal" or from "Bernardo", the son of Fernando Duran y Chávez, an early settler. In either case it was bestowed before the 1680 Pueblo Indian revolt (Chávez 1948:111).

The Bernalillo which was founded, or refounded, after the revolt, was several miles upstream of its present location and probably on the west side of the Río del Norte. Some colonists built a plaza and a church, which was dedicated to San Francisco, in 1695 (Kessell 1989:313). In his 1741 reminiscences, Juan Candelaria noted that a convent was built in Bernalillo sometime after 1698, but it was destroyed by flood in 1735-36 (Candelaria 1929:276).

**Algodones** [35 22N 106 28W]: When Wislizenus prepared to leave Santa Fe for Chihuahua on 8 July 1846, he met the caravan that he was traveling with at their camp in Agua Fria. From there, the caravan took "the usual road, by Algodones, for the Río Del Norte" (Wislizenus 1848:29).

**Keres (or Queres)**: In his Memorial of 1634, Benavides reported that the

Keres nation consisted of seven pueblos, four thousand souls, all baptized and docile, and three convents and churches in addition to one in each pueblo (Hodge, Hammond, and Rey 1945:65). After the Espejo party came up the Río del Norte in 1583 through the lands of the Tiwa, they entered the Keres and then followed the Jemez River to the north and turned west, going as far as Arizona. They returned to the Río Grande valley in the northern Tiwa area and again entered Keres. This time they exited the valley by way of the Galisteo basin and made their way to the great plains, then down the Pecos River back to Mexico. During this second stay, Luxán recorded the names of all of the Keres pueblos. The names he gave were Catiete (also Catiste and La Tiete), Gigue, Tipolti, Cochita, and Sieharan. These have been identified as follows:

Catiete = San Felipe (the native name is Katishtya).

Gigue = Gipuy (Oñate) or Santo Domingo.

Tipolti = Tamy or Tamaya (Oñate) or Santa Ana.

Cochita = Cochití.

Sieharan = Sia or a nearby pueblo (Hammond and Rey 1929:116-117).

Castaño de Sosa moved his camp from San Marcos in the Galisteo basin to near a pueblo reported to be Santo Domingo. It was at a ruined pueblo in the Keres region where he was arrested by Morlete for his illegal colonization (Hull 1916:328-329).

**La Misión de San Felipe** [Modern San Felipe Pueblo 35 26N  106 26W]: On 30 July 1598, the Oñate expedition passed "Sant Phelipe" while heading to Santo Domingo (Pacheco, Cárdenas y Torres 1871:XVI.254). Vetancurt reported in 1692, that the convent at "San Phelipe" was a well stocked infirmary. It also had a music chapel ("Capilla de musicos") and, together with the smaller Santa Ana Pueblo nearby, accounted for many faithful. There were 600 persons in the two pueblos (Vetancurt 1971:100).

On 2 June 1726, Rivera found the Keres pueblo of San Felipe five leagues from Sandia on the west side of the river (Alessio Robles 1946:51). In 1760, Bishop Tamarón located this pueblo four leagues south of Santo Domingo and on the opposite side of the Río del Norte (Adams 1953:203). A Franciscan priest ministered to "Keres" Indians in this mission which Lafora thought was two and a half leagues southwest of Santo Domingo pueblo on the right bank of the Río del Norte (Alessio Robles 1939:97).

Zebulon Pike traveled down the Río del Norte as a Spanish prisoner in 1807. On 6 March, he crossed the Río del Norte to the west bank by a wooden bridge of eight arches and entered the pueblo which he called "St. Philip's." Upon leaving, he recrossed the bridge and continued down the east side of the Río del Norte. He marked San Felipe's population as 1,000 (Coues 1895:II.616-618).

**Palomares**: The Sánchez Chamuscado party of 1581 visited this Keres pueblo. It sat across (west of) the Río Grande from "Campos," or Santo Domingo, near modern Cubero. It has also been identified as "Kat-isht-ya, or the first San Felipe," not to be confused with the Piro San Felipe cited by Gallegos (Mecham 1926:278-279;Hammond and Rey 1927:47-48).

**La Misión de Santo Domingo (Campos, Ji-py-y)** [35 30N  106 21W]: Going north from Tiwa country during their 1581 entrada, Sánchez Chamuscado entered the land of the Keres speakers at the pueblo which they called "Campos." It was found on the east side of the Río Grande in the vicinity of the pueblo of Santo Domingo (Mecham 1926:278-279; Hammond and Rey 1927:47-48). On 8 and 9 March 1591, Castaño de Sosa moved his camp from San Marcos in the Galisteo basin to near Santo Domingo, apparently being the one to give it that name. It was at a ruined pueblo near Santo Domingo and "Gipuy" that he was arrested by Morlete (Hull 1916:328-330; Schroeder and Matson 1965:142;157-160; Pacheco, Cárdenas y Torres 1871:IV.347).

On the night of 27 June 1598, Oñate came six leagues from Puaray to Jipi-y or Santo Domingo, in order to apprehend two Mexican Indians named Tomas and Xupal who and been with Castaño de Sosa. They would be used as translators. On the 28th, they were taken to Puaray. On 30 June 1598, they were returned to Santo Domingo, in whose province the "Convent de Nuestra Señora de la Asumpcion" was erected (Pacheco, Cárdenas y Torres 1871:XVI.253-254; Mecham 1926:278). On 7 July 1598, a general council of seven Indian chieftains of different New Mexico provinces was held at Santo Domingo. Each one of them pledged obedience to the Spanish king (Pacheco, Cárdenas y Torres 1871:XVI.256).

When the Oñate expedition returned to Santo Domingo on 27 July 1598, Ginés de Herrera Horta, chief auditor and legal assessor to Oñate, reported seeing about 100 Indians dancing to celebrate the coming of the Spaniards (Hammond and Rey 1953:II.643,662). Captain Alonso Gómez Montesinos, one of the settlers of San Gabriel, stated that the Indians of Santo Domingo had learned to recite their prayers at the ringing of the bell. He noted that the natives taught each other the prayers willingly and devoutly (Hammond and Rey 1953:II.711).

In the early 1660s, Governor Don Bernardo López de Mendizábal was briefly imprisoned by the Franciscan Friars in the *baptisterio* of Santo Domingo before he was transported to Mexico City for his trial before the Inquisition (Primera Audiencia de don Bernardo López de Mendizábal, 1663). In his 1692 treatise, Vetancurt wrote that the convent at Santo Domingo housed "the best of the *custodio* and noted that it was the repository of the Franciscans' archives. The church and all of its *imágenes* were burned in the 1680 rebellion and three priests were killed. He described the road to Santa Fe as flat and did not mention Cochití at this point so he probably considered the Galisteo route to be the usual one (Vetancurt 1971:100).

On 2 June 1726, Rivera found Santo Domingo, two leagues from Sandia and San Felipe, inhabited by the Keres Indians. This same day he met with the governor of this region, who was then Juan Domingo de Bustamante, governor from 1722 to 1731 (Alessio Robles 1946:51). In 1760, Bishop Tamarón wrote that Santo Domingo was located six leagues north of Sandia. He wrote that there were no settlers and that the mission priest was a Franciscan friar. He counted 67 families of Indians, totaling 424 persons (Adams 1953:203).

In 1776, Fray Domínguez described the river Las Bocas as joining the Río del Norte from the plain above the "Mission of Our Father Santo Domingo" (Adams and Chávez 1956:41). He wrote that Santo Domingo was reached by traveling about nine leagues down from Santa Fe to the southwest. It was established and located in full view of the Río del Norte. He stated that there were two churches in this mission, one old and the other new. These buildings were destroyed by a flood in 1886, the present church at Santo Domingo dates from about 1890 (Adams and Chávez 1956:137).

Fray Domínguez described a rancho (near present Peña Blanca) of a citizen and his family located one league north on the same plain. This was the "Rancho de José Miguel de la Peña" from 1777 to 1780, the "Rancho de Peña" in 1791, and from 1792 on it was "Rancho de la Peña Blanca." He wrote that the pueblo of Santo Domingo consisted of six blocks, or buildings, of dwellings. The whole pueblo was surrounded by a high adobe wall with two gates. In order to reach the pueblo one had to travel the highway going up or down. He observed abundant cultivated lands above and below the pueblo, as well as on the opposite bank, and also small peach and apricot trees and an abundance of melons and watermelons. He wrote that the Keres of this pueblo were commonly called "Chachiscos" as well. In his census, Fray Domínguez counted 136 families, totaling 528 persons (Adams and Chávez 1956:130-138).

Ten leagues from Santa Fe, New Mexico, by the main road, this "Keres" pueblo and Franciscan mission was visited by Lafora on 18 August 1766. Here, the main road left the Río del Norte for the final stretch into the capital (Alessio Robles 1939:97). On 10 November 1780, Anza left Las Golondrinas and traveled six leagues south to the pueblo of Santo Domingo, where he met two Navajo Apaches who wanted to exchange a young Spaniard from "Presidio del Paso" for a little girl who was a captive; the next day Anza turned her over to her family (Thomas 1932:197).

Zebulon Pike traveled down the Río del Norte as a Spanish prisoner in 1807. On 5 March, he arrived at the pueblo of Santo Domingo, which he reckoned contained a population of about 1,000 "Keres" Indians. Although he thought little of the buildings in the pueblo he was quite impressed by the elegant ornamentation of the paintings and statues of the patron saint in the church. He also noted the view of the river and the "St. Dies" or Sandia mountains (Coues 1895:II.615).

**Las Bocas:** On 3 June 1726, Rivera left Santo Domingo and the Río del Norte and traveled east northeast through flat land with some hills and glades, passing a narrow pass called las Bocas, which had a dimension of three leagues. He described an arroyo with some junipers and wild rosemary that ran through it (Alessio Robles 1946:52). In 1776, Fray Domínguez described how the water from the springs below Cieneguilla formed a river called Las Bocas, which took a very winding course for about two leagues to the west through a valley between mesas. He wrote that it was so broad that there was a highway through it to the missions of Río Abajo. It joined the Río del Norte from the plain above the "Mission of Our Father Santo Domingo" (Adams and Chávez 1956:41).

**El Pino**: On 3 June 1726, Rivera passed Las Bocas and stayed at an un-inhabited place called el Pino, located on the bank of the small Santa Fe River (Alessio Robles 1946:52).

**La Misión de Cochití (Medina de la Torre, Cachiti, Cachili, Cochita)** [35 36N  106 20W]: This Keres pueblo was probably the Medina de la Torre visited in 1581, by the Sánchez Chamuscado company, their descriptions conform to the locale of the modern pueblo of Cochití, on the west side of the Río Grande (Mecham 1926:278-279; Hammond and Rey 1927:47-48).

The Keres speakers Cachiti (or Cachili or Cochita) met Espejo in the area of Puaray and invited them to visit. Once there, the Spanish were given food and bartered for buffalo skins. From Cochití, they visited two other Keres pueblos which they called Los Confiados and La Milpa Llana. They followed the Jemez River north out of the Keres region and then turned west to visit the western pueblos (Hammond and Rey 1929:82-83,116-117).

Castaño de Sosa visited Cochití pueblo on 18 January 1591 (Schroeder and Matson 1965:142;157-160). In 1692, Vetancurt wrote that more than 300 Christian Indians lived there before the 1680 revolt. Many Apaches also came there to worship. He placed it on the left, or east, bank of the Río del Norte and noted that it had been burned in the 1680 revolt (Vetancurt 1971:102).

**Los Confiados**: When Espejo was chasing Tiwas in the region of Puaray, representatives of Cochití came to invite him to visit their pueblo. While there, he met other Keres speakers and visited at least two of their pueblos, which Luxán called Los Confiados and La Milpa Llana. They followed the Jemez River north out of the Keres region and then turned west to visit the western pueblos (Hammond and Rey 1929:82-83).

**La Milpa Llana**: When Espejo was chasing Tiwas in the region of Puaray, representatives of Cochiti (Luxán called it Cachiti and Cachili) came to invite him to visit their pueblo. While there, he met other Keres speakers and visited at least two of their pueblos, which Luxán called Los Confiados and La Milpa Llana. They followed the Jemez River north out of the Keres region and then turned west to visit the western pueblos (Hammond and Rey 1929:83).

**Galisteo River and Basin**: Castaño de Sosa went from the Río Grande to the Galisteo basin via the Santa Fe River and returned by way of the Galisteo, thus exploring both valleys as routes away from the Río Grande below La Bajada hill and White Rock Canyon (Schroeder and Matson 1965:142;157-160). The later *Camino Real* would turn away from the river in this same area.

In July of 1598, Oñate traveled from San Juan Pueblo to Galisteo and from there to the great pueblo of Pecos. On the 27th of July they returned to the valley of Santo Domingo, where they remained until 1 August 1598 (Pacheco, Cárdenas y Torres 1871:XVI.258-259). On 23 June 1601, a group of the Oñate expedition left San Gabriel and traveled for four days before reaching Galisteo, which was one of the first settlements (Hammond and Rey 1953:II.747). In Oñate's era, wagons left the river at Santo Domingo and headed up the Galisteo basin to Santa Fe to avoid the climb at La Bajada (Moorhead 1958:26).

Vetancurt described the area between Santo Domingo and Santa Fe as flat and noted no settlements in between the two. This probably means that, before the 1680 revolt, he thought of the route through the Galisteo basin as the usual way to Santa Fe rather than a road through Cochití and along the Santa Fe River (Vetancurt 1971:100).

**House of El Alamo**: On 24 May 1760, Bishop Tamarón reached the house of El Alamo, six leagues from Santo Domingo. He described it as large, with an upper story and many corridors (Adams 1953:203).

**La Hacienda de Don Tenorio**: The road from Santo Domingo to Santa Fe, New Mexico passed through there in an area of gentle hills and difficult ravines. On 19 August 1766, Lafora sited this hacienda four leagues short of Santa Fe (Alessio Robles 1939:97-98).

**La Bajada** [35 33N  106 13W]: Zebulon Pike left Santa Fe on 4 March 1807, as a Spanish prisoner bound for Chihuahua. His description of his route out of the capital is rather vague but was interpreted by Elliot Coues in 1895. Coues described the road as following the high ground between the Río de Santa Fe and Arroyo Hondo past Agua Fria and then forking, with both forks heading toward La Bajada and the Río del Norte (Coues

1895:II.613-614). Northbound wagons often left the river at Santo Domingo and followed the Galisteo basin to Santa Fe rather than negotiate the hill at La Bajada (Moorhead 1958:26).

**Las Golondrinas**: On 9 November 1780, Anza left Santa Fe and traveled four leagues south to the pueblo of Las Golondrinas (Thomas 1932:197).

**Tetilla Peak** [35 36N   106 12W]: As Coues interpreted Pike's 1807 description, in 1895, the road forked near Agua Fria. The right fork went past Tetilla Peak on its way to La Bajada. This was the road taken by Pike from Santa Fe (Coues 1895:II.613-614).

**Río de Santa Fe**: In 1581, Sánchez Chamuscado followed the Río Grande north all the way to the mouth of the Santa Fe River and then turned to follow it to the area of the later capital. They eventually continued further north as well as south into the Galisteo basin. Gallegos called the Santa Fe valley Atotonilco and reported finding four pueblos there: Guatitlan or Guaxitlan, La Guarda or Guarda, Valladolid, and La Rinconada (Mecham 1926:279;Hammond and Rey 1927:48).

Castaño de Sosa first encountered this river en route from Pecos to the Tewa region on 7 January 1591, near the later site of the capital. He came down the Río del Norte to the mouth of the Río de Santa Fe near Cochití on 18 January, then followed it into the Galisteo basin (Hull 1916:328-330; Schroeder and Matson 1965:142;157-160).

Rivera mentioned staying at El Pino on 3 June 1726, located on the bank of the small Santa Fe River, which joined with the Río del Norte (Alessio Robles 1946:52). In 1776 Fray Domínguez stated that the source of the Santa Fe River was Santa Fe Lake, located in the "Sierra Madre." He described the river as flowing from east to west, winding almost through the center of Santa Fe. He wrote, nonetheless, that its waters were usually insufficient for the inhabitant's needs (Adams and Chávez 1956:40). Fray Domínguez also wrote that a little below Cieneguilla there were a number of springs which were probably an outcrop of the Santa Fe River (Adams and Chávez 1956:41). In 1895, Elliot Coues also referred to the Santa Fe River as the "Río Chacito." Under guard, Pike left the capital of Santa Fe heading south down the Santa Fe River to the Río del Norte (Coues 1895:II.604-613).

**Cieneguilla** [35 38N   106 06W]: In 1776, Fray Domínguez wrote that two roads went down from Quemado like a "V" and led to two settlements or ranchos, both of which were to the southwest. They were two leagues apart and about five leagues from Santa Fe. The higher settlement was called Cieneguilla; it was in a canyon that came down from San Ildefonso Springs where it met the channel of the Santa Fe River. There were a number of springs a little below this settlement, which were probably a resurgence of the Santa Fe River. These springs ran west in little ravines (Adams and Chávez 1956:41).

Pike's 4 March 1807, description of his route south out of the capital is rather vague but as interpreted in 1895 by Elliot Coues it forked near Agua Fria. The left fork met the Santa Fe River at the town of Cieneguilla and then followed it to La Bajada (Coues 1895:II.613-614). In December 1846, Abert nearly lost his life and that of his mule when he attempted a shortcut across marshy land at Cieneguilla. Only the fact that much of the ground was frozen allowed him to escape and to save the mule (Abert 1962:139).

**Ciénega Grande** [Ciénega Creek 35 33N   106 09W]: In 1776, Fray Domínguez identified Ciénega Grande as the settlement below Cieneguilla and five leagues from Santa Fe. He wrote that it lay in a kind of nook between two cañadas, and that the outlines of ancient ruins were visible at the site of this settlement, which might have been "pagan" pueblos. From there Fray Domínguez went to another settlement called Río de Tesuque, north of Ciénega Grande, and continued north to visit other pueblos (Adams and Chávez 1956:41).

Pike's 1807 map contained a town marked "Vitior" which Coues identified in 1895 as being at or near La Bajada. However, it has also been connected to the town of Cienega or Sienega, on a creek of the same name and two miles southeast of Cieneguilla (Coues 1895:II.613-614;III.950).

**Arroyo Hondo** [35 34N   106 06W]: Pike, as interpreted by Elliot Coues, described the road south out of Santa Fe as following the high ground between the Río de Santa Fe and Arroyo Hondo past Agua Fria (Coues 1895:II.613-614).

**Agua Fria** [35 39N   106 01W]: When Pike left Santa Fe on 4 March

1807, he followed a road which took the high ground between the Río de Santa Fe and Arroyo Hondo. Just past Agua Fria it forked, with both forks eventually reaching La Bajada and the Río del Norte (Coues 1895:II.613-614). When Wislizenus prepared to leave Santa Fe for Chihuahua on 8 July 1846, he met the caravan that he was traveling with at their camp in Agua Fria. From there, the caravan took "the usual road, by Algodones, for the Río Del Norte" (Wislizenus 1848:29).

**Quemado**: In 1776, Fray Domínguez wrote that Quemado was one league west and at the very outskirts of Santa Fe. It was an Indian pueblo in the old days and had this name because it was purposely burned. The settlement near this place was later called Agua Fría (Adams and Chávez 1956:41). The burned pueblo was excavated after the Santa Fe River laid part of it bare (Adams and Chávez 1956:41).

Map 14: Route from Santa Fe to San Juan de los Caballeros

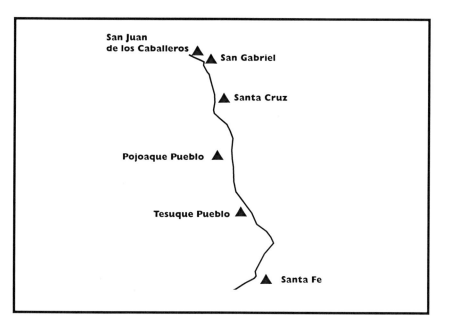

EL CAMINO REAL

**Santa Fe** [35 41N  105 56W]: Castaño de Sosa's party may have passed near the later capital on 7 January 1591, while going from Pecos pueblo to the Tewa pueblos to the north. He noted passing a river after crossing the mountains; this was probably the Santa Fe River just northwest of the present city (Hull 1916:324; Schroeder and Matson 1965:112).

The history of Santa Fe was tied to the life of the Camino Real de Tierra Adentro.  Sometime in 1599, Governor Oñate moved the capital of New Mexico from San Juan de los Caballeros to San Gabriel, closer to the confluence of the Río Grande and the Río Chama. Of historical importance, the *cabildo*, or town council, was created as the basic unit of popular government, first at San Juan, then transferred to San Gabriel. When Santa Fe was officially established as the new capital in 1610, by Pedro de Peralta, the *cabildo* was moved and housed in what came to be known as the Palace of Governors. Since 1610, Santa Fe's history merged with that of the Camino Real de Tierra Adentro.

The historical process that led to the official establishment of Santa Fe began around 1605, when, Juan de Oñate, it appears, gave approval for the establishment of an outpost called "San Francisco de Santa Fe, Real Campo de Españoles" (San Francisco de Santa Fe: Royal Spanish Outpost). That year, Juan Martínez de Montoya led a group of settlers south of San Gabriel where they they set up their encampment. In time, the location of Martinez de Montoya's outpost became blurred, but Spanish colonial chroniclers such as Friar Alonso de Benavides wrote, in 1626, that it was, indeed, Santa Fe, the Spanish capital of New Mexico. The official founding of Santa Fe, however, occurred when, in 1609, the viceroy of New Spain authorized Pedro de Peralta to proceed to New Mexico and establish a new villa, he did not mention that such a town named Santa Fe existed. Instead, he perceived that the main settlements were in the San Juan de los Caballeros-San Gabriel area. Peralta's orders called for him to establish a "villa" that would serve as New Mexico's capital. Meanwhile, Juan de Oñate, the proprietor of the colony, seeing that his fortunes were waning, resigned as governor of New Mexico. Meanwhile, the Spanish crown had already taken the Province of New Mexico under its royal wing. Thus, Oñate's tenure in New Mexico contributed to the founding of Santa Fe, the new terminus of the Camino Real de Tierra Adentro.

In the change from proprietary to royal control, Don Pedro de Peralta was appointed governor and captain general of the province. On March 30, 1609, Viceroy Luis de Velasco handed Don Pedro instructions to follow in establishing his administration as royal governor and in strengthening defenses within his jurisdiction. Upon receipt of his orders, Peralta organized his expedition and departed Mexico City sometime that summer. With Peralta and his soldiers were Fray Alonso Peinado, the new *padre comisario* of the missions, and eight friars. The caravan, numbering at least thirty *carretas*, a large herd of livestock, servants, teamsters and a mounted escort, traveled north on the Camino Real de Tierra Adentro to Nuevo México.

In his Memorial of 1634, Fray Benavides reported that Santa Fe numbered some 250 Spaniards and their wives, families, and servants, a total of about 1,000 people. The original church had collapsed but Benavides oversaw the building of a fine replacement (Hodge, Hammond, and Rey 1945:68). In Vetancurt's 1692 description of pre-revolt New Mexico, the area between Santa Domingo and Santa Fe was depicted as flat and no settlements were noted between the two. This seems to indicate that he was thinking of a route through the Galisteo basin from the Río del Norte to the capital. Vetancurt described an attractive plaza with some small artillery pieces and noted that the governor, some soldiers, and four priests had lived there before the 1680 revolt (Vetancurt 1971:100).

On 4 June 1726, Rivera traveled east from El Pino along the west bank of the Santa Fe river until he reached the *villa* of same name. He wrote that it was the capital of the "reino and provincia de la Nueva Mexico," and that its population was made up of Spaniards, mestizos and mulattoes. He stated that it served as the quarters for the *presidio's* 80 soldiers, whose salaries were paid for by the king (Alessio Robles 1946:52).

On 24 May 1760, Bishop Tamarón came four leagues east from the house of El Alamo to Santa Fe. On 25 May 1760, he visited the principal church, which he described as large, with a spacious nave and a transept adorned by altars and altarscreens, all of which he inspected. He wrote that two Franciscan friars served this *villa*. The census showed 379 families of citizens of Spanish and mixed blood, which totaled 1285 persons. But, since Bishop Tamarón confirmed 1,532 persons, he was convinced that the census was wrong. He also visited a church dedicated to the Archangel St. Michael. In the plaza, another church, dedicated to the Most Holy Mother of Light, was then being built. The chief founder of this church was the Governor,

Francisco Marín del Valle. At the time of his visit, Tamarón noted that all the buildings of Santa Fe were adobe and that there was no fortress or any formal *presidio* building. The garrison consisted of 80 mounted soldiers.

In his general description, Bishop Tamarón wrote that the *villa* lay at the foot of a *sierra*, which was east of it and ran to the north. He explained that water was scarce because the Santa Fe river dried up in the months before harvest. From Santa Fe Bishop Tamarón visited Pecos, Galisteo, Tesuque, Nambe, Pojoaque, Picurís, and Taos (Adams 1953:204-215).

In 1776, Fray Domínguez described Santa Fe as the capital of the kingdom and seat of political and military government and of a royal *presidio*. He located it about 700 leagues to the north of the "great city of Mexico" and wrote that it was established on a very beautiful site at the foot of the Sierra Madre, which was not far to the east of the *villa*. The church was almost in the center of the *villa*, its titular patron "Our Seraphic Father St. Francis' (Adams and Chávez 1956:12).

Domínguez stated that the location and site of Santa Fe was as good as he had pictured it, but that its appearance, design, arrangement and plan did not correspond to its state as a *villa*. He described it as "a rough stone set in fine metal." He also compared Santa Fe to quarter of Tlatelolco in Mexico City and described it's appearance as mournful. His opinion of the adobe houses was that they were made of earth, unadorned by "any artifice of brush or construction." Santa Fe consisted, at the time, of many small ranchos at various distances from one another, with no plan as to their location. There was a semblance of a street, which extended 400 or 500 *varas* from the west gate of the cemetery of the parish church. According to Domínguez, this "street" lacked orderly rows of houses. He wrote that the harvest of Santa Fe consisted of wheat, maize, legumes and green vegetables, and fruits such as melon, watermelon and apricots (Adams and Chávez 1956:39-41).

Lafora arrived in the capital of the kingdom of New Mexico, on a good road, on 19 August 1766. He reported that a company of eighty men guarded a population of 2,324, divided among the families of the 80 soldiers, of 274 Spanish *vecinos*, and of 89 Indians of various nations. He judged the existing fortifications unusable for defense (Alessio Robles 1939:98). On 15 August 1779, Anza described marching north from Santa Fe along the *Camino Real* to the pueblo of "Pujuaque," where he and his troop stayed the night (Thomas 1932:123). By 10 September 1779, Anza and his army had returned to Santa Fe by way of Taos Pueblo where they picked up the *Camino Real* leading to the capital (Thomas 1932:139).

Zebulon Pike entered the city of Santa Fe as a prisoner of the Spanish government on 3 March 1807, coming from the north past the present site of Fort Marcy. He described Santa Fe as being only three streets wide and extending for a mile along the banks of the Río de Santa Fe, which he called a small creek. In 1895, Elliot Coues also referred to the Río de Santa Fe as the "Río Chacito." Pike contrasted the two magnificent churches with the modest appearance of the typical houses. The soldiers were quartered to the north of the central plaza, which was surrounded by the government palace on the north and, across from it, the clergy and public officers. He reported the population of Santa Fe to be 4,500 souls. On the next day, Pike left the capital heading south down the Santa Fe River to the Río del Norte (Coues 1895:II.604-613).

German born Wislizenus found Santa Fe disappointing for a capital when he arrived from Missouri on 30 June 1846. He reported a population of 3,000 in the city itself and 6,000 including nearby settlements. He said that, aside from two churches and the Palace of the Governors, all of the houses were one-story adobes scattered along "irregular, narrow, and dusty" streets. He did, on the other hand, admire the mountainous surroundings (Wislizenus 1848:19,28-29).

The Casas Reales, or the Palace of the Governors, was believed to have been built in 1610 when Santa Fe was established. People took refuge in it during the Indian siege of August 1680. In 1731 it was recorded that Governor Bustamante "built at his own expense the Casas Reales where the governors reside today" (Adams and Chávez 1956:22). Much of Santa Fe was built between 1610 and 1612. There were later additions, including a large military compound containing arsenals, offices, a jail, a chapel, and the governor's residence and office. The outer walls of adjoining structures served as the defensive walls of the compound and enclosed two interior plazas. The dwellings in these two plazas were three and four stories high (Sánchez 1989:28). The barrio of Analco in Santa Fe was the main Mexican Indian (Nahua-speaking Tlaxcalan or other groups) settlements of New Mexico from its founding at least until the late eighteenth century (Chávez 1979:199). They built San Miguel Chapel located in the Barrio de Analco in present Santa Fe.

**Sierra Madre**: In 1776, Fray Domínguez wrote that the Sierra Madre lay to the east of Santa Fe; he described it as being abundant in firewood and timber. He also described Santa Fe Lake, the source of the Santa Fe River (Adams and Chávez 1956:40).

**San Juan de los Caballeros, Caypa, Ohke (San Juan Bautista)**: According to the itinerary of the 1598 Oñate expedition, on 4 July Oñate sent Don Juan de Zaldívar to get the rest of the settlers who had been left behind at the grave of Robledo in May. He was to bring them to the San Juan valley, which he did on 18 August (Pacheco, Cárdenas y Torres 1871:XVI.254-255) This was a reference to the area of San Juan de los Caballeros, which had been established after the ceremonies at Santo Domingo (Hammond and Rey 1953:I.320). Oñate wrote that his army caught up to him on 19 August at San Juan de los Caballeros "in this province of the Teguas" (Hammond and Rey 1953:I.481). San Juad de los Caballeros was New Mexico's first capital.

In 1779, Anza and the main troop traveled northward from San Juan de los Caballeros along the *Camino Real* and crossed the Río Grande, heading north northwest. At the deserted pueblo of Ojo Caliente, the last settlement in the area (Thomas 1932:124), Anza reported having reached the end of his "*Camino Real*"— in his terminology, the end of the road his army marched on, not the *Camino Real de Tierra Adentro*. (See also Appendix B).

**San Gabriel**: According to Joseph Brondate, captain of the cavalry on the Oñate expedition, Oñate established his army headquarters at San Gabriel. From here, the expedition explored the area 50 leagues to the north and twenty leagues to the sides. They found about 50 pueblos, the smallest with 30 houses and the largest with 400. He also explained that it was not necessary to build any forts because the Indians were so peaceful. This place was very appropriate because it had water, rivers and forests (Hammond and Rey 1953:II.626-627).

San Gabriel, the pueblo of Yunque or Yugewinge, was founded a few months after San Juan de los Caballeros. San Gabriel was located on the left bank of the Chama where it flowed into the Río Grande. It remained the capital of New Mexico until Governor Don Pedro de Peralta, Oñate's successor, founded Santa Fe in 1610. It was a town of approximately four

hundred houses and was more adequate for the needs of the Spanish settlers (Hammond and Rey 1953:I.17). After San Juan de los Caballeros was
abandoned, San Gabriel became New Mexico's capital until the founding
of Santa Fe in 1610. At that point Santa Fe became the terminus of the
Camino Real de Tierra Adento which emanated from Mexico City until the
end of the Spanish period in 1821. After Mexico achieved its independence
from Spain, the Camino Real was no longer "royal"--but the name Camino
Real continued to be used locally along its length.

EL CAMINO REAL

# Appendix A

## *El Camino Real De Tierra Adentro* National Historic Trail Establishment Act (P.L. 106-307*)*

Oct. 13, 2000
[S. 366]

El Camino Real
de Tierra
Adentro National
Historic Trail
Act.
New Mexico.
Texas.
16 USC 1241
note.
Public Law 106—307
106th Congress
An Act

To amend the National Trails System Act to designate El Camino Real
de Tierra

Adentro as a National Historic Trail.

Be it enacted by the Senate and House of Representatives of
the United States of America in Congress assembled,

SECTION 1. SHORT TITLE.

This Act may be cited as the "El Camino Real de Tierra Adentro
National Historic Trail Act".

SEC. 2. FINDINGS.

The Congress finds the following:

(1) El Camino Real de Tierra Adentro (the Royal Road of the
Interior), served as the primary route between the colonial Spanish
capital of Mexico City and the Spanish provincial capitals at San
Juan de Los Caballeros (1598-1600), San Gabriel (1600-1609) and
then Santa Fe (1610-1821).

(2) The portion of El Camino Real de Tierra Adentro that
resided in what is now the United States extended between El Paso,
Texas and present San Juan Pueblo, New Mexico, a distance of 404
miles;

(3) El Camino Real is a symbol of the cultural interaction
between nations and ethnic groups and of the commercial exchange
that made possible the development and growth of the borderland;

(4) American Indian groups, especially the Pueblo Indians of
the Rio Grande, developed trails for trade long before Europeans
arrived;

(5) In 1598, Juan de Oñate led a Spanish military expedition
along those trails to establish the northern portion of El Camino
Real;

(6) During the Mexican National Period and part of the United
States Territorial Period, El Camino Real de Tierra Adentro
facilitated the emigration of people to New Mexico and other areas
that would become the United States;

(7) The exploration, conquest, colonization, settlement,
religious conversion, and military occupation of a large area of the
borderlands was made possible by this route, whose historical period
extended from 1598 to 1882;

(8) American Indians, European emigrants, miners, ranchers,
soldiers, and missionaries used El Camino Real during the historic

development of the borderlands. These travelers promoted cultural interaction among Spaniards, other Europeans, American Indians, Mexicans, and Americans;

(9) El Camino Real fostered the spread of Catholicism, mining, an extensive network of commerce, and ethnic and cultural traditions including music, folklore, medicine, foods, architecture, language, place names, irrigation systems, and Spanish law.

37

114 STAT. 1074 PUBLIC LAW 106—307—OCT. 13, 2000

SEC. 3. AUTHORIZATION AND ADMINISTRATION.

Section 5(a) of the National Trails System Act (16 U.S.C. 1244(a)) is amended—

(1) by designating the paragraphs relating to the California National Historic Trail, the Pony Express National Historic Trail and the Selma to Montgomery National Historic Trail as paragraphs (18), (19), and (20), respectively; and

(2) by adding at the end the following:

"(21) EL CAMINO REAL DE TIERRA ADENTRO.—

"(A) El Camino Real de Tierra Adentro (the Royal Road of the Interior) National Historic Trail, a 404 mile long trail from the Rio Grande near El Paso, Texas to San Juan Pueblo, New Mexico, as generally depicted on the maps entitled 'United States Route: El Camino Real de Tierra Adentro', contained in the report prepared pursuant to subsection (b) entitled 'National Historic Trail Feasibility Study and Environmental Assessment: El Camino Real de Tierra Adentro, Texas-New Mexico', dated March 1997.

"(B) MAP.—A map generally depicting the trail shall be on file and available for public inspection in the Office of the National Park Service, Department of the Interior.

"(C) ADMINISTRATION—The Trail shall be administered by the Secretary of the Interior.

"(D) LAND ACQUISITION—No lands or interests therein outside the exterior boundaries of any federally administered area may be acquired by the Federal Government for El Camino Real de Tierra Adentro except with the consent of the owner thereof.

"(E) VOLUNTEER GROUPS; CONSULTATION—The Secretary of the Interior shall—

"(i) encourage volunteer trail groups to participate in the development and maintenance of the trail; and

"(ii) consult with other affected Federal, State, local governmental, and tribal agencies in the administration of the trail.

"(F) COORDINATION OF ACTIVITIES.—The Secretary of the Interior may coordinate with United States and Mexican public and non-governmental organizations, academic institutions, and, in consultation with the Secretary of State, the government of Mexico and its political subdivisions, for the purpose of exchanging trail information and research, fostering trail preservation and educational programs, providing technical assistance, and working to establish an international historic trail with complementary preservation and education programs in each nation..

Approved October 13, 2000.

LEGISLATIVE HISTORY—S. 366:

SENATE REPORTS: No. 106—22 (Comm. on Energy and Natural Resources).

CONGRESSIONAL RECORD:

Vol. 145 (1999): Nov. 19, considered and passed Senate.

Vol. 146 (2000): Oct. 3, considered and passed House

# Appendix B

# Toward a Definition of the Spanish *Camino Real*: *Cabañas*, *Villas*, Armies, and the Spanish Crown

by
Joseph P. Sánchez
María Luisa Pérez González
Bruce A. Erickson

The legal sources consulted for this discussion regarding *caminos reales* are compilations or codes that follow Spanish tradition. From tradition, sprang a body of laws that formed the legal practice and jurisprudence of Spanish America. The dynamics of tradition and practice are found in the *Fuero Juzgo, Fuero Real* compiled in Medieval Spain. The laws of the *Fuero Juzgo* passed to the modern age through the *Nueva Recopilación*, the *Recopilación de leyes de Indias* and the *Novísima Recopilación de 1805*. It is clear from these laws that privileges were extended only to individual Spaniards or associations of Spaniards, primarily in the Peninsular and Creole social classes. Colonial minorities performing the business of the king benefitted from certain privileges, especially if they were prescribed. To be sure, all common or public roads in the Spanish domain were protected roads.

Having consulted the referenced compilations of laws, it is clear that privileges accorded for use of certain roads, mines and roads used by associations of cart drivers and the mesta, a livestock association, for herding sheep, constitute a *regalía*, or privileges conceded by the king. In her dictionary, lexigrapher María Molinar states that the word *regalía* comes from the Latin "regalis" meaning *real* or akin to royal prerogatives. Hence the definition of *real* is "a prerogative of a kind, that like the minting of money, corresponds solely to the sovereign of a country. [Also, it is] a name given to certain privileges that the Pope concedes to the king regarding questions of ecclesiastic discipline." From these actions, the king extracted certain rights in the form of taxes and royal duties.

Throughout the Low Middle Ages, the king strengthened his control over jurisdictions, privileges of the nobility, clergy, etc. in Castile and new acquisitions as well. Thus, the Spanish word *real* grew in acceptance during the birth of modern state. Once established, however, the crown was unwilling to turn loose of its power, even in the face of opposition from the nobility. The nobility, the Church, and the towns, themselves, drew their authority from such privileged positions. They, too, were unwilling to relinquish rights granted to them by the king. The crown assured the establishment of a state income that permitted the growth of a national economy and patrimony that strengthened state controls. Therefore, even in modern times, the crown, through tradition and practice, clearly defined its spheres of influence within the state.

Within the privileges of the concept *real*, roads held a preeminent position because they were the arteries of the economy. In particular, trade, mining, and transhumance activities formed an important element of defining certain roads. Royal income was also augmented by designating certain roads as toll roads. Given that situation, all common or public roads were under the protection of the crown. Some roads, especially those that offered the crown advantages, were favored through the *regalias* of the users.

*Regalias* could be granted for one lifetime, or two lifetimes, or in perpetuity. Charters to towns were also given for indefinite periods of time. All privileges could be revoked by the crown which gave them in the first place. Usually, economic benefits were the main consideration for the granting of privileges. The crown never took its eyes off the possibility of finding minerals so it encouraged the search for mineral wealth through the granting of privileges to do so. Therefore, mines, also referred to as *reales*, received special attention from the crown.

The Spanish word "*real*", when applied to a *camino real*, is nothing more than what its status, through certain privileges, defined. That status came from the human usage and the status carried by the users. Most often, the "*real*" was granted to an individual or a group, or it attached to a place along the route such as a mine or a town by dint of the privileges conceded to it or its owners or proprietors.

In 1497, Queen Isabel reinforced the concept of royal roads when she established the *Cabaña Real de Carreteros*, the Royal Association of Cart Drivers, in the area of Granada. The privileges granted the cart drivers included a right-of-way with free pasturage and access to pasture lands during the winter, off-the-road overnight camping, with whatever needs attached to camping, and the use of the road without a toll or fee to a town it came near. In time, other privileges were extended to users of the road. Here is a case where the privileges were granted to an association of cart drivers. Whatever road the Royal Association of cart drivers used was considered the "royal road" as they were guaranteed protection and other privileges.

The function of the *Cabaña Real* was to protect cart drivers as defined by their privileges. By the middle seventeenth century, convoys were formed for protection against attacks, and eventually, special militia forces were organized to further protect the convoys. By 1671, the protective efforts had become costly and the crown allowed municipalities to construct fences near roads limiting the off-road activities of the convoys. In time, privileges became more limited to cart drivers, such that pasturing privileges were restricted as was the exemption from tolls. Apparently, tolls were charged whenever cart drivers did not carry any cargo. The towns interpreted that at that point they were carrying out the business of the king.

Appealing to the crown, which had already conceded them privileges, the cart drivers complained that their privileges had been curtailed. In a series of cases, the courts tended to favor the cart drivers in establishing some of their rights. Between 1734 and 1807, the *Cabaña Real* succeeded in codifying laws related to the privileges in Spanish law books, inclusive of the *Novísima Recopilación* (1804-07). Thus, tradition gave way to practice, and practice became law.

Similarly, there were other "royal cabañas" established that used roads to benefit the coffers of kings. Slowly, the institution of the *Cabaña Real* came into being. In 1599, the crown created a special jurisdiction for the *Cabaña Real* within the *Consejo Real* (Royal Council) to deal with carriages. A member of the *consejo* served as special judge of the *Cabaña Real*. Procurators were appointed in Madrid (1599), Granada (1607), and Murcia (1613) to oversee problems associated with the privileges. In 1629, a *Juez Conservador* was appointed to oversee the *Cabaña Real* on a national basis.

In the Americas, the crown applied the laws of Spain to its new possessions. In 1537, the crown gave the viceroy authority to take the initiative in establishing the mesta in New Spain. Evidently, the crown did not intend to repeat its errors regarding confused jurisdictions as had resulted in Spain. The crown aimed at clearly defining its prerogative of *regalía*. A *real*, therefore, could be a one time use or one granted for a limited or indefinite period. The word *real* could be used for a villa, a town, a road, a mine, an office, an army, a right-of-way, a campsite that is associated with the king's business, etc. More often than not, a *regalía* was granted for a short period to permit the advancement of a project. To that end, and keeping the *cabaña real* in mind, the crown provided that the mesta be established throughout the empire. The royal decree provided that:

In New Spain ordinances of the Mesta shall be guarded and introduced in other parts of the Indies. The benefit and utility which result from having introduced the Mesta into the Kingdom of Castile give cause for introducing it into Mexico City and the Kingdom of New Spain, by order of don Antonio de Mendoza, our Viceroy. He shall enact ordinances to benefit and increase the herds, and to remedy and punish frauds and crimes which are committed with much frequency. He shall guard mandates, which have been confirmed by us, and comply with our wish that in New Spain a start be given to this organization. These mandates shall have complete effect in nearby provinces where they have not been introduced...The viceroy, presidents, audiencias, and governors, shall bound the Mesta in order to promote the raising of all kinds of livestock...and they shall enforce the ordinances of Mexico and other laws which are contained herein. (*Recopilación de leyes*, lib. v. tit. v, ley i.)

The privileges granted the Mesta, in theory, applied to all other classes of drovers. The precedent for privileges accorded the Mesta stemmed from medieval traditions as well as the model of the *Cabaña Real*. The main point is that the privileges and protections applied to Spanish users of roads or routes. Towns also had their privileges, and as roads passed through them town officials tended to enforce their privileges over all comers. *Alcaldes mayores* (magistrates) sometimes charged fees or tolls for the use of roads passing through their towns. In 1734, for example, José de Acevedo, a cattleman from Tepic, herded cattle to Mexico City and points in between. He complained that he had suffered abuses at the hands of *alcaldes mayores* who had charged him exorbitantly for use of their roads. The Viceroy issued a special decree to bring offending officials under control. (Dussenbery, *The Mexican Mesta*, 168).

In Mexico, the *Tribunal del Consulado* attended to the upkeep of royal roads (Viceroy Branciforte to the King, 28 February 1798, Veracruz, Archivo General de Indias, Estado 27, #35). In 1798, Antonio de Basocs was the *prior* in charge of the tribunal. That year he oversaw the construction and repair of bridges on the Camino Real de Veracruz and the Camino Real de Tierra Adentro. The money for such repairs came from tolls, fees for areas occupied by herds (*contribuciones de pisage)*, and assessments made to towns along the routes. Earlier, in 1793, a new road, under the auspices of the *Tribunal del Consulado*, was approved, between Yucatan and the Villa de Nuestra Señora de los Dolores in Guatemala. That road, part of the *camino real* network, was opened by Martín de Ursúa y Arimendi, who cut the road at his own cost. The road was approved with all the proper cedulas; and, when it was opened the settlers in the 74-league long stretch of road turned out for a celebration (Autos sobre la abertura de Camino desde Yucatan hasta Guatemala, Archivo General de Indias, Patronato 237, ramo 3). Under the laws of Spain and the empire, the road, as all public roads, was protected, but because of its military, political, and economic importance for the exchange of people and things, certain associations were granted additional privileges, especially the exemption of tolls. In the eighteenth century, the Royal Corps of Engineers carried out construction projects along *caminos reales*. Similarly, activities involving the opening of roads were often a military function.

During military expeditions throughout the northern frontier in the seventeenth century, the usage of *real* is one of convention. That is, the king did not have to state the privileges, they were understood in the approval of a project. The expeditions of Alonso de León in Texas and Diego de Vargas in New Mexico, for example, used the word *real* in reference to the armies they led, the campsites they used, and the line of march they followed. In these instances, the *real* was temporary while the army explored any advantages for the crown that could be found in the area of the expedition. Once the expedition returned to its point of origin, the word *real* lost any continuous meaning in the context of the expedition and where it had been. In the eighteenth century, leaders such as Juan Bautista de Anza and Nicolas Lafora utilized the word *real* in the same way. In all such cases, the *real* was temporary.

Missionary work fell into a larger grouping of privileges under the *Real Patronato*. The granting of privileges for mission programs usually was tied to the economy, for the crown felt if an area could be pacified without military force then a given area could be open to investors--with privileges. In 1756, Bernardo de Miranda discovered a hill with iron and silver deposits north of the Río Grande at a place that would soon be known as San Sabá. The crown then approved the extension of the Franciscan mission field to San Sabá and ordered the establishment of a presidio in the area to protect the mission and the mine. Thus, the privilege was to assure the survival of a *mina real*. No royal road, other than that attached to the mine, while it lasted, was created, although the road leading to San Sabá was sometimes referred to as a *camino real*. That status only attached to the mine not the road. Sometimes, the word *real* in association with a *camino* was loosely used. Local usage did not mean official usage.

Unlike Spanish villages and Indian pueblo, villas had *reales* prescribed in their charters. The Villa de Santa Fe, for example, was given its charter in 1609. An important factor under which a town received a set of privileges was its economic importance to a region, province, or colony. Certainly, a colonial town's economic importance was measured in terms of its benefit to the metropolis. Sometimes a mine owner received a *real* and a population grew up around it. From that settlement, a town developed which in turn received a *real*. In particular, the town controlled the common lands around it in addition to the four square leagues in which it was situate. Similarly, the main road through the town, included in the privileges, could be a toll road charged to all transients. Historically, royal roads connected economically important Spanish towns, capitals of provinces, and mines that possessed a charter prescribing royal privileges.

Some royal roads were short-lived. During their active periods, they were significant, for they connected far-flung Spanish centers or capitals of remote areas. Others lasted over a longer period of time. Los Adaes, on the east Texas frontier, for example, served as the capital of Texas for the period 1721-1772. As a military outpost, Los Adaes was connected to New Spain by the *camino real* that ran northward from Saltillo. Los Adaes, therefore, was significant because it was of benefit to the king as a capital and presidio, and did, through military and missionary work, aim at pacifying the area for possible advantages to the crown. Later, when San Antonio became the capital of Texas, it became the terminus of the *camino real*.

The benefit of a person or a geographic area to the interests of the Spanish crown was a paramount consideration in the granting of royal privileges, usually referred to as a *real*. The word *real* is rooted in the word *regalía*, meaning privileges granted by the king. The word *real* in the name *camino real* does not necessarily pertain to the idea that the road was the *real* but does mean that the word attached to the holder of the *real*. In principle and in theory, as is demonstrated above, the *real* was a privilege or set of privileges conceded by the king of Spain to a person or group that carried a *real* with them. *Reales* given to villas, *cabañas* or associations such as the *mesta*, an army, or muleteers and cart drivers, for example, carried documents indicating their privileges with them. Whatever road a holder of a *real* took, it, momentarily, was designated a *camino real* while he passed along it. Armies, for example, usually referred to their route as a *camino real* or, livestock drovers passing along certain established routes, or through toll roads or through towns always declared their route to be a *camino real*. That way, they were exempt from taxes or user fees and could pasture their herds on common pasturelands, or water their animals in local watering places, or camp along a road without penalty by local officials. Likewise, between villas which held reales, roads usually carried the name *camino real*, demonstrating the tradition of the *regalía*.

# Sources

Autos sobre la abertura de Camino desde Yucatan hasta Guatemala, Archivo General de Indias, Patronato 237, ramo 3.

Ramón Carande, *Carlos V y sus Banqueros* (Barcelona: Edición Crítica, 1990). Carande discusses the rise of the modern state in relation to the obligations, needs, and prerogatives of the crown from its antecedents in the Low Middle

Ages that extended to Europe as well as the Americas. See, especially pp.31-45, 166-175, 235-239.

Diez Navarro, ed. *Quaderno de leyes y privilegios del Honrado Conçejo de la Mesta* (Madrid: 1731).

William H. Dussenberry, *The Mexican Mesta* (Urbana: University of Illinois Press, 1963).

"Fuero Viejo de Castilla (1356, Pedro I)" in *Los Codigos Españoles* (Madrid: Imprenta dela Publicidad M. Rivadeneyva, 1847-51).

Julius Klein, *La Mesta: Estudio de la Historia Económica Española, 1273-1836* (Madrid: Alianza Editorial, 1985).

David Ringrose, *Los transportes y el estancamiento economico de España* (Madrid: Edición Tecnos, 1972). See especially, pp. 129-143.

*Repertorio de la Nueva Recopilación de las leyes del reino hecho por el licenciado Diego de Atiença* (Impreso en Alcalá de Henares en casa de Andrés de Angulo. Año de 1571).

Rodríguez de San Miguel, *Pandectas hispano-megicanas* (Mexico: Universidad Autónoma, 1980).

"Tercera Partida. Título XXVIII, Ley VI," in *Códigos españoles concordados y anotados* (Madrid: Imprenta de la publicidad, M. Rivadeneyva, 1847-51).

Suarez Arguello, Clara, *Trabajo y Sociedad en la Historia de Mexico, Siglos XVI-VIII* (Mexico: Coleccion Miguel Othón de Mendizábal, 1992).

Viceroy Branciforte to the King, 28 February 1798, Veracruz, Archivo General de Indias, Estado 27, #35e Veracruz and the Camino Real de Tierra Adentro.

José Maria y Coronado, *Biblioteca de Legislación Ultramarina en forma de diccionario* (Madrid: Imprenta de J. Martín Algería, 1846).

# Selected Bibliography

1994 "El Viaje: A Planning Study for El Camino Real Interpretive Center." Report prepared for Museum of New Mexico State Monuments.

2001 "El Camino Real Historic Corridor Management Plan for the Rio Abajo." Museum of New Mexico State Monuments Division. May 2001.

Abel, Annie Heloise (ed.). *The Official Correspondence of James S. Calhoun While Indian Agent at Santa Fe and Superintendent of Indian Affairs in New Mexico.* Washington D. C.: Government Printing Office, 1915.

Abert, James William. *Abert's New Mexico Report, 1846-47.* Albuquerque: Horn and Wallace, 1962.

Adams, Eleanor B. (ed.). "Bishop Tamarón's Visitation of New Mexico, 1760," *New Mexico Historical Review*, Vol. XXVIII, No. 2. (April 1953), Pages 81-114; No. 3. (July 1953), Pages 192-221; No. 4. (October 1953), Pages 291-315; Vol. XXIX, No. 1. (January 1954), Pages 41-47.

Adams, Eleanor B. and Fray Angelico Chavez (eds.). *The Missions of New Mexico, 1776: A Description by Fray Francisco Atanasio Dominguez.* Albuquerque: University of New Mexico Press, 1956.

Aiton, Arthur Scott. *Antonio de Mendoza: First Viceroy of New Spain.* Durham: Duke University Press, 1927.

Alatriste, Oscar. *Desarrollo de la industria y la comunidad minera de Hidalgo del Parral durante la segunda mitad del siglo XVII (1765-1810).* México: Universidad Autónoma de México, 1983.

Alessio Robles, Vito (ed.). *Pedro Tamarón y Romeral: demostración del vastísimo obispado de la Nueva Vizcaya-1765.* México: Antigua Librería Robredo, de José Porrúa e Hijos, 1937.

Alessio Robles, Vito (ed.). *Diario y derrotero de lo caminado, visto y observado en la visita que hizo a los presidios de la Nueva Espana septentrional el brigadier Pedro de Rivera.* México, D.F.: Taller Autográfico, 1946.

Alessio Robles, Vito (ed.). *Nicolás de Lafora, relación del viaje que hizo a los presidios internos situados en la frontera de la América septentrional.* México D.F.: Editorial Pedro Robredo, 1939.

Alessio Robles, Vito (ed.). *Viaje de indios y diario del Nuevo México por el rev. fray Juan Agustín de Morfí.* México: Antigua Librería Robredo de José Porrúa e Hijos, 1935.

Almada, Francisco. *Gobernadores del estado de Chihuahua.* México: Imprenta Cámara de diputados, 1950.

Almada, Francisco. *Guía histórica de la ciudad de Chihuahua.* Chihuahua: Gobierno del estado de Chihuahua, 1984.

Altamirano, Graziella and Guadalupe Villa (trans. and eds.). "Personal Narrative of Explorations and Incidents in Texas, Nuevo Mexico, California, Sonora, y Chihuahua, 1850-1853," By John Russell Bartlett, *Chihuahua: textos de su historia, 1824-1921.* México: Gobierno del estado de Chihuahua, Instituto Mora, Universidad Autónoma de Ciudad Juárez, 1988. Pages 594-643.

Alvarez, Salvador. "Minería y poblamiento en el norte de la Nueva España. Los casos de Zacatecas y Parral," *Actas del I congreso de historia regional comparada.* Ciudad Juárez: Universidad Autónoma de Ciudad Juárez, 1989. Pages 105-139.

Alvarez, Salvador. "Tendencias regionales de la propiedad territorial en el norte de la Nueva España. Siglos XVII y XVIII," *Actas del II congreso de historia regional comparada,* Ciudad Juárez: Universidad Autónoma de Ciudad Juárez, 1990. Pages 141-179.

Alvarez, Salvador. "Chiametla: una provincia olvidada del siglo XVI," *Trace,* no. 22 (December 1992). Pages 5-23.

Arregui, Domingo Lázaro de. *Descripción de la Nueva Galicia (1623).* Guadalajara: Gobierno del estado de Jalisco, 1980.

Bailey, Jessie Bromilow. *Diego de Vargas and the Reconquest of New Mexico, 1692-1704.* Albuquerque: University of New Mexico Press, 1940.

Bakewell, Peter. *Minería y sociedad en el México colonial: Zacatecas 1546-1700.* México: FCE, 1976.

Bancroft, Hubert Howe. *History of Arizona and New Mexico, 1530-1888.* Albuquerque: Horn and Wallace, 1962.

Bandelier, Adolph F. *Final Report of Investigations Among the Indians of the Southwestern United States, Carried on Mainly in the Years from 1880 to 1885. Part II.* Cambridge: John Wilson and Son, 1892.

Bandelier, Adolph F. *Historical Introduction to Studies among the Sedentary Indians of New Mexico.* Boston: A. Williams and Co., 1881.

Bargellini, Clara. *La arquitectura de la plata. Iglesias monumentales del centro-norte de México.* México: Universidad Autónoma de México, Instituto de Investigaciones Estéticas, c. 1991.

Bloom, Lansing B. "The Chihuahua Highway," *New Mexico Historical Review*, Vol. XII, No. 3. (July 1937). Pages 209-217.

Blumenschein, Helen G. "Historic Roads and Trails to Taos," *El Palacio*, Vol. 75, No. 1. (Spring 1968). Pages 9-19.

Blumenschein, Helen G. "The Old Trail to Taos," *New Mexico Magazine*, Vol. 43, No. 3. (March 1965). Page 33.

Bolton, Herbert E. *Coronado: Knight of Pueblos and Plains*. Albuquerque: University of New Mexico Press, 1990.

Bolton, Herbert E. (ed.). *Spanish Exploration in the Southwest, 1542-1706*. New York: Charles Scribner's Sons, 1916.

Borah, Woodrow. "Early Colonial Trade and Navigation between Mexico and Peru," *Ibero Americana*, No. 38 (1954).

Burton, E. Bennett. "The Taos Rebellion," *Old Santa Fe*, Vol. I, No. 2. Pages 176-209.

Calkins, Hugh G. *Notes on Community-Owned Land Grants in New Mexico*. Albuquerque: United States Department of Agriculture Soil Conservation Service, Region Eight, 1937.

Candelaria, Juan. "Information Communicated by Juan Candelaria, Resident of the Villa de San Francisco Xavier de Alburquerque, Born 1692- Age 84," Translated by Isidoro Armijo, *New Mexico Historical Review*, Vol. IV, No. 2. (July 1929). Pages 274-297.

Carroll, H. Bailey and J. Villasana Haggard (trans. and eds.) *Three New Mexico Chronicles: the Exposicion of don Pedro Bautista Pino 1812; the Ojeada of lic. Antonio Barreiro 1832; and the Additions of don Jose Augustin de Escudero, 1849*. Albuquerque: The Quivira Society, 1942.

Chance, John K. *Race and Class in Colonial Oaxaca*. Stanford: Stanford University Press, 1978.

Chávez, Fray Angélico. "Don Fernando Durán de Chávez," *El Palacio*, Vol. 55, No. 4. (April 1948). Pages 103-121.3

Chávez, Fray Angelico. "Genizaros," in *Handbook of North American Indians*, Volume 9: Southwest, Alfonso Ortiz (ed.). Washington D.C.: Smithsonian Institution, 1979. Pages 198-200.

Chávez, Fray Angélico. *Origins of New Mexico Families: A Genealogy of the Spanish Colonial Period*. Santa Fe: Museum of New Mexico Press, 1992.

Cheetham, F.T. "El Camino Militar," *New Mexico Historical Review*, Vol. XV, No. 1. (January 1940). Pages 1-11.

Chevalier, François. *Land and Society in Colonial Mexico: The Great Hacienda*. Berkeley: University of California Press, 1963.

Cobarruuias Orozco, Don Sebastian de. *Tesoro de la lengua castellano, o espanola*. Madrid: Luis Sánchez, Impressor del Rey N.S., 1611.

Cordell, Linda S. *A Cultural Resources Overview of the Middle Rio Grande Valley, New Mexico*. Albuquerque: USDA Forest Service, 1979.

Coues, Elliot (ed.). *The Expeditions of Zebulon Montgomery Pike, to Headwaters of the Mississippi River, through Louisiana Territory, and in New Spain, during the Years 1805-6-7.* New York: Francis P. Harper, 1895.

Cramaussel, Chantal. *Juan Rangel de Biesma. Un descubridor en problemas.* Serie Chihuahua: Las épocas y los hombres. Ciudad Juárez: Meridiano 107, Gobierno del estado de Chihuahua, Universidad Autónoma de Ciudad Juárez, 1992.

Cramaussel, Chantal. *La provincia de Santa Bárbara en la Nueva Vizcaya (1567-1631).* Ciudad Juárez: Universidad Autónoma de Ciudad Juárez, 1990.

Cramaussel, Chantal. "La urbanización primitiva del real de Parral," *Trace*, no. 22 (December 1992). Pages 37-54.

Crosby, Harry. *Antigua California: Mission and Colony on the Peninsular Frontier, 1697-1768.* Albuquerque: University of New Mexico Press, 1994.

Crosby, Harry. *The King's Highway in Baja California.* Salt Lake City: Copley Books, 1974.

Dalager, Rudolph Levin. *The Espejo Expedition into New Mexico, 1582-1583.* Los Angeles: M.A. Thesis, University of Southern California, 1929.

*Diccionario Porrúa de historia, biografía y geografía de México, tercera edición.* México: Editorial Porrúa, S.A., 1970.

Drumm, Stella M. (ed.). *Down the Santa Fe Trail and into Mexico: the Diary of Susan Shelby Magoffin, 1846-1847.* New Haven: Yale University Press, 1926.

Dunham, Harold H. *Spanish and Mexican Land Policies and Grants in the Taos Pueblo Region, New Mexico.* Prepared for Pueblo de Taos v. United States, Docket No. 357, Indian Claims Commission, 1959.

Encinias, Miguel Alfred Rodríguez and Joseph P. Sánchez (Trans. and eds.). *Gaspar Pérez de Villagrá's historia de la Nueva Mexico, 1610.* Albuquerque: University of New Mexico Press, 1992.

Espinosa, J. Manuel. *Crusaders of the Rio Grande.* Chicago: Institute of Jesuit History, 1942.

Espinosa, J. Manuel. "Governor Vargas in Colorado," *New Mexico Historical Review*, Vol. XI, No. 2. (April 1936). Pages 179-187.

Fireman, Janet R. *The Spanish Royal Corps of Engineers in the Western Borderlands: Instrument of the Bourbon Reform 1764-1815.* Glendale: The Arthur H. Clark Company, 1977.

Florescano, Enrique. *Descripciones económicas generales de Nueva España: provincias del norte (1790-1814).* México: SEP-INAH, 1976.

Florescano Mayet, Sergio. *El camino Mexico-Veracruz en la epoca colonial* (Su importancia económica, social y estratégica). Xalapa: Universidad Veracruzana, 1987.

Forrestal, Peter P. and Cyprian J. Lynch (trans. and ed.). *Benavides' Memorial of 1630.* Washington D.C.: Academy of American Franciscan History, 1954.

Frazer, Robert W. (ed.). *Mansfield on the Condition of the Western Forts, 1853-54.* Norman: University of Oklahoma Press, 1963.

Frobel, Julius. *Siete años de vaje en Centroamérica, norte de México y lejano oeste de los Estados Unidos*. Edited by Luciano Cuadra. San José, Managua: Colección cultural del Banco de América, Editorial y Litografía, 1978.

Fugate, Francis L. and Roberta B. Fugate. *Roadside History of New Mexico*. Missoula: Mountain Press Publishing Company, 1989.

Gallegos, José Ignacio. *Historia de Durango 1563-1910*. Durango: Banco Nacional de México, 1983.

García Cubas, Antonio. *Diccionario geográfico, histórico y biográfico de los Estados Unidos Mexicanos*. México: Oficina Tipográfica de la Secretaría de Fomento, 1889.

*Gazateer Number 15: Mexico*. Washington D.C.: Office of Geography, Department of the Interior; U.S. Government Printing Office, 1956.

Gerhard, Peter. *The North Frontier of New Spain*. Norman: University of Oklahoma Press, 1993.

Gilbert, Rafael. "La paz del camino en el derecho medieval español," *Anuario de Historia del Derecho Espanol*, Vols. XXVII-XXVIII (1957-58). Pages 831-852.

Góngora, Don Carlos de Siguenza y. *The Mercurio Volante*. Translated and edited by Irving Albert Leonard. Los Angeles: The Quivira Society, 1932.

Greenleaf, Richard E. "Atrisco and Las Ciruelas 1722-1769," *New Mexico Historical Review*, Vol. XLII, No. 1. (January 1967). Pages 5-25.

Greenleaf, Richard E. "The Founding of Albuquerque, 1706: An Historical-Legal Problem," *New Mexico Historical Review*, Vol. XXXIX, No. 1. (January 1964). Pages 1-15.

Gregg, Josiah. *Commerce of the Prairies: The Journal of a Santa Fé Trader*. Dallas: Southwest Press, 1933.

Gregg, Kate L. (ed.). *The Road to Santa Fe*. Albuquerque: University of New Mexico Press, 1952.

Griffen, William. *Apaches at War and Peace: The Janos Presidio, 1750-1858*. Albuquerque: University of New Mexico Press, 1988.

Griffen, William. *Indian Assimilation in the Franciscan Area of Nueva Vizcaya*. Tucson: University of Arizona Press, 1979.

Hackett, Charles Wilson (ed.). *Historical Documents Relating to New Mexico, Nueva Vizcaya, and Approaches Thereto, to 1773*. Three volumes. Washington D.C.: Carnegie Institution of Washington, 1923-1937.

Hackett, Charles Wilson. "The Location of the Tigua Pueblos of Alameda, Puaray, and Sandia in 1680-81," *Old Santa Fe*, Vol. II, No. 4. (April 1915). Pages 381-391.

Hackett, Charles Wilson. "The Retreat of the Spaniards from New Mexico in 1680, and the Beginnings of El Paso," *The Southwestern Historical Quarterly*, Vol. XVI, No. 2. (October 1912). Pages 137-168.

Hackett, Charles Wilson and Charmion Clair Shelby (eds.). *Revolt of the Pueblo Indians of New Mexico and Otermín's Attempted Reconquest 1680-1682.* Albuquerque: The University of New
Mexico Press, 1942.

Hackett, Charles Wilson. "The Revolt of the Pueblo Indians of New Mexico in 1680," *The Quarterly of the Texas State Historical Association*, Vol. XV, No. 2. (October 1911). Pages 93-147.

Haley, James L. *Apaches: A History and Culture Portrait.* Garden City: Doubleday & Company, Inc., 1981.

Hallenbeck, Cleve. "The King's Highway," *New Mexico Magazine*, Vol. 23, No. 10. (October 1945). Pages 16-17;39-41.

Hammond, George P.(ed.). *Don Juan de Onate and the Founding of New Mexico.* Santa Fe: El Palacio Press, 1927.

Hammond, George P. and Agapito Rey (eds). *Don Juan de Onate: Colonizer of New Mexico, 1595-1628.* Albuquerque: University of New Mexico Press, 1953.

Hammond, George P. and Agapito Rey (eds.). *Expedition into New Mexico Made by Antonio de Espejo, 1582-1583.* Los Angeles: The Quivira Society, 1929.

Hammond, George P. and Agapito Rey (eds.) "The Gallegos Relation of the Rodríguez Expedition, 1581-2," *New Mexico Historical Review*, Vol. II; No. 3, Pages 239-268. (July 1927); No. 4, Pages 334-362. (October 1927).

Hammond, George P. and Agapito Rey (eds.). *Narratives of the Coronado Expedition of 1540-1542.* Albuquerque: University of New Mexico Press, 1940.

Hammond, George P. and Agapito Rey (eds.). *New Mexico in 1602: Juan de Montoya's Relation of the Discovery of New Mexico.* Albuquerque: The Quivira Society, 1938.

Hammond, George P. and Agapito Rey (eds.). *Obregon's History of 16th Century Explorations in Western America.* Los Angeles: Wetzel Publishing Company, Inc., 1928.

Hammond, George P. and Agapito Rey (eds.). *The Rediscovery of New Mexico, 1580-1594.* Albuquerque: University of New Mexico Press, 1966.

Hassig, Ross. *Trade, Tribute, and Transportation: The Sixteenth-Century Political Economy of the Valley of Mexico.* Norman: University of Oklahoma Press, 1985.

Hendrickson, James and Richard M. Straw. *A Gazeteer of the Chihuahuan Desert Region: A Supplement to the Chihuahua Desert Flora.* Los Angeles: California State University Los Angeles, 1976.

Hodge, Frederick Webb (ed.). *Handbook of American Indians North of Mexico.* Washington: Government Printing Office, 1910.

Hodge, Frederick Webb. "The Six Cities of Cibola: 1581-1680," *New Mexico Historical Review*, Vol.I, No.4. (October 1926). Pages 478-488.

Hodge, Frederick Webb, George P. Hammond and Agapito Rey (eds.). *Fray Alonso de Benavides' Revised Memorial of 1634.* Albuquerque: University of New Mexico Press, 1945.

Hodge, Frederick Webb and Theodore H. Lewis (eds.). *Spanish Explorers in the Southern United States, 1528-1543*. New York: Barnes and Noble, Inc., 1965.

Hughes, John T., A.B. *Doniphan's Expedition; Containing an Account of the Conquest of New Mexico; General Kearney's Overland Expedition to California; Doniphan's Campaign Against the Navajos; His Unparalleled March Upon Chihuahua and Durango; And the Operations of General Price at Santa Fe: With a Sketch of the Life of Col. Doniphan. Illustrated with Plans of Battle Fields and Fine Engravings.* Cincinnati: U.P. James, 1847.

Hulbert, Archer Butler (ed.). *Southwest on the Turquoise Trail: the First Diaries on the Road to Santa Fe.* Denver: The Stewart Commission of Colorado College and The Denver Public Library, 1933.

Hull, Dorothy "Castaño de Sosa's Expedition to New Mexico in 1590," *Old Santa Fe*, Vol. III, No. 12. (October 1916). Pages 307-332.

Humboldt, Alejandro de. *Ensayo político sobre el reyno de Nueva España, 1808.* Madrid: Imprenta de Nuñez, 1818.

Jackson, Donald Dean (ed.). *The Journals of Zebulon Montgomery Pike* (With Letters and Related Documents). Norman: University of Oklahoma Press, 1966.

Jackson, W, Turrentine. *Wagon Roads West: A Study of Federal Road Surveys and Construction in the Trans-Mississippi West.* Berkeley: University of California Press, 1952.

Jenkins, Myra Ellen. "Taos Pueblo and its Neighbors: 1540-1847," *New Mexico Historical Review*, Vol. XLI, No. 2. (April 1966). Pages 85-114.

Jones, Oakah L. *Nueva Vizcaya: Heartland of the Spanish Frontier.* Albuquerque: The University of New Mexico Press, 1988.

Kenaston, Monte R. "Fresnillo, Zacatecas: población y sociedad en el siglo XVII," *Anuario de Historia*, no. 2, Centro de Investigaciones Históricas, Universidad Autónoma de Zacatecas, 1979. Pages 219-214.

Kenaston, Monte R. "Testimonios de Fresnillo Zacatecas desde el siglo XVI," *Zacatecas*, no. 1, Universidad Autónoma de Zacatecas (1978). Pages 259-279.

Kessell, John L. and Rick Hendricks (eds.). *By Force of Arms: The Journals of don Diego de Vargas, 1691-1693.* Albuquerque: University of New Mexico Press, 1992.

Kessell, John L. (ed.). *Remote Beyond Compare: Letters of don Diego de Vargas to his Family from New Spain and New Mexico, 1675-1706.* Albuquerque: University of New Mexico Press, 1989.

Lopez de Gonzalez, Lorenzo Esteban. *Taos Valley: A Historical Survey.* Self-published, 1985.

Lummis, Charles F. (Trans. and ed.). "Geronimo de Zarate-Salmeron, Relating all of the things that have been seen and known in New Mexico as well by sea as by land from the year 1538 till that of 1626," *Land of Sunshine*, Vol. XI, No. 6, Pages 337-346. (November 1899) and Vol. XII, No. 3, Pages 180-187. (February 1900).

Lummis, Charles F. *The Man Who Married the Moon and Other Pueblo Indian Folk-Stories.* (New York: The Century Co., 1894).

Marshall, Michael P. 1991 "El Camino Real de Tierra Adentro: An Archeological Investigation. The 1990 New Mexico Historic Preservation Division Survey." Prepared by El Camino Real Project and Cibola Research Consultants for the New Mexico Historic Preservation Division.

Marshall, Michael P. *Excavations at Nuestro Señora de Dolores Pueblo (la 677), a Prehistoric Settlement in the Tiguex Province.* Albuquerque: Office of Contract Archaeology, University of New Mexico, 1982.

Marshall, Michael P. and Henry J. Walt. *Rio Abajo: Prehistory and History of a Rio Grande Province.* Santa Fe: Historic Preservation Division, 1984.

Martínez, Oscar. *Ciudad Juárez: el auge de una ciudad fronteriza a partir de 1848.* México: FCE, 1982.

McCall, Colonel George Archibald. *New Mexico in 1850: A Military View.* Edited by Robert W. Frazer. Norman: University of Oklahoma Press, 1968.

Mecham, J. Lloyd "Antonio de Espejo and his Journey to New Mexico," *The Southwestern Historical Quarterly*, Vol. XXX, No. 2. (October 1926). Pages 114-138.

Mecham, J. Lloyd. *Francisco de Ibarra and Nueva Vizcaya.* Durham: Duke University Press, 1927; and New York: Greenwood Press, 1968.

Mecham, J. Lloyd "The Second Spanish Expedition to New Mexico," *New Mexico Historical Review*, Vol. I, No.3. (July 1926). Pages 265-291.

Mecham, J. Lloyd "The Martyrdom of Father Juan de Santa María," *The Catholic Historical Review*, Vol. VI, No. 3. (October 1920). Pages 308-321.

Menéndez Pidal, Gonzalo. *Los caminos en la historia de Espana.* Madrid: Ediciones Cultura Hispanica, 1951.

Metzgar, Joseph V. "The Atrisco Land Grant, 1692-1977," *New Mexico Historical Review*, Vol. LII, No. 4. (October 1977). Pages 269-296.

Moorhead, Max L. *New Mexico's Royal Road.* Norman: University of Oklahoma Press, 1958.

Moorhead, Max L. "Spanish Transportation in the Southwest, 1540-1846," *New Mexico Historical Review*, Vol. XXXII, No. 2. (April 1957). Pages 123-150.

Murphy, Dan. *New Mexico, The Distant Land: An Illustrated History.* Northridge: Windsor Publications, Inc., 1985.

Murphy, Lawrence R. "Cantonment Burgwin, New Mexico, 1852-1860," *Arizona and The West*, Vol. XV, No. 1. (Spring 1973). Pages 5-26.

Naylor, Thomas H. and Charles W. Poltzer (eds.). *Pedro de Rivera and the Military Regulations for Northern New Spain, 1724- 1729.* Tucson: The University of Arizona Press, 1988.

Naylor, Thomas H. and Charles W. Poltzer (eds.). *The Presidio and Militia on the Northern Frontier of New Spain, Volume I, A Documentary History: 1570-1700.* Tucson: The University of Arizona, 1986.

*New Mexico Geographical Names Information System Alphabetical Listing* 1990. Vienna, Va.: Geographic Names Information Section, Branch of Geographic Names, Office of Geographic and Cartographic Research, National Mapping Division, U.S. Geological Survey, 1990.

Ortiz, Alfonso, Ed. 1979 Southwest. Handbook of American Indians, Vol. 9. General Editor, William C. Sturtevant. Washington, D.C.: Smithsonian Institution, 1979.

Pacheco, Joaquín Francisco, Francisco de Cárdenas y Espejo, and Luis Torres de Mendoza (eds.). *Colección de documentos ineditos, relativos al descubrimiento, conquista y organización de las antiguas posesiones españolas de América y Oceania, sacados de los archivos del reino, y muy especialmente del de Indias. Competemente autorizada.* Madrid: Ministerio de Ultramar, 1864-84.

Pacheco, Joaquín Francisco, Fermín de la Puente y Apezechea, Pedro Gómez de la Serna, Francesco de Paula Díaz y Mendoza, and Gregorio López. *Códigos españoles concordados y anotados.* Madrid: Antonio de San Martín, 1872-1873.

Pacheco, José De La Cruz and Sánchez, Joseph P, editors. 2000 *Memorias del Coloquio Internacional El Camino Real de Tierra Adentro.* Instituto Nacional de Antropología e Historia (Mexico D.F.: 2000)

Palmer, Gabrielle G., Comp., June-el Piper and LouAnn Jacobson, Eds. 1993 El Camino Real de Tierra Adentro, (Volume One). Santa Fe: Bureau of Land management, Cultural Resources Series No. 11.

Palmer, Gabrielle G. and Stephen L. Fosberg, Comps., June-el Piper, Ed. 1999 El Camino Real de Tierra Adentro, Volume Two. Santa Fe: Bureau of Land management, Cultural Resources Series No. 13.

Paso y Troncoso, Francisco del. *Epistolario de Nueva España.* Tomo 15, no. 851. México: 1940. Pages 50-54.

Peñafiel, Antonio. *Nomenclatura geográfica y etimológica de México.* México: Oficina Tipográfica de la Secretaría de Fomento, 1897.

Ponce de León, Jose María. *Reseñas históricas del estado de Chihuahua, tomo 1.* Chihuahua: Imprenta del Gobierno, 1909.

Porras Muñoz, Guillermo (ed.). *Diario y derrotero de lo caminado, visto y observado en el discurso de la visita general de precidios, situados en las Provincias Ynternas de Nueva Espana, que de orden de su magestad executo d. Pedro de Rivera. brigadier de los reales exercitos.* Mexico: Sociedad Chihuahuense de Estudios Históricos, 1945.

Porras Muñoz, Guillermo. *La frontera con los indios de Nueva Vizcaya en el siglo XVII.* México: BANAMEX, 1980.

Porras Muñoz, Guillermo. *Iglesia y estado en Nueva Vizcaya (1562-1821).* México: Universidad Autónoma de México, 1980.

Porras Muñoz, Guillermo. *El nuevo descubrimiento de San José del Parral.* México: Universidad Autónoma de México, 1988.

Powell, Philip Wayne. "The Chichimecas: The Scourge of the Silver Frontier in Six-teenth-Century Mexico," *The Hispanic American Historical Review*, Vol. XXV, No. 3. (August 1945). Pages 315-338.

Powell, Philip Wayne. "The Forty-Niners of Sixteenth-Century Mexico," *Pacific Historical Review*, Vol. XIX, No. 3. (August 1950). Pages 235-249.

Powell, Philip Wayne. "Franciscans on the Silver Frontier of Old Mexico," *The Americas: A Quarterly Review of Inter-American Cultural History*, Vol. III, No. 3. (January 1947). Pages 295-310.

Powell, Philip Wayne. "Genesis of the Frontier Presidio in North America," *The Western Historical Quarterly*, Vol. XIII, No. 2. (April 1982). Pages 125-142.

Powell, Philip Wayne. "Peacemaking on North America's First Frontier," *The Americas: A Quarterly Review of Inter-American Cultural History*, Vol. XVII, No. 3. (January 1960). Pages 221-250.

Powell, Philip Wayne. "Presidios and Towns on the Silver Frontier of New Spain, 1550-1580," *The Hispanic American Historical Review*, Vol. XXIV, No. 2. (May 1944). Pages 179-200.

Powell, Philip Wayne. *Soldiers, Indians and Silver: the Northward Advance of New Spain, 1550-1600*. Berkeley: University of California Press, 1952.

Powell, Philip Wayne. "Spanish Warfare Against the Chichimecas in the 1570's," *The Hispanic American Historical Review*, Vol. XXIV, No. 4. (November 1944). Pages 580-604.

Powell, Philip Wayne (ed.) and María L. Powell (transcriber). *War and Peace on the North Mexican Frontier: A Documentary Record. Volume I: "Crescendo of the Chichimeca War" (1551-1585)*. Madrid: Ediciones José Porrúa Turanzas, 1971.

Pratt, Boyd C. and David H. Snow. *The North Central Regional Overview: Strategies for the Comprehensive Survey of the Architectural and Historic Archaeological Resources of North Central New Mexico*. Santa Fe: New Mexico Historic Preservation Division, 1988.

Rae, Steven V., Joseph E. King and Donald R. Abbe. *New Mexico Historical Bridge Survey*. Santa Fe: New Mexico State Highway and Transportation Department, 1987.

Ramírez Cabañas, Joaquin (ed.). *Descripción geográfica de los reinos de Nueva Galicia, Nueva Vizcaya y Nueva Leon por d. Alonso de la Mota y Escobar*. México D.F.: Editorial Pedro Robredo, 1940.

Rees, Peter W. "Origins of Colonial Transportation in Mexico," *The Geographical Review*, Vol. 65, No. 3. (July 1975). Pages 323-334.

Rees, Peter William. *Route Inertia and Route Competition: An Historical Geography of Transportation Between Mexico City and Vera Cruz*. Berkeley: Ph.D. Dissertation, University of California, Berkeley, 1971.

Reeve, Frank D. *History of New Mexico*. New York: Lewis Historical Publishing Company Inc., 1961.

Reff, Daniel T. *Disease, Depopulation, and Culture Change in Northwestern New Spain, 1518-1764*. Salt Lake City: University of Utah Press, 1991.

Rittenhouse, Jack D. *The Santa Fe Trail: A Historical Bibliography*. Albuquerque: University of New Mexico Press, 1971.

Roca, Paul. *Spanish Jesuit Churches in Mexico's Tarahumara*. Tucson: University of Arizona Press, 1979.

Roca Chávez, Rubén. *Breve monografía de Santa Bárbara al cumplir su IV centenario*. México: JUS, 1967.

Rose, Jeffrey Lee. *The New Camino Real: New Mexico's Subregional Highway Development, 1903-1943*. Albuquerque: M.A. Thesis, University of New Mexico, 1992.

Rowland, Buford (ed.). "Report of the Commissioners on the Road from Missouri to New Mexico, October 1827," *New Mexico Historical Review*, Vol. XIV, No. 3. (July 1939). Pages 213-229.

Ruxton, George. *Adventures in Mexico and the Rocky Mountains*. London: John Murray, 1847.

Sánchez, Joseph P. *Between Two Rivers: The Atrisco Land Grant in Albuquerque History* (Norman: University of Oklahoma Press, 2008)

Sánchez, Joseph P. and Larry D. Miller, *Martineztown 1823-1950: Hispanics, Italians, Jesuits & Land Investors in New Town Albuquerque* (Albuquerque: Río Grande Books, 2008), pp. 50-51.

Sánchez, Joseph P. "The Peralta-Ordóñez Affair and the Founding of Santa Fe," in David Noble Grant (ed.). *Santa Fe: History of an Ancient City*. Santa Fe: School of American Research Press, 1989. Pages 27-38.

Sánchez, Joseph P. *The Rio Abajo Frontier 1540-1692: A History of Early Colonial New Mexico*. Albuquerque: The Albuquerque Museum History Monograph Series, 1987.

Sánchez, Joseph P. *Spanish Bluecoats: The Catalonian Volunteers in Northwestern New Spain, 1767-1810*. Albuquerque: The University of New Mexico Press, 1990.

Sánchez, Joseph P. "Twelve Days in August: The Pueblo Revolt in Santa Fe," in David Noble Grant (ed.). *Santa Fe: History of an Ancient City*. Santa Fe: School of American Research Press, 1989. Pages 39-52.

Saravia, Atanasio G. *Apuntes para la historia de la Nueva Vizcaya*. Obras, tomo 2, México: Universidad Autónoma de México, 1979.

Saravia, Atanasio G. *Apuntes para la historia de la Nueva Vizcaya*. Obras, tomo 3, México: Universidad Autónoma de México, 1980.

Sauer, Carl. *The Road to Cibola*. Berkeley: University of California Press, 1932.

Scholes, France V. "Documents for the History of the New Mexican Missions in the Seventeenth Century," *New Mexico Historical Review*, Vol. IV, No. 1. (January 1929) Pages 45-58.

Scholes, France V. "The Supply Service of the New Mexico Missions in the Seventeenth Century," *New Mexico Historical Review*, Vol. V; No. 1, Pages 93-115. (January 1930); No.2, Pages 186-210. (April 1930); No.4, Pages 386-404. (October 1930).

Scholes, France V. *Troublous Times in New Mexico 1659-1670*. Albuquerque: The University of New Mexico Press, 1942.

Schroeder, Albert H. and Dan S. Matson. *A Colony on the Move: Gaspar Castano de Sosa's Journal, 1590-1591*. Santa Fe: The School of American Research, 1965.

Schurz, William Lytle. *The Manila Galleon*. New York: E.P. Dutton and Co., 1939.

Secosse, Federico. "Zacatecas en 1550," *Artes de México*, no. 194-195 (1975). Pages 4-8.

Secretaría de Gobernación y Gobierno del Estado de Durango. *Los Municipios de Durango. Colección: Enciclopedia de los Municipios de México*. México, D.F.: Secretaría de Gobernación y Gobierno del Estado de Durango, 1988.

Seligman, Arthur. "El Camino Real (The King's Highway)," *New Mexico Magazine*, Vol. 10, No. 10. (October 1932). Pages 6-12.

Sharp, Jay W. "Jornado del Muerto," *New Mexico Magazine*, Vol. 63, No. 1. (January 1985). Pages 18-20.

Simmons, Marc. 1983 "Carros y Carretas: Vehicular Traffic on the Camino Real." In Hispanic Arts and Ethnohistory in the Southwest, edited by Martha Weigle, pp. 325-334. Ancient City Press, Santa Fe. U.S. Department of Agriculture, National Resource Conservation Service

Simmons, Marc. "Governor Cuervo and the Beginnings of Albuquerque, Another Look," *New Mexico Historical Review*, Vol. LV, No. 3. (July 1980). Pages 188-208.

Simmons, Marc. *The Last Conquistador*. Norman: University of Oklahoma Press, 1991.

Simmons, Marc. *The Little Lion of the Southwest: A Life of Manuel Antonio Chaves*. Chicago: The Swallow Press Inc., 1973.

Simmons, Marc. *New Mexico: A Bicentennial History*. New York: W.W. Norton and Company, Inc., 1977.

Simmons, Marc. *Spanish Government in New Mexico*. Albuquerque: University of New Mexico Press, 1968.

State Highway Commission of New Mexico. *Through New Mexico on the Camino Real*. Santa Fe: State Highway Commission, 1915.

Swann, Michael M. *Tierra Adentro: Settlement and Society in Colonial Durango*. Boulder: Westview Press, 1982.

Tainter, Joseph A. and Frances Levine. *Cultural Resources Overview: Central New Mexico*. Albuquerque: USDA Forest Service, 1987.

Tenorio, Oclides. *Los caminos de Nuevo Mejico/Trails of New Mexico*. Taos: Title VII, ESEA Bilingual Project, Taos Public Schools, 1975.

TePasque, John J. and Herbert S. Klein. *Ingresos y egresos de la real hacienda de Nueva España*. Vol. 1. México: Instituto Nacional de Antropología e Historia, Colección Fuentes, 1988.

Teresa de Jesús, Santa. *Camino de perfección*. Rome: Tipografia Poliglotta Vaticana, 1965.

Timmons, W.H. *El Paso: A Borderland History*. El Paso: The University of Texas, 1990.

Thomas, Alfred Barnaby (ed.). "Documents Bearing Upon the Northern Frontier of New Mexico, 1818-1819," *New Mexico Historical Review*, Vol. IV, No. 2. (April 1929). Pages 146-163.

Thomas, Alfred Barnaby (ed.). *Forgotten Frontiers: A Study of the Spanish Indian Policy of don Juan Bautista de Anza, Governor of New Mexico 1777-1787*. Norman: University of Oklahoma Press, 1932.

Twitchell, Ralph Emerson. *The Leading Facts of New Mexican History*. Cedar Rapids, Iowa: The Torch Press, 1911.

Udall, Stewart L., Photographs by Jerry Jacka. *To the Inland Empire: Coronado and Our Spanish Legacy*. Garden City, New York: Doubleday and Company, Inc., 1987.

United States Department of the Interior/National Park Service. *Coronado Expedition: National Trail Study and Environmental Assessment*. Denver: Denver Service Center, 1992.

Vetancurt, Fray Agustin de. *Chronica de la Provincia del Santo Evangelio de Mexico. Quarta Parte del Teatro Mexicano de los Successos Religiosos*. México: Editorial Porrúa, S.A., 1971.

West, Robert C. *The Mining Community in Northern New Spain: The Parral Mining District*. Berkeley: University of California Press, 1949.

Wheat, Carl I. *Mapping the Transmississippi West, 1540-1861*. San Francisco: The Institute of Historical Cartography, 1959.

Winship, George Parker. "The Coronado Expedition, 1540-1542," *Fourteenth Annual Report of the Bureau of Ethnology, 1892-1893*. Washington: Government Printing Office, 1896. Pages 339-615.

Winship, George Parker (ed.). *The Journey of Coronado, 1540-1542*. New York: Allerton Book Co., 1922.

Wislizenus, Frederick A. *Memoir of a Tour to Northern Mexico Connected with Col. Doniphan's Expedition in 1846 and 1847*. Washington: Tippin and Streeper, Printers, 1848.

Worcester, Donald E. (trans. and ed.) "Notes and Documents: Advice on Governing New Mexico, 1794; by Gov. Col. Don Fernando de la Concha," *New Mexico Historical Review*, Vol. XXIV, No. 3. (July 1949). Pages 236-254.

Zavala, Silvio. *El servicio personal de los indios en la Nueva España*. Vol. 3 (1576-1599). México: El Colegio de México y El Colegio Nacional, 1987.

# EL CAMINO REAL

# Index

Hacienda del Gallinero 59-60
Hacienda de Los Diegos 65-66
Hacienda de los Gachupines 61-62
Hacienda de Los Sauces 70
Hacienda del Palo Blanco 168
Hacienda de Luis López 215
Hacienda de Muleros 90
Hacienda de Nuestra Señora de Aran-
    zazú 141
Hacienda de Pozo Bravo 71
Hacienda de San Antonio de Ramada
    140-141
Hacienda de San Bartolomé 70
Hacienda de San Diego 65, 73, 90, 100
Hacienda de San Lucas 158-160
Hacienda de San Miguel 96
Hacienda de San Pedro 72
Hacienda de San Salvador 101-102
Hacienda de Santa Catarina 104,-107
Hacienda de Santo Domingo de la
    Boca 102
Hacienda de Sauceda 116
Hacienda of Mariano Chávez's Widow
    225
Horse Mountain 207
House of El Alamo 245
Huehuetoca 4, 48-50
Humboldt, Alejandro de (Alexander
    von Humboldt) 2-4, 26

**I**

Ibarra, Francisco de 65, 80, 84-85, 87-
    88, 92, 98, 103, 116, 125
Indé 124-127
Indehe 124, 131

**J**

Jarales 222
Jilotepec 5, 51

Jornada del Muerto xi, 9, 19-21, 23-24,
    28, 39, 189, 192, 201, 203-205,
    207-208, 210-211, 216
Jueves de las Comadres 211
Junta de los Ríos 152

**K**

Keres 11, 211, 225, 236, 239-244

**L**

La Alamedilla 153-154
La Bajada 245-248
La Barranca 137, 147, 156
La Barranca de las Vueltas 156
La Barreta 145, 149-150
La Bufa 15, 74-75, 120
La Calera 79
La Cañada 34, 36, 121-122, 186
La Cañada de Agostadero 121-122
La Carretada 162
La Chorrera 145, 149
La Ciénaga Grande 155
La Ciénaga Helada 156-157
La Ciénaga Llana 145, 150
La Cieneguilla 114-115
La Cruz 143-144
La Cuesta del Corral de los Dueños
    121-122
La Cuesta de San Felipe 61
La Daga 153
La Deseada 154
La Elona 152
La Estancia de San Pedro de Alamo
    107
La Fonda 81-82
Lafora, Nicolás de 27, 49-55, 66-75,
    79-86, 88, 90-97, 99, 101-108,
    110-114, 118-119, 124, 127,
    129-130, 136, 139-142, 158-
    160, 162-163, 166-168, 173,
    175-180, 183, 185, 191, 193-

## Z

# About the Authors

Dr. Joseph P. Sánchez is superintendent of Petroglyph National Monument and the Spanish Colonial Research Center at the University of New Mexico. Dr. Sánchez is also founder and editor of the *Colonial Latin American Historical Review (CLAHR)*. He has served as Acting Superintendent at Fort Davis National Historic Site in Texas, and at Pecos National Historical Park in New Mexico. Before his career with the National Park Service, Dr. Sánchez was a professor of Colonial Latin American history at the University of Arizona, Tucson. He was also director of the Mexican-American Studies and Research Center. He has taught at the University of New Mexico, Santa Ana College in Southern California and at the Universidad Autónoma de Guadalajara in Mexico. Additionally, he has taught seminars in history at the Universidad de Sevilla, and the Universidad Internacional de La Rábida in Spain. Dr. Sánchez has presented numerous papers at professional conferences in the United States, Canada, Sweden, Spain, and Mexico. Throughout his career, he has researched archives in Spain, Mexico, France, Italy, and England, and has published several studies on the Spanish frontiers in California, Arizona, New Mexico, Texas, and Alaska. Internationally recognized, in May 2000, he was awarded the *Medalla de Acero al Mérito Histórico Capitán Alonso de León by the Sociedad Nuevo-leonesa de Historia, Geografía y Estadística*, Monterrey, Mexico, for his lifelong work in Colonial Mexican history. In April 2005, he was inducted into the prestigious knighthood order of the *Orden de Isabel la Católica* by King don Juan Carlos of Spain. In 2006 he was appointed to the History Commission of the Instituto Panamericano de Geografía e Historia that is headquartered in Mexico City and affiliated with the Organization of American States in Washington, D.C. His many publications include: *Explorers, Traders, and Slavers: Forging the Old Spanish Trail, 1678-1850* (1997); *Don Fernando Duran y Chaves's Legacy* (1999); *Memorias del Coloquio Internacional El Camino Real de Tierra Adentro,* co-edited by Joseph P. Sánchez and José de la Cruz Pacheco, Mexico City (2000); *Exploradores, comerciantes y tratantes de esclavos: la forja de la Vieja Ruta Española, 1678-1850,* Barcelona (2001); *Between Two Countries: A History of Coronado National Memorial,* co-authored by Joseph P. Sánchez, Bruce Erickson, and Jerry Gurulé (2007); *Between Two Rivers: The Atrisco Land Grant in Albuquerque History, 1691-1968* (2008); *Martineztown 1823-1950: Hispanics, Italians, Jesuits & Land Investors in New Town Albuquerque,* co-authored by Joseph P. Sánchez and Larry D. Miller (2009); *All Trails Lead to Santa Fe: An Anthology Commemorating the 400th Anniversary Founding of Santa Fe, New Mexico in 1610,* co-edited with Editing and Publications History Committee for the Santa Fe 400th (2010).

Dr. Bruce A. Erickson is assistant Professor of History at Le Moyne College in Syracuse, New York. Originally from Chicago, he has lived in Bisbee, Arizona, near Coronado National Memorial. In 1991, Dr. Erickson received his M.A. in Latin American Studies and, in 2001, his Ph.D. in Latin American History, both from the University of New Mexico. He has taught at Western New Mexico University and Eastern Michigan University. For eight years, he served as a research historian at the Intermountain Spanish Colonial Research Center. Dr. Erickson also served as a contract research historian for the National Park Service. His research interests cover a range of topics from gender on the Spanish Colonial frontier to historic trails dealing with the Spanish Colonial period. He has contributed to studies published by the National Park Service. Additionally, his research interests include contemporary efforts to sustain peace and guarantee Human Rights.

CPSIA information can be obtained at www.ICGtesting.com
Printed in the USA
LVOW010759220911

247378LV00003B/6/P